W9-BKK-565

HE 8697.8 .S77 1997

Street, Nancy Lynch.

Messages from the
  underground

DATE DUE

NEW ENGLAND INSTITUTE
OF TECHNOLOGY
LEARNING RESOURCES CENTER

MESSAGES FROM
THE UNDERGROUND

MESSAGES FROM THE UNDERGROUND

*Transnational Radio in
Resistance and in Solidarity*

Written and Edited by
Nancy Lynch Street
and Marilyn J. Matelski

NEW ENGLAND INSTITUTE
OF TECHNOLOGY
LEARNING RESOURCES CENTER

PRAEGER

Westport, Connecticut
London

2\98

35298445

Library of Congress Cataloging-in-Publication Data

Street, Nancy Lynch.
    Messages from the underground : transnational radio in resistance
and in solidarity / written and edited by Nancy Lynch Street and
Marilyn J. Matelski.
       p. cm.
    Includes bibliographical references and index.
    ISBN 0–275–95602–4 (alk. paper)
    1. Radio in politics.   2. International broadcasting—Political
aspects.   3. Radio in propaganda.   I. Matelski, Marilyn J. 1950–.
HE8697.8.S77   1997
302.23′44—DC20   96–41545

British Library Cataloguing in Publication Data is available.

Copyright © 1997 by Nancy Lynch Street and Marilyn J. Matelski

All rights reserved. No portion of this book may be
reproduced, by any process or technique, without the
express written consent of the publisher.

Library of Congress Catalog Card Number: 96–41545
ISBN: 0–275–95602–4

First published in 1997

Praeger Publishers, 88 Post Road West, Westport, CT 06881
An imprint of Greenwood Publishing Group, Inc.

Printed in the United States of America

∞™

The paper used in this book complies with the
Permanent Paper Standard issued by the National
Information Standards Organization (Z39.48–1984).

10 9 8 7 6 5 4 3 2 1

Copyright Acknowledgments

The author and publisher gratefully acknowledge permission for use of the following material:

From Ernest G. Bormann, "Symbolic Convergence: Organization Communication and Culture," in
Linda L. Putnam and Michael E. Pacanowsky (Eds.), *Communication and Organization: An Inter-
pretive Approach*, Beverly Hills, CA: Sage Publications, 1983. Permission to publish granted by
Linda L. Putnam.

From *The Four Days of Courage: The Untold Story of the People Who Brought Marcos Down* by
Bryan Johnson. Copyright © 1987 by Bryan Johnson. Reprinted with permission of The Free Press,
a division of Simon & Schuster.

Every reasonable effort has been made to trace the owners of copyright materials in this book, but in
some instances this has proven impossible. The author and publisher will be glad to receive information leading to more complete acknowledgments in subsequent printings of the book and in the
meantime extend their apologies for any omissions.

To Harry, Wayne, and Kate

Contents

Acknowledgments

This book is the result of several journeys to transnational radio services in Europe and in the United States, as well as interviews and contributions from scholars and professionals in Great Britain, France, Cuba, the Philippines, China, Korea, Italy, Germany, Poland, Hungary, and the Czech Republic. We thank them all for their time, their wisdom, and their frankness. Most especially, we'd like to acknowledge the following people for their insightful case study material and conceptual development: James Dunton (our editor), Br. Miguel Quiachon Rapatan, Fr. Federico Lombardi, Dr. John J. Michalczyk, Dr. John Spicer Nichols, Kevin Klose, Gene Pell, Kim Andrew Elliott, Betty Tseu, Richard Richter, and John Harbaugh.

For aiding and abetting the cause: Dr. Jadwiga Smith, Dr. Indra deSilva, Bronislaw Wildstein, Anna Krzyzak-Maslaniec, Andrzej Adamczyk, Robert Fielding, Andrzej Matla, Alan Heil, Joseph Buday, Sherwood Demitz, Harry Heintzen, Melissa Fleming, Peter Baumgartner, Robert Gillette, Yuri Handler, Gene Parta, Peter Hermann, Mark Rhodes, Ted Lipien, Jim Brown, Sam Lyon, William Marsh, J. B. de Weydenthal, Peter Hebblethwaite, Myra Ozaeta, Fr. Kevin Kersten, Fr. Kevin R. Locke, Fr. Anton Weerasinghe, Joe O'Connell, John Lindburg, Carolyn Matelski, the CART Center at Bridgewater State College, and the ORA at Boston College.

Finally, we thank our families and friends for allowing us the time and space to go "underground" for the message.

Introduction

To some observers, the dissolution of the USSR, the fall of the Berlin Wall, and the liberation of Eastern Europe from the Soviet Union in 1989 signaled the demise of "godless" communism and the triumph of the good--that is, capitalism and democracy. To many governments and their peoples however, the battle will not be won until communism is crushed everywhere in the world, signaling the total triumph of Christianity and capitalism.

The primary target in this new "crusade" now appears to be the Third World (principally Asia, Africa and South America), while keeping a watchful eye out for backsliding on the former Soviet Union (now in some disarray) and the equally struggling Eastern Europe. To reach this target audience (both technologically and rhetorically), one of the most available means is through transnational radio.

MARCONI'S LEGACY: "WIRING" THE WORLD

British journalist G. K. Chesterton once characterized the first decades of the twentieth century in this way:

It is the fashion to divide recent history into Pre-War and Post-War conditions. I believe it is almost essential to divide them into the Pre-Marconi and Post-Marconi days. It was during these agitations upon that affair that the ordinary English citizen lost his invincible ignorance: or, in ordinary language, his innocence. . . . I think it probable that centuries will pass before it is seen clearly and in its right perspective; and that then it will be seen as one of the turning-points in the whole history of England and the world.[1]

Chesterton was referring not only to the technological revolution set forth by Guglielmo Marconi's invention of the wireless telegraph; he meant also the political, social, and economic turmoil that would necessarily follow. No single device since Gutenberg's printing press would influence a world population so profoundly. The possibilities for information, education, propaganda, and international diplomacy would be infinite, limited only by the philosophical direction of the institution using the technology.

MARCONI'S EARLY YEARS

Guglielmo Marconi was born on April 25, 1874, to an affluent Bolognese business family. At the time of his birth, the world was in the midst of great industrial, economic and social change. Transportation had improved markedly with the growing availability of railway and steamship routes throughout Europe and the United States; telegraphic communication provided the means to connect nations and peoples instantaneously from around the globe; and innovations in material production and management would ultimately lead to new political and social world orders.

Marconi himself came from a particularly colorful mixture of culture, economics, and politics. His father (Giuseppe) was an Italian landowner, and his Scotch-Irish mother (Annie) was an heiress of a family brewery. Although he was baptized in his father's Roman Catholic Church, his mother (a staunch Protestant) was most influential in her son's religious upbringing. Marconi's mother was also among the first to recognize his unique potential and encouraged him to conduct scientific experiments in his own laboratory at the family estate, Villa Grifone. In addition, she encouraged him to develop business skills and language fluency (especially in English) so that he might later turn his genius into a profitable enterprise. For many years, however, Marconi's father remained unimpressed with his son's talent, as were many of the townspeople. In fact, according to the inventor's daughter, Degna:

One incident precipitated a real crisis. The whole family was at Porretta, Annie out of the house each day at the sulfurous springs, Giuseppe visiting with old friends, the older boys off on their own. . . . Villagers saw the boy [Guglielmo] at the edge of the stream with a series of dinner plates he had contrived to line up like vertebrae through an elaborate arrangement of string. When they were all in place he shot high-voltage electricity into the string, sending the plates crashing onto the brook's stones. The passers-by thought the younger Marconi boy was crazy and so did his father. . . . From that day onward his father systematically ruined Guglielmo's mechanical apparatuses whenever he found them. Mother and son conspired to keep them from him.[2]

Despite these obstacles, Marconi's tenacity prevailed. After years of studying on his own as well as with professors at the University of Bologna,[3] he acquired enough knowledge to construct a crude wireless telegraph. In 1894, he was able to send electric signals across a small room. Within a few months, Marconi modified his invention to allow signals to travel over longer distances. He also began to enjoy the support of his father and the local villagers. By 1896, however, Marconi realized that he could go no further with his experiments without great financial investment. He first offered to sell his new invention to the Italian Ministry of Posts and Telegraphs but was flatly refused. Shortly after his rejection, Marconi's mother (whose family had powerful contacts in the British Parliament) suggested that he cross the Channel to her native England. There, he made the same offer to the British Post Office.

The British were slightly more interested than the Italians and offered him a small amount of money for his patents--smaller than his mother thought he should accept. As a result, in July 1897, Marconi (with the financial help of his mother and her family) created a private company, known as the Wireless Telegraph and Signal Company, Ltd. (which was later changed to the Marconi Wireless Telegraph Company, Ltd.). The British Marconi Company, armed with all of Marconi's shrewdly acquired patents, rose quickly in recognition; within a year, it was the first company to achieve successful transatlantic communication between Europe and the United States.[4] Thus, it was only a matter of time before Marconi's company became influential in Canada and America, as well as in other areas of southern and central Europe.[5] This influence would later become evident as heads of state contemplated the powers of international communication.

MARCONI AND GREAT BRITAIN

Though Marconi had initially approached the Italian government with his plans to construct a national system for wireless communication, he was not tied solely to his country of birth. After being rejected by the Italian ministry, Marconi traveled to England to negotiate with the British Post Office for similar status. As he soon discovered, though, he was not alone. Years before, the English had begun work on their own system of wireless communication, which, incidentally, was quite unlike Marconi's blueprints. Instead of using Hertzian waves, the British designed their equipment based on electromagnetic induction, a concept developed by Sir William Preece in 1896. Despite these differing perspectives, however, Marconi was greeted warmly (if not enthusiastically) when he crossed the English Channel.

Before being able to demonstrate his innovations to the British, Marconi was required to apply for the appropriate patents as well as to reconstruct the equipment that had been damaged on his voyage to England. For months, he worked diligently on both tasks, relying on the help of his mother's cousin, Henry Jameson-Davis. Within four months he was ready to set up his operation.[6] Many physicists, including Preece, were impressed with the new apparatus and suggested that it be tested further.

Marconi was not without his detractors, however. During his first year in England, some scientists, including Oliver Lodge, remained skeptical about the young Italian's claims of uniqueness and originality. Lodge described an 1896 British Association meeting:

Preece came there, knowing nothing of Hertz, but interested in space methods of telegraphy and told us in Section A of a remarkable discovery which had just been brought over from Italy. It was stale news to me and [another scientist] Fitzgerald, and to Lord Kelvin and to a few others; but, whereas we had been satisfied with the knowledge that it could be done, Mr. Marconi went on enthusiastically and persistently, at first with the help of Preece and the resources of the British P.O. Department, till he made it a practical success.[7]

Debates over the veracity of Marconi's claims and ethical conduct, including the legitimacy of his patents, continued for many years. By 1912 the inventor was embroiled in a huge controversy over monopolistic influence in Britain's Imperial Chain of wireless stations. He never really recovered from it. G. K. Chesterton coined the episode as "the Marconi scandal" and attributed Marconi's excessive political power to his relationship with Sir Rufus Isaacs, Britain's Attorney-General:

Everybody knows the record of Isaacs and his father, and his uncle, and in general of the whole family. Isaacs' brother is Chairman of the Marconi Company, it has therefore been secretly arranged between Isaacs and [Postmaster-General Herbert] Samuel that the British people shall give the Marconi Company a very large sum of money through the agency of the said Samuel, and for the benefit of the said Isaacs. Incidentally, the monopoly that is to be granted to Isaacs No. 2, through the ardent charity of Isaacs No. 1 and his colleague the Postmaster-General, is a monopoly involving antiquated methods, the refusal of competing tenders far cheaper and far more efficient, and the saddling of the country with corruptly purchased goods. . . . Another reason why the swindle, or rather theft, impudent and barefaced as it is, will go through is that we have in this country no method of punishing men who are guilty of this kind of thing.[8]

Even in the midst of controversy, however, the Marconi Wireless Telegraph Company (first established in 1897) became a powerful force by providing the technological standard of wireless communication in Britain as well as in other Western governments, including Italy (which had rejected Marconi's offer years before).

Within a short while, the United States government joined its European counterparts in soliciting Marconi's expertise. In September 1899 the Italian inventor sailed to New York to expand his horizons--both technologically and financially--and formed the American Marconi Company. Soon after he arrived, a young scientist named Lee de Forest approached him for a job. De Forest's letter of introduction was intelligent, enthusiastic, and candid:

Knowing that you are about to conduct experiments for the US Government in the wireless telegraphy I write you begging to be allowed to work at that under you. It may be that some assistants well versed in the theory of Hertz waves will be desired in that work, if so may I not be given the chance? . . . At present I am working for the Western Electric Company of this City [Chicago] in telephone work. As a young man you will I know fully appreciate the desire I feel in just starting out, to get a start in the lines of that fascinating field, so vast in extent, in which you have done so much. It has been my greatest ambition since first working with electric waves to make a life work of that study. If you can, signor, aid me in fulfilling this desire, you will win the lasting indebtedness, as you have already the admiration of Your obedient servant.[9]

De Forest was inadvertently denied the job; Marconi never even responded to his request. The young physicist later formed several of his own companies, claiming innovations that rivaled those found in Marconi's operation,[10] and vying for the title, "Father of Radio." De Forest also became a worthy opponent in subsequent legal cases similar to those filed against the Italian inventor in England.

AMERICAN MARCONI, DAVID SARNOFF, AND RCA

After successfully transmitting a signal across nine miles of English landscape in 1897,[11] Marconi dreamed of adding to his wireless empire by building an experimental laboratory for future entrepreneurial opportunities in the United States. By 1899 the American Marconi Company had established itself firmly in the New World, selling telegraphic equipment to many shipping businesses and employing scores of young men to send and receive "Marconi grams" throughout the country. Further, Marconi was gaining more recognition as the scientific leader in transatlantic communication. In 1901 he was able to transmit a signal (the Morse code "S") from Newfoundland to England, setting the stage for even more ambitious experimentation.

In 1906 Marconi was fated for further good fortune, although he didn't know it at the time. One day, as he toured the facilities of his American company, he was greeted by one of its newest employees--a sixteen-year-old Russian immigrant named David Sarnoff. The two got along well almost immediately, and before long, Sarnoff was promoted from office boy to Marconi's personal messenger. The young immigrant went on to receive an even greater amount of recognition six years later, when he was hailed as "the boy wonder of radio"[12] after telegraphing countless messages to anxious friends and family members during the Titanic disaster of 1912.

Sarnoff continued to be promoted at American Marconi in the years that followed; and through this experience, he began to see greater potential for wireless communication than had been recognized previously. In 1906 Lee de Forest's development of an audion vacuum tube had become available, expanding on Marconi's concept of point-to-point transmission and making it possible to send voices and music to several points of reception at once. Sarnoff was among the first to recognize the commercial possibilities of such an invention. In 1916 he proposed the idea of a "radio music box" to Marconi--a set (without headphones) that would allow many people at the same time to listen comfortably to signals sent from a central location. (This concept would later be referred to as *broadcasting*.) Ironically, Marconi was indifferent to his idea; but Sarnoff was not discouraged. He continued to work at the company until he was called into active military service for World War I. After the war, a subsidiary of General Electric, the newly-formed Radio Corporation of America (RCA), purchased American Marconi for $3.5 million.[13] Sarnoff was subsequently hired as RCA's general manager, and his vision of the "radio music box" became a reality soon afterwards.

Despite Marconi's lack of vision in the area of broadcasting, Sarnoff continued to have great respect for his former employer. Years later, in 1933, when Marconi was invited to tour the broadcast facilities of RCA's new Radio City Music Hall, he was greeted warmly by its Chairman of the Board, the former immigrant telegrapher,[14] who still believed the Italian inventor to be the true "Father of Radio." Marconi's impact on electronic communications was not finished, however. And as the world found itself bracing once again for international conflict, he turned his attention to his homeland for yet another scientific experiment.

MARCONI AND THE VATICAN

Guglielmo Marconi's specific involvement with Vatican Radio (the world's oldest transnational broadcast system) evolved from a unique combination of spiritual need, national pride, and marital stability. And, given world affairs at the turn of the century, the Catholic Church was anxious for his help.

In 1929 Pope Pius XI signed the Lateran Treaty with Benito Mussolini, guaranteeing papal sovereignty in the newly established Vatican State. However, as Fascism spread throughout Italy, Church officials became unsettled over certain portions of the Treaty, most specifically Article 12, which seemed unclear about the Pope's diplomatic powers during times of war. Although the Article acknowledged the right of the Holy See to *send* papal nuncios throughout the world at any time, it was less definitive about the rights to *receive* embassies during periods of crisis. Mussolini's interpretation of the pact's wording was characteristically rigid: He felt that the Pope had no guaranteed rights during political conflict. Thus, he warned Pius that future envoys might be captured should they cross over enemy soil to reach Vatican City.

The Pope, quite understandably, feared for the Vatican's safety and independence under such conditions. He consulted with many advisors to seek the best means to preserve papal world diplomacy, regardless of the temporal whims of Italy's politicians. After intense discussion, radio seemed to be the clear answer to his problem. At this point, he asked his Secretary of State, Cardinal Eugenio Pacelli,[15] to implore Guglielmo Marconi for help.

By 1930 Marconi, a middle-aged Protestant, had returned to Roman Catholicism after his second marriage--to Christina Bezzi-Scali, herself a staunchly religious woman. According to author W. P. Jolly:

Marconi's marriage to his Italian bride marked the start of a spiritual withdrawal into his home country. He traveled abroad still, but his interests were in Italy. He had administrative work in Rome in his government posts as Senator, President of the National Research Council, and President of the Royal Academy; his research interests moved towards radar and television which are systems of relatively short range so that experiments did not require him to move many miles from home; and his new family life bound him closely to Italy and also prompted him to push his old family further away--after the first two years of his marriage to Cristina the [three] children of his first marriage were no longer invited to spend summer holidays with him.[16]

After hearing Cardinal Pacelli's plea for technological help, Marconi was only too willing to serve his new Church. He also was delighted with the opportunity to test for himself the transnational limits of radio broadcasting. By the end of 1930 Marconi was often found in the Vatican gardens, personally supervising the construction and installation of (what would become) the world's first international broadcast operation. The facilities included four towers, with seven transmitters. At first glance, the Church grounds did not look markedly different; that, too, was part of Marconi's grand design:

Every effort has been made to harmonize as far as possible the transmitting building and aerial towers with the graceful surroundings of the Vatican City. The transmitting building is of sober but pleasing architectural design. The tops of the masts are finished off to give a Bishop's miter effect, which greatly enhances their appearance in silhouette. The transmitting building contains a spacious transmitting room with land line control tables, amplifier control room, receiving room, accumulator room, machine room, general store and general office.[17]

Only three months after conferring with Cardinal Pacelli and Pius XI, Marconi introduced his new system at the February 12, 1931, inaugural ceremonies for Vatican Radio--the world's first transnational broadcast station. Unlike the American and British radio systems, Vatican Radio's mission seemed relatively uncomplicated at first: "[to spread] the Gospel, in its specific religious meaning as the revealed word of God and in its wider meaning of the Christian view of the whole of reality and all aspects of human life."[18] But like the other two, VR would also experience great change and growth as the century evolved.

MARCONI'S LEGACY TO WORLD BROADCASTING

Within 20 years (1931--Vatican Radio; 1932--the British Broadcasting Company's Empire Service; 1942--the Voice of America; 1950--Radio Free Europe; and 1951--Radio Liberty), Marconi's historic vision linking the Western world through international communications had come to fruition. Despite commonalities in technological authorship, however, these countries had quite unique and differing perspectives on the functions of transnational broadcasting, as evidenced by their original charters. At first, governmentally supported operations (such as VOA and the BBC) perceived their primary mission to be disseminating nationalistic views and values to citizens in faraway places. Privately owned systems, like RFE and RL, saw themselves instead to be surrogate broadcasters, serving those who could not transmit news and information themselves. In contrast to the secular systems, religious groups such as VR were committed solely to propagating their own religious doctrine.

As technologies and political diplomacy became more complex toward the second half of the century, transnational broadcasters realized that the world was quickly becoming a "global village." The original goals and objectives of these diverse groups were thus rejected as somewhat simplistic, outdated, and in need of reform.

RESEARCHING TRANSNATIONAL RADIO

Though many nation states maintain transnational media systems, in this book, we focus on the structure and the impetus for the transnational radio systems of three sovereign states--the Vatican, Great Britain, and the United States. First, utilizing the journalistic five-part canon of "who, what, when, where, and why" in its Burkean "action" form (act, scene, agent, agency purpose), we look at two Christian radios--Vatican Radio (VR) broadcasting from inside the Vatican, as well as Radio Veritas (DZRV) broadcasting from the Philippines. Second, we discuss Great Britain's BBC, formerly (in 1932) the "Empire Service" and now in 1996 (one year before the end of its major emblems of imperialism--the return of Hong Kong to China in 1997), the "World Service." Third, we look at the fragmented array of American radios: Radio Free Europe/Radio Liberty (RFE/RL) with headquarters in Prague; Voice of America (VOA), broadcasting from Washington, D.C.; the anti-Castro Radio Marti, broadcasting from Washington, D.C., and the newly created Radio Free Asia (RFA was mandated by Congress in 1994). Viewed as too confrontational by many, principally American businesspeople with investments in China and U.S. Senators and Representatives with a vested interest in keeping these businesspeople happy, the radio's name was changed to Radio Free Asia/Asia Pacific Network (APN). Broadcasting from Washington, D.C. to China in Mandarin began in September 1996.

With the exceptions of RFA/APN and Radio Marti, the radios we will focus on have been credited by eveyone from Vaclav Havel to Boris Yeltsin with playing a significant role in the demise of the Soviet Union, the dissolution of the Eastern Bloc, and the subsequent formation of independent nation states. With this in mind, we set about attempting to ascertain the validity of this perception of transnational radio's effectiveness as a player in the Cold War.

Our first direct encounter with transnational radio perceived as a serious influence upon the so-called democratization of the Soviet Bloc occurred in August 1990. In Poland, we visited the Shrine of the Black Madonna at the Jasna Gora Monastery in Czestochowa, arguably the most sacred site in all of Poland. Following the viewing of the Black Madonna, we exited the chapel to find ourselves in a room overflowing with Solidarity memorabilia, heightening our awareness of the partnership between the Church and the media in the triumph of the Solidarity Movement in Poland. Later, as we traveled throughout Hungary, the Czech Republic, Slovakia, and East Germany, we were able to validate our first impressions, noting the importance of racial and ethnic identities (through religion, music, folklore and language) to bond people together. Tied inextricably with cultural identity was the impact of underground radio in unifying groups toward social movement. Whether through religious ceremony coupled with news (Vatican Radio), surrogate news reporting (Radio Free Europe/Radio Liberty), or the so-called Western democratic role models (VOA, the BBC), transnational broadcasting created a vision of freedom that seemed realistic and attainable. How well--and accurately--this vision was portrayed and ultimately achieved is illustrated through the case studies in this book.

The methodology used in Phase 1 of this study began with the historical-critical approach coupled with computer mediated research and communication. In Phase 2, we utilized descriptive methodology, conducting audiotape-assisted team interviewing at various sites in Eastern Europe, beginning this process at Solidarity headquarters in Gdansk, Poland. There we interviewed Andrzej Adamczyk, International Secretary, Solidarity Trade Union; Andrzej Matla, Head, International Department, Solidarity Trade Union; and, Robert Fielding, former interpreter for President Lech Walesa. Travelling by train, we then went to Krakow, Poland, where Dr. Jadwiga Smith (graduate of the Jagellonian University in Krakow and now Associate Professor of English at Bridgewater State College) had arranged several interviews for us, including one with well known former dissident Bronislaw Wildstein (formerly a Paris-based RFE/RL correspondent), now head of Radio Krakow. We then spent a week in Munich, Germany, at RFE/RL headquarters conducting team interviews (14), utilizing the open-ended question technique.

Whereas the historical-critical phase of our research seemed to confirm our initial impression in Czestochowa--that is that transnational radio must have had significant impact upon the democratization of Eastern Europe--our work at RFE/RL headquarters in Munich, Germany, led to a somewhat different perspective and the need to develop new questions. This new direction was in large part due to our findings at the very well endowed RFE/RL Research Institute (located in Munich), which was not founded until 1989. Until that time, doing well-conducted audience research was not possible within Eastern Europe or the former Soviet Union. Subsequent field work at VOA headquarters in Washington, D.C., in May 1994 revealed that VOA also did not (and unlike RFE/RL, still does not) conduct significant audience research. Personnel at both VOA and RFE/RL praised the audience research conducted by the BBC.

Thus, we have a dilemma. There appears to be a lack of a reliable statistical database to substantiate many of the claims made by both RFE/RL and the VOA regarding the impact of transnational radio upon the democratization of the former communist states. Perhaps this work will be done later; although in the interim, circumstances have changed, and the research institute will serve RFE/RL, the VOA, and the newly mandated Radio Free Asia/Asia Pacific Network.

Our research program further evolved when, by the time we reached Munich in August, 1993, it then seemed (the situation is now different) that only one American transnational radio system would survive congressional economic cutbacks. In the quest for survival, RFE/RL and VOA were jousting rhetorically, each backed by the positive claims of former dissidents and current heads of state in Eastern (or Central) Europe, in the media and in the Congress.

In our interviews with the management staff at the three Radios--including William Marsh (RFE/RL Executive Vice President, Programs and Policy), Kevin Klose (Director, Radio Liberty) and Robert Gillette (Director, Radio Free Europe) as well as Ted Lipien (Affiliate Relations, VOA-Europe)--a clear distinction was drawn between RFE/RL and the VOA (prior to 1989). Like

CNN (and unlike RFE/RL), VOA is a worldwide service and VOA-Europe broadcasts in English only with "programming based upon scripts centrally written by Americans." Unlike RFE/RL, it was not meant to be a surrogate facility, "to speak for those who cannot speak," nor has it ever taken on that role. Merging these two divergent broadcast facilities and philosophies may, in fact, diminish them both. As Kevin Klose, former Moscow correspondent for the *Washington Post* and present director of Radio Liberty, puts it,

Journalism, well done, is very powerful and very fragile, you start messing with it, its sense of self, its independence from the people who pay its way and things start changing in the cadres' head and pretty soon, very quickly, it's up the antenna and out. These are people [in the recently released countries of the former Soviet Union] who have spent the last 75 years struggling with the poison of government run media, they are very, very, sensitive to the issue of how it sounds, is it credible enough.[19]

Perception and credibility are serious issues. For years Americans have railed against government controlled media everywhere, advocating the free press approach followed in the United States. Why then is the American government proposing (in 1996) more invasive government control over information dissemination *in other countries?* Phasing a federalized RFE/RL into the VOA under the aegis of the United States Information Agency increases the propaganda quotient, diminishing journalistic integrity. As Vaclav Havel, president of the Czech Republic, said in a letter to President Clinton in March 1993, "This radio station (RFE) is helping the citizens of our country as well as in the whole Eastern Europe, to create a democratic awareness and conduct. . . . Its journalistic standards are a model for our mass media."

In our quest thus far, these points seem clear to us:

1. Transnational radio reflects/shapes the world(s) it serves;
2. Different political/ideological forces drive each of the models;
3. Models are in flux due to political/technological changes;
4. Transnational radio systems differ in approach/extent of propaganda;
5. After the fall of the Wall, policy changes in Western transnational radio systems still reflect the Cold War "Star Wars" rhetorical vision of democracy/capitalism versus communism in the "emerging world order;"
6. Journalistic integrity and ethics are central issues in all the above.

The latter two points were clearly at issue when we conducted interviews in Washington, D.C., in April 1994. With Radio Free Asia (RFA) about to become reality (at that time the legislation had been passed authorizing the creation of Radio Free Asia), many were concerned about the means and goals of the new service. As in some of our interviews at RFE/RL, during our China Branch interview at VOA we were asked to turn the tape recorder off, for the issue of using mainland Chinese dissidents to program the service is a complicated one. As Betty Tseu explained,

"Dissident service" depends on how you define dissidents. Do you mean the dissidents in the United States, or do you mean the dissidents left in China? These are becoming two quite different groups. The Radio Free Asia project is immensely popular with the dissidents in the United States, because everyone would be 120 percent for it.[20]

After mandating Radio Free Asia in 1994, Congress was forced to rethink the project, because RFA's name and purpose was considered by many (in response to outrage from the People's Republic of China and American businesspeople doing business in the PRC) to be "too confrontational." In our 1994 interview China Branch personnel said, "So certainly we try to provoke people's minds. But VOA's policy and the Chinese branch policy has never been to incite rebellion. We want people to think about their lives, to think about their society, and to think about their systems."[21]

In a June 1996 telephone conversation Richard Richter, newly selected president of the Asia Pacific Network, asserted that, unlike the VOA, the Asia Pacific Network (APN) "is not the official voices of the U.S. government." Indeed, he states that APN will be "similar in content and tone to NPR and not an agent for instant provocation."[22] Clearly, the sting of assertions and charges following in the wake of VOA participation in the Tiananmen media event remains. But close reading of "The Role of the Chinese National News Media and the Voice of America in the 1989 Chinese Pro-Democracy Movement" reveals that the BBC (discussed in Chapter 2) may have, from time to time, been even more aggressive than the VOA during the Tiananmen crisis of 1989.

In our 1994 interview at VOA in Washington, D.C., we asked Kim Elliott, head of audience research at VOA, about his perception of the creation/structure of Radio Free Asia, as well as his perceptions regarding the structure of the BBC. Acknowledging that "the BBC usually rates highest in credibility," Elliott pointed out that the BBC World Service management "is able to stay around and build up expertise, whereas often times VOA front office management, and RFE/RL too, is just people with good political connections without any particular expertise."[23] Unlike the BBC World Service, which can hire and fire based upon expertise, or the lack thereof, the VOA is staffed with civil servants. Further, Elliott's final arguments on the primacy of the BBC in the world of transnational radio had to do with the economics of the two systems.

Elliott claims that the addition of RFA (now APN) will be "the downfall of the American transnational radio system,"[24] because, unlike the BBC organizational structure, VOA, RFE/RL, and RFA/APN are separate entities, not a single unitary organization. Add to this the fact that the American radios are staffed with civil servants, and one understands why the United States spends twice as much as Britain on international broadcasting. Elliott went on to say that the BBC world service has

more listeners than VOA, twice as many as VOA, more than VOA and RFE/RL combined. They are very efficient and we are not. They are unitary . . . and can make adjustments for the mix in each target area, and ours are divided, thus we are not competing well with other countries' international broadcasting.[25]

Further illuminating differences between the American models and the British model for transnational radio takes one into the realm of the origins and original mission statements of the various services. In contrast to RFE/RL, the BBC was created as an independent corporation, its news insulated from government control, whilst RFE/RL was created to be an anticommunist organization, dispensing anticommunist propaganda. A common theme emerging from all our interviews is that people receiving broadcasts from other nations now want hard news--not propaganda. Someone has observed that, after all, if listeners want propaganda, they can tune in to their domestic programming.

During our field work, several issues developed that we will deal with in some depth in this book. First, our original premise--that RFE/RL and VOA had impact on the democratization of Eastern Europe--is a complicated one, difficult to research, perhaps impossible to prove. Second, given the restructuring of the American transnational system (unless the gods intervene), there is scant hope for Western-style journalism to prevail in this system, so long as the primary purpose is not to deliver hard news but, to a large extent, propaganda intended to create dissent in countries such as China. The driving force of the existing transnational model is to spread our brand of capitalism/democracy, at any cost, despite the rhetorical stance of RFE/RL and VOA. On the other hand, the BBC World Service model both meets minimal journalistic standards and is economically viable.

In the following pages, we examine the rhetoric of each of the transnational radios systems under scrutiny here: Vatican Radio, Radio Veritas, the BBC World Service, Radio Free Europe/Radio Liberty, Voice of America, Radio Martí, and Radio Free Asia/Asia Pacific Network. We critically analyze the statements of personnel of each service and its audience, contrasting mission statements with action. We also employ and use case studies by other scholars to develop our arguments. Concepts such as journalistic integrity/ethics and the utility/futility of propaganda are key issues in this discussion, as well as the development and trajectory of such central concepts as freedom and democracy.

NOTES

1. G. K. Chesterton, *Autobiography* (London: Hutchinson, 1936), 202.

2. Degna Marconi, *My Father, Marconi* (New York: McGraw-Hill, 1962), 15.

3. According to historians, one of the most renowned scientific scholars at the University of Bologna during these years was Augusto Righi. Righi also happened to be a neighbor of the Marconis. Annie Marconi tried for years to forge a solid relationship between Guglielmo and Professor Righi, but the physicist discouraged it. Finally, after much discussion, Righi agreed to let young Marconi audit his classes, without credit.

4. Andrew F. Inglis, *Behind the Tube: A History of Broadcasting Technology and Business* (Boston: Focal Press, 1990), 33-35.

5. Frances Donaldson, *The Marconi Scandal* (New York: Harcourt, Brace & World, Inc., 1962), 13.

6. W. P. Jolly, *Marconi* (New York: Stein and Day, 1972), 34-35.

7. Ibid., 42.

8. Donaldson, 23.

9. Jolly, 74.

10. Like Marconi, de Forest was not without his detractors. Critics claimed that the American had not only taken ideas for his inventions from other scientists; many times he didn't even understand the principles of physics behind them. Most notable among his accusers was inventor Edwin Howard Armstrong, who successfully sued de Forest for the latter's assertions that Armstrong had taken too much credit for his improvements on de Forest's patented vacuum audion tube. During court testimony, Armstrong was exonerated, however, because de Forest had trouble explaining simple concepts behind the tube, much less the intricate innovations added to it.

11. Jolly, 37. This series of experiments actually took place on Salisbury Plain, and had begun almost a year before the successful nine-mile transmission.

12. "Empire of the Air," aired on PBS, 29 January 1992.

13. Inglis, 54.

14. Marconi, 293-294.

15. Cardinal Pacelli later succeeded Pius XI, to become Pope Pius XII.

16. Jolly, 261-262.

17. "Pope to Dedicate Radio Tomorrow," *New York Times.* 11 February 1931, 28.

18. James J. Onder, "The Sad State of Vatican Radio," *Educational Broadcasting Review* (August 1971): 45.

19. RFE/RL Director Kevin Klose, interview by authors, 7 August 1993, tape recording, Munich, Germany.

20. Betty Tseu, Chief, Mandarin Service, Chinese Branch, VOA and John Harbaugh, Special Assistant, Chinese Branch, VOA, interview by authors, 28 April 1994, tape recording, Washington, D.C.

21. Ibid.

22. Richard Richter, President, Asia Pacific Network, phone interview by Street, 14 June 1996, Boston/Washington, D.C.

23. VOA Audience Analysis Division Officer Kim Andrew Elliott, interview by authors, 28 April 1994, tape recording, Washington, D.C. Elliott made it clear that his comments were personal opinions only and not necessarily reflective of the Voice of America.

24. Ibid.

25. Ibid.

Part I

BRIEF OVERVIEWS OF VATICAN, BRITISH, AND AMERICAN TRANSNATIONAL SERVICES

1

Vatican Radio: Papal Visions for Propagating the Faith

Marilyn J. Matelski and Nancy Lynch Street

Vatican Radio, established in 1931, is recognized as the world's first truly transnational radio system. However, shortly after its inception, Catholic ecclesiastical leaders recognized hidden complexities within the new technology. On the one hand, broadcast communication would create heretofore unimagined opportunities for instantaneous message dissemination; conversely, the messages chosen for this medium would now be required to reflect a more universal diplomatic reality. The "global village" of Roman Catholicism had now entered into a new era.

ORIGINS OF THE MEDIUM

The original mission for Vatican Radio can be traced back as early as 1870, when the Papal States were invaded by the new Italian army. This act of aggression drove Pope Pius IX into exile in Vatican City, essentially depriving him of all temporal power and status in the Western world. In fact, from 1870 until the adoption of the Lateran Treaty (1929), the Pope, although Bishop of Rome, was for all intents and purposes a prisoner within his own country.

After the Lateran Pact was signed, Vatican City was established as an independent, sovereign entity from Italy, with separate laws, currency, and even postage stamps. The Pope (now Pius XI) was also free to travel wherever and whenever he wanted. As tensions began to grow between Pius XI and Italy's fascist dictator, Benito Mussolini, the implicit threat of future repression lingered. Because the Catholic Church wanted never again to repeat its recent record of defeat in modern world politics, members of the ecclesiastical hierarchy sought ways to strengthen the Vatican's power--both within and without.

Cardinal Eugenio Pacelli, then Vatican Secretary of State (and later Pope Pius XII) was a leader among those who proposed ways of avoiding any hint of future papal exile. Pacelli suggested that the Holy See investigate the possibilities of incorporating a new medium--radio--into Church propagation. Through radio, no pope could ever be driven into isolation again; geographic and political borders had become virtually meaningless when confronted by the "airwaves" of broadcast technology.[1] Pius XI listened intently to the Secretary of State's arguments and later supported his proposal to build a transnational system for the Catholic Church. Accordingly, in 1930, Pacelli began negotiations with inventor Guglielmo Marconi to create a powerful shortwave radio system, as well as an efficient telephone operation for Vatican use.

With the technological blueprints of Vatican Radio in place, the Pope began to consider the operational responsibilities of this potentially powerful communicative force. The new transnational broadcast system, he reasoned, would require a certain knowledge, dedication, and commitment to the goals of the pope and of the Catholic Church through the next millennium. At the time, Father Giuseppe Gianfranceschi, S.J., President of the Pontifical Academy of Sciences, seemed to be a natural choice. As a result, on September 21, 1930, the Holy See named Father Gianfranceschi as director of the newly constructed "Vatican Radio" station. The Society of Jesus, quite naturally, became the religious order appointed to run the facility.

Construction of the Vatican radio facility went quickly and smoothly. On February 12, 1931, within months of his original discussions with Cardinal Pacelli, Pope Pius XI blessed the world's first transnational radio system, Vatican Radio. Giugliemo Marconi was accorded the honor of introducing his newest creation to the world. Despite a few transmissional imperfections,[2] Marconi's enthusiasm was received clearly by all who listened:

It is my very great honor and privilege to announce to you that within a few moments the supreme Pontiff, his Holiness, Pius XI will inaugurate the radio station of the State of Vatican City. The electric ways will carry his august words of peace and benediction throughout the world.

For nearly twenty centuries the Roman Pontiffs have given their inspired messages to all people, but this is the first time in history that the living voice of the Pope will have been heard simultaneously in all parts of the globe. With the help of Almighty God, who places such mysterious forces of nature at mankind's disposal, I have been able to prepare this instrument that will give to the faithful throughout the world the consolation of hearing the voice of the Holy Father.[3]

Following Marconi's inaugural remarks, Pius XI continued the historic broadcast by praising the Italian radio inventor, commending the new medium, and asking God to bless both:

Having in God's mysterious designs become the successor of the Prince of the Apostles, those Apostles whose doctrine and preaching were by Divine command destined for all nations and for every creature, and being the first Pope to make use of this truly wonderful Marconian invention, we, in the first place, turn to all things and all men and we say to them: Hear, O ye Heavens, the things I speak, let the earth give ear all ye of my mouth; hear these things all ye nations; give ear all ye inhabitants of the world both rich and poor together; give ear ye islands and harken ye people from afar to Almighty God.[4]

Those who heard the Pontiff's unabashed delight to be "the first Pope to make use of this truly wonderful Marconian invention"[5] were amazed at the technical clarity of his message on shortwave. In fact, many executives at NBC (the primary American recipient of Vatican Radio's historic transmission) characterized its inaugural ceremony as one of the twelve most dramatic events of its decade.[6]

Thus began a new era in Roman Catholic propagation. In Radio Vaticana's first decade of broadcast, its mission seemed relatively uncomplicated. The Jesuits, charged with managing the station, were told to spread "the Gospel, in its specific religious meaning as the revealed word of God and in its wider meaning of the Christian view of the whole of reality and all aspects of human life."[7] They accepted the challenge gladly.

THE GOLDEN YEARS

Within six months of broadcast operation, Vatican Radio had become a significant force in Church propagation, programming portions of its content to diverse audiences in seven languages.[8] One of the most significant broadcasts of this era occurred on May 15, 1931, during the 40th anniversary of Pope Leo XIII's famous encyclical, *Rerum Novarum*. In an hour-long sermon over Vatican Radio airwaves, Pope Pius XI used the occasion to emphasize religious institutionalism (i.e., allegiance to the pope, professed faith in the Catholic Church, and recognition of the importance of sacramental practice) within the contexts of socialism and the labor movement. He also took the opportunity to introduce a new encyclical, *Quadragesimo Anno*. Unfortunately, however, the Pontiff mixed too many metaphors from his encyclical and that of Pope Leo, causing listeners to be confused over the Church's religious teachings versus its political stance within fascist Italy. This confusion was later augmented by some curious twists in papal diplomacy (such as the 1933 Concordat with Hitler and the 1935 declaration of support for Mussolini's conquest of Ethiopia). Before long, the Holy See was faced once again with the tumultuous challenge of "walking the line" between sacred and secular issues. Ecclesiastical leaders looked to Vatican Radio, among other propaganda sources, to help the Pope through many stormy days ahead.

In 1938, Pius XI attempted to further clarify his position as Church leader by instituting a "Catholic Information Service" via Vatican Radio airwaves, managed by the Jesuits, and created solely to attack the atheistic propaganda coming from Germany, Italy, Japan, and Russia. With added broadcast power (now transmitting in 10 languages on both short- and mediumwave), this act clearly established radio as a primary medium for the Pontiff's anticommunist message. The "new" propaganda campaign continued through the last days of Pius XI's life, as well as during the reign of his successor, Cardinal Pacelli (Pope Pius XII).

On March 12, 1939, Cardinal Eugenio Pacelli became Pius XII, the new Bishop of Rome. Vatican Radio aired the entire ceremony, reaching a large portion of the world's 300 million Catholics. Many churches (including those in the United States) stayed open throughout the night so that the faithful could experience together all the speeches and musical performances related to the new Pontiff's spiritual inauguration. After the ceremonial fanfare, Pius XII recruited Vatican Radio's help for a much more serious cause--transmitting his spiritual and temporal messages during World War II.

Pius XII quickly ascertained the importance of radio as a message disseminator to vast territories instantaneously and hence reaching far greater numbers of people within a shorter period of time than any other medium in the late 1930s and early 1940s. Further, radio voices often communicated more emotionally, dramatically, and persuasively than most other informational sources. Because of this efficacy, radio was used extensively not only by the Vatican but by all major powers as the world prepared itself for war. Author Julian Hale quotes former German radio executive Eugene Hadamowski on the medium's potential for his nation and others:

We spell radio with three exclamation marks because we are possessed in it of a miraculous power--the strongest weapon ever given to the spirit--that opens hearts and does not stop at the borders of cities and does not turn back before closed doors; that jumps rivers, mountains, and seas; that is able to force peoples under the spell of one powerful spirit.[9]

Radio Vaticana's policy began as one of neutrality during the war years. Pius XII had reemphasized the Roman Catholic Church's traditional position, one of supramorality and universality, throughout the years of prewar skirmishes. When aggression became more severe and global battle seemed to be inevitable, diplomatic neutrality was not an easy policy to maintain. For example, when Italy declared war on France and Great Britain, both Allied envoys moved to the Vatican enclave. Ironically, when the tides of war began to favor the Allied Forces, Pius XII found himself obligated to offer the same safe harbor to the Axis countries. Amid this backdrop, personnel at Vatican Radio were asked to do many things, which involved covert activities as well as humanitarian assistance. Some of the most courageous broadcasts aired by Radio Vaticana at this time were those that unveiled the horrors of the Nazi Holocaust. On January 20, 1940, an American Jesuit became the first announcer in world radio to report the imprisonment of Jewish and Polish prisoners in "sealed ghettos." From that point on, Vatican Radio continued to feature stories on concentration camps and other Nazi torture chambers. From 1940 to 1946, Vatican Radio also ran an Information Office, transmitting almost 1.25 million shortwave messages to locate prisoners of war and other missing persons. Later the radio system combined its information services with the International Refugee Organization, forming a team "Tracing Service" to reunite war-torn families and friends.

By 1949 Vatican Radio returned to its prewar programming schedule, broadcasting in 19 languages throughout the world[10] and competing for transnational listenership with such networks as the Voice of America, Radio Moscow, and Radio Peking. The onset of the Cold War (and Stalin's growing number of "godless communism" messages) brought with it a renewed commitment to boost the Church's radio service. Underground radio had become one of the only ways to communicate with countries such as Hungary and Poland--largely Catholic populations that had been placed behind the Iron Curtain of the USSR.

Thus, in 1950, in order to combat the "Moscow-inspired atheistic propaganda being poured into the ears of bewildered Catholics in Iron Curtain countries,"[11] Vatican Radio officials asked for contributions from the faithful to expand the transnational system's facilities. With this money, Pius XII proposed to use Vatican Radio vigilantly, broadcasting 24 hours each day, in at least 28 languages. The "free world" responded to this announcement enthusiastically, contributing almost $2.5 million to the cause. The new facilities took almost six years to build. In 1957, Radio Vaticana introduced its newly finished, high-powered station to the world. The renovated system now sent its signal via two new 10-kilowatt shortwave transmitters (to add to the shortwave tranmission power of its 100-kw transmitter), one 250-kw mediumwave transmitter (augmenting the earlier 100-kw mediumwave transmitter), a 328-foot multidirectional antenna for medium-wave broadcasts to Southern, Central, and Eastern Europe, and 21 additional antennas. Pius XII visited the transmitter site, pressed two buttons to start the broadcast, and used his first minutes of airtime for an appeal for peace in the Middle East and in other world hot spots.

In addition to circumventing the Russians' attempt to jam the signal, the new transmission power of Vatican Radio reached new areas in North and South America and much of Asia. Coupled with the establishment of a Pontifical Commission for Cinematography, Radio and Television, the Holy See clearly established its commitment to transnational media propagation.

As mass communication technology continued to grow during the late 1940s and early 1950s, public figures from all areas of the world assumed a new dimension of celebrity recognition, enhanced by a powerful media spotlight, ever-focused upon their words, actions, and associations. Pope Pius XII was no exception to this rule: His election to the papacy had consumed the pages and airtime of most Western media sources in 1939; and his subsequent interviews, speeches, encyclicals, acts of diplomacy, political alliances, and personal vulnerabilities over the next two decades continued to draw the attention of newspapers and radio, as well as the "newest media kid on the block," television. Pius XII's experiences with the secular media served to underscore his commitment to Vatican Radio, firmly defining its broadcast policy in the late 1950s.

By 1958, however, the Pontiff had reigned for almost twenty years, leading his Church through a major global war as well as through a dramatically changing technological, theological, and diplomatic world. In October of that year, unfortunately, Radio Vaticana had the unhappy task of broadcasting the last days of his life. Several of the radio reports turned out to be false and ill-founded, due to some confusion between Curia officials, the Church media, and the secular press. Despite the inaccuracies, though, one fact was painfully clear: Pius XII had finally succumbed to ill health on October 9.

Shortly after Pope Pius' death, Vatican Radio programmers (along with the rest of the world) wondered aloud about the choice of a new Pontiff and his political leanings. Their doubts and fears about the fate of Vatican Radio were soon allayed, with the election of Cardinal Angelo Giuseppe Roncalli (adopting the papal name, John XXIII) as the new Bishop of Rome. Pope John XXIII was modern, liberal, and extremely media literate. Immediately after his election, the new Pontiff announced plans for a Second Vatican Council.

According to British author (and former Jesuit) Peter Hebblethwaite, however, Roman Curia conservatives were not particularly pleased with Pope John's proposed new direction for the Council and attempted to construct as many roadblocks to its success as possible along the way. Such obstacles began shortly after the Pontiff's opening convocation to Vatican II (broadcast via Vatican Radio), which was later "edited" for the permanent collection of official papal documents. His actual speech was recorded as follows:

Our task is not merely to hoard this precious treasure [the Catholic Church], as though obsessed with the past, but to give ourselves eagerly and without fear to the task that the present age demands of us--and in so doing we will be faithful to what the Church has done in the last twenty centuries. So the main point of this Council will not be to debate this or that article of basic Church doctrine that has been repeatedly taught by the Fathers and theologians old and new and which we can take as read. You do not need a Council to do that. But starting from a renewed, serene and calm acceptance of the whole teaching of the Church in all its scope and detail as it is found in Trent and Vatican I, Christians and Catholics of apostolic spirit all the world over expect a leap [balzo] forwards in doctrinal insight [penetrazione] and the education of consciences [la formazione delle conscienze] in ever greater fidelity to authentic teaching. But this authentic doctrine has to be studied and expounded in the light of the research methods and the language [formulazione letteraria] of modern thought. For the substance of the ancient deposit of faith is one thing, and the way in which it is presented is another.[12]

Those in the Curia who held a more traditional view of the Church objected to the last sentence and later "edited" it for publication in *Acta Apostolicae Sedis* (the official record of papal documents). The term, "substance of faith," was eliminated and was replaced by other, more qualified phrases. The final "draft" for official publication reads like this (italics added for the Curia-inspired modifications):

For the . . . deposit of faith *itself, or the truths which are contained in our venerable doctrine*, is one thing, and the way in which *they are expressed* is another, *retaining however the same sense of meaning.*[13]

Further, there was no mention of doctrinal "movement" of any kind, much less the "leap forwards" encouraged by the Pontiff.[14]

As Hebblewaite reports in *Pope John XXIII: Shepherd of the Modern World,*

When the pope discovered these outrageous changes in late November 1962, he was too canny to sack the editor of *Acta Apostolicae Sedis* [the repository of official Vatican papers]. He simply quoted himself, in the original nonedited version, in important speeches.[15]

Many of these speeches were given on Vatican Radio, with the help of many Jesuits. They complied gladly with his wishes, especially those liberal forces who had been unleashed through Vatican II. Thus, the Pontiff's position on Church modernization, though stymied in a formal way, nevertheless found a platform informally through speeches, interviews, letters, and broadcasts on Vatican Radio (which, of course, was run by the Jesuits).

Following the Council's convocation (in 1962), Pope John solicited help from the Jesuits and Vatican Radio to make certain that his vision for the Church was recorded accurately. He also used Vatican Radio airwaves in 1962 to mediate in the Soviet-American standoff over missiles found in Cuba, broadcasting pleas to both Khruschev and Kennedy. The crisis was later aborted, due in part to the efforts of Pope John and Vatican Radio.

Because a great part of John XXIII's plan for papal diplomacy and ecumenical reform involved message dissemination through Radio Vaticana, the Pope set out to improve the technology that would accommodate his increasing need for extensive broadcast coverage. To this end, Vatican Radio underwent tremendous growth in the late fifties and early sixties. In 1960, the Pontiff announced plans to build and operate more powerful stations in Asia[16] and Africa,[17] reaffirming the missionary responsibilities of his holy office:

The Roman Catholic Church has a doctrine that permits her to answer the grave problems of men. She moreover places at their disposal in a disinterested fashion principles of action most useful to the development of individual, family, professional, civil and international life.[18]

Recurrent themes of spiritual values and international unity pervade in many of John XXIII's broadcasts at this time. On February 12, 1961, for example, the Pope used the occasion of Vatican Radio's 30th anniversary to impart his apostolic blessing to "the whole human family,"[19] as well as to use radio "to overcome the barriers of nationality, of race, [and] of social class."[20] Vatican Radio responded to his wishes repeatedly, most notably in Christian-Jewish relations, as evidenced (just a few months later) in the Adolph Eichmann trial.

During the Eichmann trial, it became apparent that many Catholics, especially in Germany, resisted any suggestion of a connection between Christian-based anti-Semitism and Nazi racism prior to World War II. In point of fact, most scholars would agree that a link between the two perspectives, though certainly correlational, was not necessarily causal. However, Jewish survivors and their families from around the world insisted that without admitting to this link, future relations between Christians and Jews would be tenuous at best. Realizing the enormity of this problem, John XXIII called upon Vatican Radio to make this statement--an apology for German Christians:

[Although] the existence of the concentration camps was no secret, skilled propaganda and the impossibility of direct contact with prisoners made the masses believe Propaganda Minister Joseph Goebbels' description of them as "educational establishments.". . . The want of foresight, resolution, and unity among [the clergymen at this time] involves them to a certain degree in responsibility and should make them bow in humble confession under God's judgment. In spite of exceptions, however, the general attitude of Christians was so clear, outspoken and perceptible, that the Nazis recognized in believing Christians their most confessed adversaries.[21]

With these statements, the Pope was able to mend a few immediate fences between Christians and Jews, as well as to acknowledge anti-Semitism as a serious world concern and to place the issue on his Vatican II agenda.

By 1962, through experiences like the fence-mending incident just mentioned above, John XXIII had reestablished Vatican Radio as "a living and concrete expression of the universality of the Church."[22] The world's oldest transnational broadcast system now beamed programming in 30 languages, 17 of which were specifically intended for nations behind the Iron Curtain. And, according to Vatican officials, its purpose was both political and religious:

The delicate phase of the rapid evolution towards full political and social status through which so many countries of Africa and Asia are going, an evolution which is being followed by the Holy Father with special attention and interest, has rendered all the more necessary a service from the Vatican Radio. It is a service that has been requested for a long time by the faithful and by the Hierarchies of these continents. The remarkable number of radio stations in Latin America which link themselves daily with the Vatican Radio to relay its programmes, shows the utility and the interest that these have for the Catholics of the entire continent.[23]

Thus, by its 30th anniversary in 1961, Vatican Radio had truly experienced a golden age. Soon after the construction of its new transmitters, however, the world's oldest transnational radio system began to decline--first, by the loss of its visionary pope; and later, by a sharp reduction in perceived power and credibility at the Vatican.

THE DECLINE OF A "RADIO INSTITUTION"

On Monday, June 3, 1963, at 7:53 p.m., Vatican Radio gave this brief announcement: "With a soul profoundly moved, we give this following sad announcement: The Supreme Pontiff, John XXIII, is dead."[24] After one of the shortest reigns in modern papal history--just four years, seven months, and six days--one of the most universally loved and respected pontiffs had succumbed to his bout with stomach cancer.

As the historic conclave began, at least six cardinals were nominated as potential successors to the Papal Throne. Of these, Cardinal Archbishop Giovanni Battista Montini of Milan was the name mentioned most often by both liberals and conservatives alike. Montini had been a close associate to Pope John in such important matters as the Second Vatican Council and the Moscow-Vatican Pact; but he had also built a strong reputation as a traditionalist, having served Pius XII from 1939 to 1954 and having managed one of the most complex archdioceses in Italy for over eight years. Many remembered his qualifications from the papal election five years earlier, where he was lauded as a brilliant diplomat, a linguistic genius, and an organizational wizard. He was also a widely traveled scholar, knowledgeable about Catholic dogma as well as the Roman Curia. At 66 years old, he also seemed to be the right age for the position--for unlike the previous election, many cardinals were anxious for a papal candidate with a potentially long life span. After only five ballots were cast, white smoke billowed from the chimney at the Vatican Palace: a new pope had been elected. Cardinal Giovanni Battista Montini, adopting the pontifical name Paul VI, greeted the crowds with warmth and promise.

Montini's first official act as Pope was to reconvene the Second Vatican Council, promising "to this main work we will devote all Our powers."[25] Accordingly, on September 19, 1963, the new Pontiff re-opened Vatican II with this brief summary of its goals: "1) The notion, or if you prefer, the awareness of the Church; 2) Her renewal; 3) The restoration of unity among all Christians; 4) The Church's dialogue with the men of our own day."[26] Pope Paul went on to say that while the Church needed rejuvenation (both in doctrine and in ecclesiastical structure), this "facelift" should not be taken as a departure from the original vision of its founder. Care must be taken to redefine the role of Roman Catholicism without destroying its basic tenets.

However, whereas John XXIII had also viewed the members of the Society of Jesus as strong allies for Catholic modernism at the Second Vatican Council, Paul VI became somewhat dubious over the Order's ultimate goals in post-Vatican II, especially after listening to reports from several sources. To confirm (or allay) his suspicions, Pope Paul allegedly compiled an extensive dossier on the Jesuits, which, Malachi Martin reports, suggested a lack of commitment to Church values and its hierarchy.[27]

Clearly, by the mid-1970s, the Society of Jesus had sown its seeds of discontent with Paul VI, leaving the future of the management of Vatican Radio in jeopardy. Sensing the breakdown in the Order's relationship with the Pope, other groups emerged, campaigning aggressively for this esteemed position. Among the contenders was a relatively new, yet impressive lay organization named "Opus Dei."

The origins of Opus Dei (a worldwide Catholic lay organization) are sketchy in detail, although most authors would agree that there is little doubt about its power,[28] its hierarchical structure, its recruitment practices, and its goals (along with the prescribed means to achieve them).[29] Author Penny Lernoux adds that "asceticism, anticommunism, a rigid hierarchy, and religious militancy"[30] have also become distinguishing characteristics of Opus Dei, as well as a controversial element of secrecy.

In short, during the late 1960s and early 1970s, the Jesuit management at Radio Vaticana seemed uncertain about the reciprocation of their dedication to the Pontiff. Even though three new 100-kilowatt transmitters, another 150-kilowatt booster, and four additional directional antennae were added to the facility by 1970, station personnel suffered from a serious case of low morale. Scholar James J. Onder reflected on the strengths and weaknesses of the medium, as Radio Vatican approached its 40th anniversary:

Tied to no national ideology, Vatican Radio is the world's only independent editorial voice. Vatican Radio has the potential for avoiding the ideological credibility gap which affects every other international broadcasting system from Radio Peking to

Voice of America. Yet, Vatican Radio is suffering from a deep institutional malaise which can be traced to its very beginnings.[31]

Onder's concern was representative of many media critics, including Robert R. Holton, who made these caustic remarks:

Take a multi-million-dollar, international radio network; sprinkle it liberally with well-meaning but largely unqualified personnel; mold them into dainty language and geographical cubes and garnish each with a thick coating of autonomy. Then blindfold the chef, put the mixture into an oven set for a thirty-nine-year slow broil and allow it to simmer in its own juices of discontent. When the timer bell rings, remove the concoction and you have Radio Vaticana 1970. Or as one veteran New York broadcasting executive once described it: "The most colossal misuse of airlane potential since Marconi invented the radio."[32]

Technically speaking, the facilities at Vatican Radio were beyond reproach. Programmatically, however, the transnational superstation had become a broadcast laughingstock, consistently airing such foibles as stomach rumbles, sneezes, snorts, and long periods of silence (while anxiety-ridden announcers presumably tried to find their places in the scripts). Even without the occasional stutter, stammer, and audible paper shuffle, the program schedule was singularly noncreative, filling valuable broadcast time with organ recitals, sacred choral presentations, and detailed announcements of minor papal appointments.[33] Vatican Radio had indeed entered into a mid-life crisis.

The lack of access, creativity, and professionalism in Radio Vaticana's program schedule during much of the 1970s is traceable to several well-known facts and many educated guesses. Among the facts are these:

1. The original mission statement for the station--"to spread the Gospel, in its specific religious meaning as the revealed word of God and in its wider meaning of the Christian view of the whole of reality and all aspects of human life" [34]--was overly general and vague.
2. After the mission of the station (however general) was established, no financial provisions were made for personnel, audience research, professional training, or program production/acquisition.[35]
3. The number of shortwave voice broadcast transmitters had risen over fourfold from 1950 to 1972, creating more programmatic competition, frequency interference and signal-jamming on the airwaves.[36]
4. The final authority for the station rested not in the hands of the Society of Jesus but instead with the Vatican Secretariat of State. In short, the Jesuits had all of the responsibility but none of the authority to run the station.

These facts can be placed within several contexts (which only the Vatican can verify), namely:

1. The possibility that Radio Vaticana fell victim to other shortwave competition (especially in Soviet bloc countries, where potential listeners struggled to hear daily newscasts from such sources as Radio Free Europe, Radio Liberty, and the BBC), or to the newer, technologically more seductive medium of television;

2. The possibility that the Pope had more access to the secular media (especially during his extensive international travel) thereby minimizing Vatican Radio's influence;

3. The possibility that the Vatican, not unlike most corporate entities, recognized the importance of good technology, but failed to see the creative value of programming;

4. The possibility that the events of the 1960s and 1970s, while historically significant, were not as "media-friendly"[37] as those reported in earlier years (most specifically, during World War II);

5. The possibility that Paul VI, in the wake of Vatican II, wanted more direct control over the media;

6. The possibility that the Pope had grown to mistrust the Jesuits and the areas of their influence;

7. Some or all of the above.[38]

Clearly, the Pope felt a mistrust of the secular media, citing its failure to provide complete and accurate information about sacred pronouncements, as well as their propensity to report Vatican unpleasantries rather than good news:

Not infrequently they [the media] present such items in a one-sided manner, and possibly slightly altered and dramatized in order to add to their interest and sting. Thus they accustom their readers [or listeners] not to an objective and calm judgment, but on the contrary, to a negative point of view, to a systematic distrust, to a preconceived lack of esteem for persons, for institutions, and for activities pertaining to the Church. . . . Such actions are not inspired by haste to obtain exact and complete information, or for a desire to impart fraternal correction when it is needed. Instead, they are prompted by a taste for the sensational, for complacency with an attitude of denunciation and conflict which spurs on certain types of experts in publicity, thereby sowing unrest and intractability in the minds of so many otherwise good Catholics. Indeed, some priests and more than a few fervent young people allow themselves to be affected in their outlook by exactly these means.[39]

This adversarial relationship between the Pope and secular media undoubtedly had an effect on Vatican Radio, which suffered a period of inertia during most of the decade of the 1970s. Fortunately, however, the dark era at the Catholic station was temporary and would later be reversed by an increase in professional station management and creative programmatic direction, as well as a more media-wise pope.

RISING FROM THE ASHES?

The "golden age" of Vatican Radio as the primary broadcast medium for Church propagation had clearly begun to erode after the death of Pope John XXIII in the early 1960s. The internationally recognized Catholic radio network had experienced a tenuous (at best) relationship with Paul VI, due in part to his access to other transnational media, as well as to his growing mistrust of the Jesuit Order. Paul's immediate successor, Pope John Paul I, was equally mistrustful of some of the Jesuits' programming decisions at Vatican Radio, despite his extremely short term of office (thirty days).[40] However, John Paul I's successor, Pope John Paul II, has seemed to be more mixed in his feelings toward the transnational radio service.

On the one hand, Pope John Paul has received Radio Vaticana's full support during his pilgrimages to Poland; regarding his diplomatic overtures in China, Mexico, Zaire, and the Philippines; and regarding his "muscle strategy"[41] toward the Soviet Union. Furthermore, during the frightening assassination attempt on his life, Radio Vaticana served as a credible voice to rest of the world. Author Paul Hofmann observes:

When he was shot down in St. Peter's Square on May 13, 1981, Vatican Radio, which had routinely been covering his general audience, went right on reporting the attack, the pontiff being rushed to the hospital, and the surgery. Networks in many countries took on the running broadcast from the Vatican in one of the greatest radio hookups ever achieved. Vatican Radio, which does not often have a chance to make money, later put out a recording of the dramatic May 13 broadcast as a cassette, which was widely sold.[42]

However, from time to time, the programming on the Holy See's transnational radio system seemed entirely too liberal for the Pontiff's traditionalist tastes. According to author David Willey, part of his consternation was based in fact, but a large portion was due to Pope John Paul's negative perception of media in general:

Wojtyla [Pope John Paul II] neither likes nor trusts the media. He finds its values shallow and its behaviour intrusive. He scans a wide range of daily and weekly newspapers from many countries. He is usually disappointed by journalists. He cannot see why they should not be glad to act as evangelizers.[43]

In 1979, John Paul grew particularly concerned about his lack of influence over the media when Radio Vaticana supported (through editorials) the views of controversial theologians Hans Küng and Edward Schillebeeckx.[44] At that time, the Pope ordered the entire Society of Jesus to "clean house of doctrinal dissent."[45] He also suggested the need for greater control over Jesuit-run Vatican Radio, because, as Willey notes:

[The Pope's] authoritarian side abhors the lack of control he has over the media, despite the fact that his activities have probably filled more column inches in the secular written press and have certainly received more air time on TV and radio than those of any other pontiff in history.[46]

By 1982, still clearly frustrated by some of the editorial policies of Radio Vaticana and other Vatican journalists, the Pope attempted to "rein in" the media by joining his predecessors in the suggestion that the service be run by Opus Dei. The Vatican Secretariat of State also felt that the $3 million annual cost of broadcasting in 35 languages could be better managed by a more conservative management. Opus Dei demurred when questioned about John Paul's intent. As one member commented, "Of course, we could handle it, if we were asked to do it."[47]   According to author David Willey, however, Opus Dei was openly delighted about the prospect of running Vatican Radio because, "Opus Dei men are good courtiers. Pressmen are not."[48]

Jesuit reaction to the rumored transfer of power at Vatican Radio was understandably different. First of all, the clerics argued that "talk about a removal at this stage . . . appear[ed] to be just that--talk."   However, as one churchman suggested, "even as malevolent gossip, it is a little scary to the Jesuit order right now."[49]

The "crisis" over a transfer in power at Vatican Radio never went far beyond the rumor and innuendo that had begun in 1982. Personnel reappointments and different programming strategies as well as tighter management and editorial control apparently subdued Pope John Paul's concern over the fate of the world's oldest transnational medium. In 1991 Radio Vaticana celebrated its 60th year of operation, still intact as a Jesuit instrument of propagation.

VATICAN RADIO AFTER SOLIDARITY

With the democratization of the Soviet bloc, Vatican Radio lost its primary recipients of papal diplomacy. No longer was the Pontiff required to step in as a political adversary; instead he could renew his pastoral commitment to "spread the word of Christ." As a result, the service looked to new areas of the world for missionary expansion as well as to new technologies and programming strategies to enlarge their listening audiences.

While still broadcasting primarily on shortwave,[50] the program content on the Church's international radio system after the collapse of the Berlin Wall contained such diverse offerings as

1. Daily Mass from St. Peter's Basilica;
2. Classical, jazz and pop music (including artists like Frank Sinatra, Ella Fitzgerald, Dionne Warwick and Elvis Presley);[51]
3. An innovative news/commentary program entitled, "Four Voices;"
4. Byzantine Slavic Church services.[52]

In addition, much of this programming was relayed to over ten million Catholics in 34 languages, by a staff comprised of 425 employees.[53] Paul Hofmann further notes,

Many nationalities are represented among the . . . employees of Vatican Radio; the majority of them are lay people. The core, however, is made up of 35 Jesuits who live at the headquarters of their order in a separate unit along with the official historians of the Society of Jesus. There is no formal rule that all clerics who work at Vatican Radio must be Jesuits, and indeed some of them aren't. But up to now, the director general of Vatican Radio; the technical director; and the heads of the program, music, and news sections have always been Jesuits.[54]

Perhaps the most revealing portrait of Radio Vaticana on its 60th anniversary was described in a 1991 *Variety* article entitled, "Spreading the News: A Day in

the Life."[55]   In it, the author recounted a typical 24-hour news day, complete
with 7 wire services, 120 stringers, and a dozen news editors. When compared
with Robert Holton's 1970 characterization of Vatican Radio as "the only radio
network of anywhere near its range and listener potential that in many sections
of the world has twenty-three hours and thirty minutes of dead time each day,"[56]
most media critics agreed that Vatican broadcasts had definitely improved.

Despite their praise of general programming strategies, most critics were quite
negative about Vatican Radio's editorial stance, noting that its tone had become
too conservative in recent years, especially when addressing important issues like
abortion, contraception, and euthanasia.[57]   Responding to these charges,
Information Director Reverend Ignazio Arregul explained:

We are not the official radio of Vatican City. Ours is not a civil society but a spiritual
brotherhood. More than just being the voice of the Pope, Vatican Radio is the voice
of 900 million Catholics all over the world.[58]

Once again, the centuries-old debate over the Church's role in secular society had
been raised . . . and responded to . . . on the side of traditionalism and
spirituality.

Thus, in 1991 the immediate fate of Vatican Radio was resolved. Opus Dei,
though still looming in the background, was out of the station's management
picture for the moment. In addition, Pope John Paul approved plans for
technological improvement and staff and scheduling expansion, and a formalized
(i.e., written) set of institutional statutes,[59] as well as new formatic direction,
especially for audiences in Asia and Africa.[60]   By 1995, Vatican Radio began
broadcasts on its new satellite network. Combined with newly developed
cooperative programming efforts on AM and FM stations throughout the world
and an internet home page, the oldest transnational broadcast service is also the
most well-connected.[61]

NOTES

1. The term broadcasting is used throughout this text as a synonym for any form of
radio or television transmission. Though some critics might argue that the word is
technically incorrect when referring to shortwave signals, the book adopts a larger
context for "broadcasting," which is taken from its foundations in agriculture, that is,
creating a form of seed distribution in order to cover large areas of land.

2. In "Station Here Helps London to Hear Pope," *New York Times*, 13 February
1931, reporters indicated that several cities, including London, Madrid, and Manila,
had trouble receiving the signal because of faulty receivers. London, however, solved
its problem quickly by some quick-thinking BBC engineers, who repatched the
signal through Schenectady, New York.

3. "Pope Pius XI Addresses and Blesses the World in his First Radio Broadcast,"
New York Times, 13 February 1931, 14.

4. Ibid.

5. Ibid.

6. James J. Onder, "The Sad State of Vatican Radio," *Educational Broadcasting
Review* (August 1971): 44.

7. Ibid.

8. Not all of Vatican Radio's programming was distributed in seven languages. This accomplishment required more time, personnel, and technological expertise. However, 1931 does mark the year in which VR began its attempt to be multilingual.

9. Julian Hale, *Radio Power* (Philadelphia: Temple University Press, 1975), 1.

10. From 1946 to 1951, Vatican Radio added 11 new languages to its programming service. Most of these were Eastern European and included Hungarian, Romanian, Czech, Russian, Slovene, Slovak, Latin, Bulgarian, Croatian, Belorussian, and Albanian.

11. Camille Cianfarra, *The Vatican and the War* (New York: E.P. Dutton, 1944), 42.

12. Peter Hebblethwaite, *Pope John XXIII: Shepherd of the Modern World* (New York: Doubleday, 1985), 431-432.

13. Ibid., 432.

14. This story was disputed by Vatican Radio Program Director, Father Federico Lombardi, S.J., in June 1996. In his response to Hebblethwaite's assertions, Fr. Lombardi replied: "The thing is absolutely groundless. John XXIII's speech, delivered in Latin, perfectly corresponds to what was published on *Acta Apostolicae Sedis* (and *Osservatore*). I verified it myself from the recording, having been requested to do so by an Oxford professor (J. Finnis), who rightly contested Hebblethwaite's assertions." Because Peter Hebblethwaite passed away in December 1994, he could not respond to these comments.

15. Ibid., 432-433.

16. "Vatican Will Operate Radio in the Far East," *New York Times*, 3 May 1960, 12. The article went on to describe future construction sites in either Hong Kong or the Philippines, with the target goal of reaching Communist China.

17. "African Advance Greeted by Pope," *New York Times*, 6 June 1960, 9.

18. Ibid.

19. "Pope Hails Radio Aid," *New York Times*, 13 February 1961, 5.

20. Ibid.

21. Religious News Service, 15 April 1961.

22. Ibid.

23. Walter B. Emery, *National and International Systems of Broadcasting* (East Lansing: Michigan State University Press, 1969), 530. A point of clarification should be inserted at this point. When Emery uses the term "relay" in this quote, he obviously is not discussing satellite relays (satellites were not used by Vatican Radio at this time). Rather, he is referring to the "bicycling" of taped programming to Latin American radio station for later rebroadcast to its audiences.

24. William E. Barrett, *Shepherd of Mankind: A Biography of Pope Paul VI* (New York: Doubleday, 1964), 15.

25. F. Peter Wigginton, *The Popes of Vatican Council II* (Chicago: Franciscan Herald Press, 1983), 112.

26. Ibid., 112-113.

27. Malachi Martin, *The Jesuits: The Society of Jesus and the Betrayal of the Roman Catholic Church* (New York: Simon & Schuster, 1987), 42. This dossier became crucial in later papal efforts to disband the order.

28. According to 1982 data, there were over 70,000 Opus Dei members throughout the world at this time. Less than 2 percent were members of religious orders.

29. Many books have been written about Opus Dei. The following texts give a much more detailed description of the organization: Michael Walsh, *Opus Dei* (New York: HarperCollins, 1992); Penny Lernoux, *People of God* (New York, Penguin Books, 1989); Malachi Martin, *The Jesuits* (op. cit.); and Eric O. Hanson, *The*

Catholic Church in World Politics (Princeton, N.J.:   Princeton University Press, 1987).

30. Lernoux, 303-304.

31. Onder, 46.

32. Robert R. Holton, "Vatican Radio," *The Catholic World*, April 1970, 7.

33. Onder, 44.

34. Ibid., 45.

35. To articulate this point more specifically, Robert Holton quotes a Jesuit communications expert, who states, "All we ever got and still get today is the order to provide a body. We are never given the money or the time to train anyone for the posts. We were told to assign a man and the Vatican would put him on the payroll" (p. 8).

36. Julian Hale, *Radio Power: Propaganda and International Broadcasting* (Philadelphia: Temple University Press, 1975), xii.

37. "Media friendly," in this context, is used to describe events that are immediate, dramatic, and affect the audience in a highly personal way.

38. Because no specific policy statements were issued at this time, the apparently strained relationship between the Pontiff and the Society of Jesus is open to interpretation and several viewpoints.   To provide another perspective, Father Federico Lombardi gives this analysis of Vatican Radio during the reign of Paul VI: "The whole epoch of Paul VI appears as a time of crisis, both in the relationship between the Pope and the Jesuits, as well as in the life of Vatican Radio.   As far as reality goes, under Paul VI the reorganization of the Radio took place, in the sense that priority was given to the radio programming as opposed to the technical equipment.   This is clearly set out by Paul VI in his speeches (1966); the same trend is also shown by the appointment (for the first time) as Director General of such Fathers as Fr. Martegani and, later, Fr. Tucci, who were men of culture, whereas beforehand they had always been men of science (Fr. Gianfranceschi, Fr. Soccorsi, Fr. Stefanizzi); this is furthermore demonstrated by the direction, given by an *ad hoc* Commission, following which the funds allotted in the budget to the production of programs were to be proportionally increased.   (All of this can be proved by documentary evidence.)   Paul VI lays therefore the ground for the requalification of Vatican Radio in the content itself of its broadcasts; he does that through the appointment of Jesuits he trust[s]."

39. Wigginton, 92-93.

40. Author David A. Yallop reviews some of these experiences in his book, *In God's Name* (New York: Doubleday, 1991). Among them: Vatican Radio's failure (along with *L'Osservatore Romano* and some off-the-record briefings by members of the Roman Curia) to provide a full, accurate portrayal of the new Pontiff's views on artificial birth control to the world press, thereby creating further false impressions (p. 192); and VR's failure (again, along with *L'Osservatore Romano*) to represent adequately John Paul I's views on liberation theology (p. 227).

41. The Pontiff's "muscle strategy" refers to his diplomatic concentration on anticommunism in the former Soviet Union. John Paul II's mission was to break the Eurocommunist bloc through church-state relations. For more information on this strategy, read Eric O. Hanson's *The Catholic Church in World Politics* (op. cit.).

42. Paul Hofmann, *O Vatican! A Slightly Wicked View of the Holy See* (New York: Congdon & Weed, 1983), 268-269.

43. David A. Willey, *God's Politician* (New York: St. Martin's Press, 1992), 195-196. Director of Vatican Radio, Fr. Federico Lombardi disagrees, however: "In my opinion, a great many journalists who know and follow the Pope do not share [this view]. At least all those who have seen him give a number of press conferences and

personal direct answers during plane trips (never before has a Pope given press conferences and answers to single questions), those who have heard him thank them for their work at the end of each trip, etc. This is only an example as to the Pope's attitude towards the media."

44. Marjorie Hyer, "Vatican Rules Küng Guilty of Heresy," *Washington Post*, 19 December 1979.

45. Ibid.

46. Willey, 196.

47. Paul Hofmann, "The Jesuits," *New York Times*, 14 February 1982, 24.

48. Willey, 198.

49. Hofmann, "The Jesuits," 24.

50. Erik Amfitheatrof, "'Spiritual Fruits from the Science of Radio,'" *Variety*, 18 February 1991, 62.

51. In 1991, hard rock was not allowed on the service.

52. Amfitheatrof, 62.

53. Ibid.

54. Hofmann, *O Vatican!*, 269.

55. "Spreading the News: A Day in the Life," *Variety*, 18 February 1991, 62.

56. Holton, 7.

57. "Mixing Credibility with Caution," *Variety*, 18 February 1991, 64.

58. Ibid.

59. Portions of these statutes can be found in Appendix A at the end of this book.

60. Erik Amfitheatrof, "Vatican Wants Radio to Be a Vital Voice," *Variety*, 18 February 1991, 64.

61. For a more detailed perspective on Vatican Radio's current facilities and plans for the future, read Chapter 6--an interview with VR's director of programming, Fr. Federico Lombardi.

2

The BBC World Service: Extending "The Empire"

Marilyn J. Matelski and Nancy Lynch Street

The British Broadcasting Corporation enjoys probably the best reputation in the world for its transnational radio service, despite distinct periods of loss in credibility. The BBC "Empire Service" (as it was first named) began in December of 1932--ten years after the inception of its domestic service--and met with great enthusiasm, especially by King George V, who inaugurated his new technology with these words:

Through one of the marvels of modern science, I am enabled this Christmas day to speak to all my peoples throughout the Empire. . . . I speak now from my home and from my heart to you all, to men and women so cut off by the snows and deserts or the seas that only voices out of the air can reach them.[1]

The idea for a British transnational radio service was originally proposed by Sir John Reith, with the express purpose of "bringing the scattered dominions closer to the mother country and of seeing that British expatriates were not deprived of the benefits derived from listening to the Home Service."[2] As suggested by its mission statement, the Empire Service carried with it an elitist, parochial tone, loyal to British government, culture, and values. It was funded by user license fees (like the BBC Home Service) and, at first, shared its news department with its domestic counterpart. After two years, however, the services assumed different identities and, ultimately, different goals, marking the first of many evolutionary phases in the BBC's long history.

During its first five years of operation, the BBC Empire Service tried to avoid controversial issues, for the most part. Instead, it focused on providing anglophilic information and cultural assimilation to a targeted global audience. In short, the programming schedule for BBC radio was often not nearly so impressive as the technology upon which the broadcasts were sent to far-reaching pockets of the world.

The BBC was not alone in its endeavors to broadcast by shortwave at this time, however. France, Germany, Italy, and the United States had also established their presence in the ether by the mid-1930s. Even the Holy See recognized the importance of propagation through the airwaves; Vatican Radio, the world's oldest transnational broadcaster, had been established in 1931. Clearly, the decade of the 1930s brought with it the realization that the presence of an international radio service was as much a competitive factor in world power as the actual need for global communication.

THE BIRTH OF A "WORLD SERVICE"

In 1938, critics like Sir Walter Citrine (from the trades union) and Felix Greene (a New York-based BBC employee) led the charge for redefining the broadcast philosophy behind the British Empire service. Their argument was simple: Transnational radio was maturing quickly in both technology and listenership; programmers must now address these new challenges. Further, with the specter of impending world war, the BBC should adopt a leadership role in international broadcasting.

In fact, World War II was the single most important factor in bringing organizational as well as programmatic changes to British radio. As the conflict escalated, both the national and international services came under the auspices of the Ministry of Information. Then, after several "false starts" in cross-cultural propaganda and endless debate between the Political Warfare Executive, the Ministry of Information, the Foreign Office, and the BBC hierarchy, a new "World Service" emerged, defined by its universal dedication to honesty, objectivity, and professionalism.[3] Broadcast scholar Walter B. Emery describes the BBC world radio *persona* that resulted:

As the Nazis and other belligerents stepped up their propaganda broadcasts via short-wave, the BBC became increasingly active in the war of words. Its newscasts and commentaries, however, were more factual and less vituperative than those from Berlin, Rome and other communication centers then under the control of the Nazis. With false, abusive and conflicting messages flooding the airways, the BBC endeavored to preserve the image of accuracy and reliability which it had established. Throughout the world, especially in German-occupied territory, it was regarded as the most dependable source of news about the war.[4]

In the early days of conflict, as Emery states, BBC broadcasters simply reasserted their intentions to win the War and invited the United States and other neutral countries to join in their victory. After the Battle of Flanders in 1940, however, the BBC stepped up its propaganda campaign by urging the rest of the "free world" to unite in the fight against Nazi domination. Some broadcasts were geared especially toward the United States, with announcers making strong arguments for American alliance to the "greater" cause. The following radio editorial provides a good example of such an appeal:

I don't believe that the American people can share in a world with Nazidom, especially not with a triumphant, all-conquering Nazidom. And even if they wanted to, they wouldn't be allowed to. This is not a European struggle. It is a world conflict or it is nothing. We regard ourselves as the first line of defense for the other side of the Atlantic.[5]

In addition to world appeals to join the anti-Axis movement, the British shored up their domestic audience's morale by providing vivid word pictures of both victory and defeat, by holding broadcast rallies that featured patriotic celebrities like Vera Lynn with songs such as "Kiss Me Goodnight Sergeant Major" and "There'll Always Be an England," and by incorporating "in the trenches" wartime themes in radio comedy and drama series.

The BBC also adopted a "Tokyo Rose" type strategy (as put forth by the Japanese); they infiltrated German radio ether and, posing as a Nazi station, produced programming with commentary that was intended to undermine the foundations of Hitler's political machine. These clandestine broadcasts appeared to support the Fuehrer. As author Lawrence C. Soley asserts, their true purpose was to sabotage Hitler's instrumental leadership by turning the military against Nazi party leaders as well as the leaders against themselves.[6] Soley provides an instance of such rhetoric with this excerpt from a radio editorial entitled, "Der Chef" ("The Chief"):

If it should be a question of choosing between Göring or Himmler, then, by God and all the Saints, let us have 30,000 hundred-weight of Hermann, rather than one milligram of this scheming political out-house flower, of this anemic inflated windbag, Heinrich Himmler. . .[7]

As for its overall impact on World War II, reactions toward the BBC are mixed. Some historians feel that the BBC played an invaluable role, especially to those members of the French Resistance. Media scholar John Michalczyk makes a persuasive argument on behalf of the BBC through an in-depth analysis of the BBC's role as a weapon of propaganda in his case study (found in Chapter 7 of this book). Other critics, including author Julian Hale, however, take a more negative view, raising questions about the BBC's wartime *persona* being more mythical than real. Hale writes:

That the BBC's reputation has lasted so long is due first of all to the Allied military victory, no less surely than it was the defeat of the Nazis which destroyed the effectiveness of their propaganda. The propaganda war in Europe was itself evenly fought. Even the famous V campaign--in which the V symbol for *Victoire* and *Vrijheid*, dreamt up by the BBC's Belgian Programme Organizer, Victor de Laveleye, was dunned into the enemy through slogans, signature tunes and the famous Churchillian gesture--was only a qualified success. The Germans appropriated it, proclaiming the V as their own victory symbol, and so weakened its impact that the BBC had to scale down plans to exploit it all over Europe.[8]

In any case, figures show that at the War's inception, BBC's international service was programming in 39 languages--more than any other radio service in the world. Even though the language numbers fluctuated throughout the next few years, the World Service still maintained its reputation in broadcasting the largest number of hours with the greatest number of languages in the world. By the end of the War, the BBC actually claimed a 45-language distribution of programming throughout the world. However, before long, this dominance was to diminish, as other services emerged and expanded.[9] In addition, the BBC was soon to come into hard budgetary times with the onset of the Cold War and a necessary redistribution of resources.

THE COLD WAR YEARS

Despite its reduction in funding during the 1950s and 1960s, however, the BBC World Service still enjoyed the support of Parliament and its listeners. Throughout its three decades of existence, the BBC had become associated with a level of civility and precision unparalleled in other parts of the world. Scholars often studied "the BBC manner,"[10] a prescribed code of language, demeanor, and social custom that defined the Corporation's infrastructure as well as its actual delivery of news, information and entertainment. In short, the BBC represented British society at its most profound level--a sort of "stiff upper lip" attitude in the face of both triumph and tragedy. Sociologist Tom Burns, having interviewed almost 60 BBC employees during the 1960s and 1970s, likens the "code" to that of the British Parliament and its people:

The code allowed for sizeable differences in attitude, opinion and aspiration: indeed these differences, and the conflicts they engender, formed much of the content of the Corporation's internal business and social life. The manner, in fact, was a way of defining the "rules of the game" according to which the internal and external business of the Corporation and all the manifold social intercourse to which this business gives rise should be conducted. The most dangerous conflicts, consequently, were those which were expressed, in almost ritualistic terms, by a deliberate departure from the BBC manner, signifying, as they did, a challenge to the "rules of the game" themselves.[11]

Thus, as the Cold War evolved, the "BBC manner" also became its new focus for broadcast. As described in a 1972 report of the Select Committee on Nationalized Industries, the BBC was no longer recognized for its programs; rather, it was seen as "chief public-impression former."[12] As such, its mission was redefined, its authority reassigned, and its organization restructured to meet new goals and objectives (see Figure 2.1).

Under the new organizational plan, the Board of Governors had some power over transnational broadcasts such as language types and numbers of broadcast hours.[13] However, it possessed no control over newscasts or other material. Scholar Natalie Doyle-Hennin elaborates further:

Unlike the Voice of America, the BBC produce[d] no official editorial commentary on behalf of the British government. Rather, commentaries [were] solicited from outside the organization in order to conserve the BBC's self-imposed role of objective observer and reporter of world events.[14]

In fact, Doyle-Hennin asserts that the BBC (as well as the VOA) enjoyed such a good reputation for objectivity, "enemy nations" like the Soviet Union refrained from signal jamming to guarantee access to information not covered by their own media.[15] In 1979, the BBC received funding for its World Radio Service from the nation's Foreign Office;[16] and by 1982, its programming was distributed in 35 foreign languages,[17] and it continued to build a constituency throughout the world linguistically, journalistically, and editorially.

Figure 2.1
The British Broadcasting Corporation

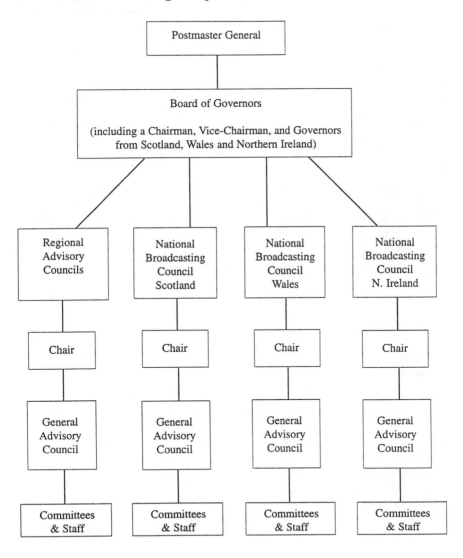

POST-COLD WAR BLUES

After the "fall" of the Berlin Wall, however, the world of transnational broadcasting changed as dramatically as the political climate on which it reported. The BBC World Service found itself to be no exception in this new configuration. For one thing, the need for shortwave broadcasts in the former Soviet bloc dropped dramatically in the early 1990s. In addition, the need for special receivers hidden behind fruit cellar doors was quickly replaced by the desire for CD players and AM/FM car radios. In short, covert programming had given way to top-ten playlists and national news capsules. As a result, previously revered broadcast "surrogates"--programmers who spoke for those who could not do so themselves--were now seen as "outsiders" and somewhat extraneous, to say the least.

The BBC World Service, like other transnational radio broadcasters, tried once again to adapt to this newly democratized world. In 1993 it expanded its radio service to 39 language divisions, which in turn attracted more than 120 million listeners. Satellite television coverage was also enhanced. To date, reactions to this reorganization have been mixed.

According to most research studies, both quantitative and qualitative, the BBC World Service still maintains a certain credibility, albeit somewhat diminished, from its golden age in Central and Eastern Europe.[18] Data compiled at the RFE/RL Institute in that year compared listenership to the BBC with that of RFE/RL and VOA in the former Soviet Bloc. Assuming an obvious bias, Table 2.1 nevertheless illustrates a close transnational competition.

Table 2.1
Regular Listening (at least once a week) in Eastern Europe

	RFE/RL%	VOA%	BBC%
Bulgaria	3	2	3
Czech Republic	13	5	4
Slovakia	10	6	2
Hungary	3	5	2
Poland	6	2	5
Romania	7	4	5

Total Listening in Eastern Europe

	RFE/RL%	VOA%	BBC%
Bulgaria	9	5	7
Czech Republic	26	16	8
Slovakia	24	14	6
Hungary	8	8	4
Poland	11	6	9
Romania	15	10	7

Taken from Appendix II: Comparative Listening to RFE/RL, VOA and BBC--Surveys Commissioned by Media and Opinion Research, *RFE/RL Audience Handbook* (March 1993): 44.

Despite the relative comparability between services, however, these figures seem to reflect a reduction in world standing between the "old" BBC and the "new" one. This observation becomes especially evident when reading anecdotal comments.

Sometimes a loss in listenership can be due to changing politics in target areas, as evidenced by these comments from residents of some former Soviet Bloc countries. For example, a Prague doctor observes that

The revolution was a stimulus for being interested in the news. But now, even if I was interested, there's not much happening. Well, lots of things are happening but there aren't so many changes now compared to November 1989. We were swallowing news.[19]

A Brno engineer adds "1989 was a watershed. Until then I listened more or less exclusively to RFE, VOA and BBC. Then, in 1989 Czechoslovak radio began to bring objective, high quality information."[20]

Sometimes criticism of BBC World Radio seems more stylistic than content-based, as articulated by a Prague housewife:

RFE is for everyone. The BBC requires more educated listeners, experts, people who have more information. RFE presents itself to the man on the street so it's very popular whereas the BBC is very British and exudes British behaviour.[21]

More specifically, says a Prague manager,

If you listen to RFE you'll get what you want to get, while the BBC is very staid and non-partisan but you must concentrate on it and know what you want to listen to. It isn't for entertainment, while you can listen to RFE just for background.[22]

But a Bulgarian listener from Sofia is far less tactful in his critique of the BBC's lack in competitive edge when compared with other radio services: "The BBC may have fallen behind because this desire for pure information makes the programmes slightly colourless and dull, I usually fall asleep."[23] Still, most critics acknowledge the BBC as the best available model of broadcast journalism in the world. In the Czech Republic, for example, a Prague doctor praises its standards for excellence: "Many stations refer to the BBC because it seems to be a guarantor of the news. . . . When someone, even RFE, says that they said it on the BBC then this is a verification of the truth."[24] A Bulgarian listener concurs:

I still share the opinion that people keep listening to the BBC as a form of double checking the information provided by Bulgarian radio. That's my personal opinion. We still rely on the BBC for verification, at least the people I know do.[25]

The BBC World Service's reputation for high-quality reporting is due, in no small part, to its basic operational structure, which leaves little room for stagnation or indifference. This point was made very clear during a 1994 conversation with VOA's Kim Elliott. When asked why the BBC could maintain its standards in a constantly changing world, Elliott described what he saw as the essential differences between the politics of the BBC versus that of its competitors, most especially the Voice of America and RFE/RL:

Street: What are the major ways in which the present RFE/RL-VOA model differ from the British model?

Elliott: U.S. international broadcasting is centrally planned, just like the Soviet economy. The VOA has predetermined that it will talk about U.S. and world affairs, and it has predetermined that RFE/RL will do target country affairs. It forces the audience then to tune in to two different stations to get a complete newscast. . . . The BBC simply provides the mix that is appropriate for each of its target countries and goes about it. The other thing that is advantageous about the BBC is that it has corporate independence, that it can make a little bit of its own money through its auxiliary enterprises. It can conduct the business. It is ruthless; it hires and fires people with impunity, but it gets the job done. . . . Then the BBC has its domestic partner, the BBC domestic services, and they can borrow a lot from their resources. The VOA has no such thing; RFE/RL really doesn't either. In fact, we both have a sort of pariah status among U.S. domestic media. If we had a domestic partner such as NPR and PBS, I think we would be able to do a better job. . . . BBC World Service management is [also] able to stay around, build up expertise, whereas oftentimes VOA front office management, and RFE/RL to a large extent too, is just people with good political connections.

Matelski: You said that the BBC will fire its employees with impunity. Who does it--who fires them?

Elliott: Their senior managers do. A lot of BBC employees now are just contract employees; they are not people with full benefits. They are not building up pension privileges or anything like that. Their big news program is "News Hour." Everybody there is on a six-month contract. The competition is so keen in London for journalists to find work [especially to work for the BBC], the talent is great.

Matelski: On the other hand, if you are an employee at RFE/RL, you could go on for twenty years?

Street: Aren't they civil service?

Elliott: Most of us are civil service.

Street: So you cannot really be fired.

Elliott: It would be really difficult. You would have to do something really pretty awful [at VOA or RFE/RL] to get fired.[26]

Unfortunately, after several decades of being a standard-bearer however, the BBC World Service, like other transnational radio services, once again faces the challenge of creating a new mission for the twenty-first century. Its future will depend on its adaptability to new boundaries, technologies, and perceptions--in short, a new world--with funding limitations. In 1993, for example, the British Foreign Service proposed future monetary cuts that totaled over $15 million (USD) each year.[27] These reductions amounted to an 8 percent decrease in its annual $265 million (USD) budget. To date, however, the World Service still broadcasts to the world in 48 languages even with its reduced annual budget of $250 million (USD).[28] With limited grants-in-aid from the government, the issue becomes "target programming." At present, while the English Language Service is still the most heavily funded, the BBC World Service devotes its next strongest efforts to those speaking Arabic.[29] China is also an important focus, with an estimated 120 million regular listeners.[30]

In addition to the economic downsizing and redirection, there exists the equally important factor of global image rebuilding. As *Guardian* columnist Hugo Young explains:

The World Service fields no legions of political power. But it is one place where Britain's world leadership happens not to be based on fantasy or pretension. It dominates the field--that of information and ideas--where, in the 2000s, international competition will be greatest. Its intrinsic values make Britain admired in corners that British industry will never reach. It speaks for the liberal world society in which Britain will feel more comfortable. It needs to be left alone, to do what it does better than anyone. It needs to be told, for a start, that its work won't be savaged to save a few outposts that this medium-sized power no longer needs.[31]

In short, the BBC World Service finds itself in yet another crisis period. However, its past history suggests that it might be able to turn adversity into advantage with creative investment, organization, and programming. Only time will reveal whether the BBC continues to participate in world history or becomes a footnote to it.

NOTES

1. Graham Mytton, ed., *Global Audiences: Research for Worldwide Broadcasting, 1993* (London: John Libbey, 1993), 2.

2. Julian Hale, *Radio Power: Propaganda and International Broadcasting* (Philadelphia: Temple University Press, 1975), 49.

3. Hale, 50.

4. Walter B. Emery, *National and International Systems of Broadcasting: Their History, Operation and Control* (East Lansing: Michigan State University Press, 1969), 87.

5. Harold N. Graves, "European Radio and the War," *Annals of the American Academy of Political and Social Science* (January 1941): 79.

6. Lawrence C. Soley, *Radio Warfare: OSS and CIA Subversive Propaganda* (New York: Praeger Publishers, 1989), 33.

7. Ibid.

8. Hale, 51.

9. Ibid., 53.

10. Tom Burns, *The BBC: Public Institution and Private World* (London and Basingstoke: The Macmillan Press, Ltd., 1977), xii.

11. Ibid., xiii.

12. Ibid., 13.

13. Natalie Doyle-Hennin, *The World according to International Radio* (Ph.D. diss., SUNY Buffalo, 1991), 67.

14. Ibid.

15. Ibid., 69.

16. Tom O'Malley, *Closedown? The BBC and Government Broadcasting Policy, 1979-1992* (London: Pluto Press, 1994), x.

17. Sydney Head, *World Broadcasting Systems: A Comparative Analysis* (Belmont, Calif.: Wadsworth, 1985).

18. According to *Global Audiences: Research for Worldwide Broadcasting 1993*, the BBC is still the leading transnational radio broadcaster in many other areas of the world including Ghana (p. 13), Mozambique and Angola (p. 57), Zambia (p. 70), Argentina (p. 166), Nepal (p. 208), and India (p. 219).

19. Mytton, 136.

20. Ibid.

21. Ibid., 141.

22. Ibid., 141-142.

23. Ibid., 125.

24. Mytton, 140.

25. Ibid., 125.

26. VOA Audience Research Officer Kim Andrew Elliott, interview by authors, 28 April 1994, tape recording, Washington, D.C. Elliott went on to describe the BBC's varied "enterprises"--books, tapes, and research data.

27. Andrew Culf, "World Service Fears Decline over Fresh Cuts," *Guardian*, 21 April 1993, 6. The actual figures in British monies are as follows: 1) a 5-million pound decrease each year from 1994 to 1997, with possible additional cuts of 2.5-5 percent, or 4.3-8.6 million pounds annually; 2) the BBC World Service budget, which is 175 million pounds each year. The dollar figures are based on estimates of the dollar exchange value in 1993.

28. Brian T. Evans, "United Kingdom," in *The International World of Electronic Media*, Lynne Schafer Gross, ed. (New York: McGraw-Hill, Inc., 1995), 119.

29. Ibid.

30. Ibid., although Evans acknowledges that this figure is somewhat unreliable because it is difficult to gather accurate data in China at the present time.

31. Hugo Young, "Marring a World Class Service," *Guardian*, 28 January 1993, 18.

3

America's Voices: Radio Free Europe/ Radio Liberty, Voice of America, Radio Marti, and Radio Free Asia

Marilyn J. Matelski and Nancy Lynch Street

Marconi once remarked that radio might ultimately be viewed as "the greatest weapon against the evils of misunderstanding and jealousy."[1] Little did he know that quite the opposite could also be true. Radio, unlike the print media, relies on the spoken word and thus communicates more directly and personally with its intended audience. Moreover, the transmission and reception of information via radio is immediate, allowing large numbers of people to receive messages quickly, unencumbered by such "boundaries" as literacy, economics, or social class.

SENDING THE "VOICE OF AMERICA" TO EUROPE

During World War II, both the Allied and Axis forces recognized radio's power and potential and tried to use it to their best advantage. Compared to its European counterparts (the BBC, Vatican Radio, Deutsche Welle, and Radio Moscow), however, the Voice of America (VOA) came into existence rather late in media history. It also evolved quite differently from its predecessors, primarily because of its roots in a free market economy. This "distinction" of operating a government-run service within a capitalist society not only delayed VOA's entry into the world of transnational broadcasting, it most probably has continued to affect VOA (both positively and negatively) more than any other factor since its inception.

Transnational broadcasting from the United States, like its domestic radio system, actually began as a private industry. Technical experiments were begun in the 1920s by some entrepreneurial visionaries; by 1941, several companies (including CBS and NBC) had already developed fledgling operations.[2] In 1942, however, all privatized transnational broadcast stations in the US were taken over by the Office of War Information (specifically, the "Overseas Branch," later to become the CIA)[3] as an emergency response to the Japanese attack on Pearl Harbor. Almost immediately the combined technological expertise from these formerly private operations were combined and reconstituted into a governmental service known as the "Voice of America."

VOA was "radio" unlike most Americans had ever known before. It did not broadcast for profit; and its programming choices were based upon neither domestic public interest nor advertising revenues. In addition, the Voice of America was not regulated by the Federal Communications Commission (FCC); instead, it often found itself wedged between the Presidential administration, the military, and commercial media needs.

VOA AND WORLD WAR II

On February 24, 1942, announcer William Harlan Hale inaugurated the first of many 15-minute "voices from America" to anxious European listeners. To calm their fears over Hitler's next possible invasion and to give them assurance of continuity within an unsettled world, VOA pledged that "the news may be good or bad,"[4] but people would be told the truth. At first, VOA had only 12 shortwave transmitters to carry out their mission; but they were helped by the BBC in some initial broadcasts, and later were able to capture transmitter sites from enemy territory (in Tunis, Palermo, Bari, and Luxembourg).[5]

John Houseman (a well-known actor, director, and producer at the time) was asked to manage this mammoth effort. He described his mission as terribly difficult from time to time, especially at VOA's beginning stages:

The news that the Voice of America would be carrying to the world in the first half of 1942 was almost all bad--we would have to report our reverses without weaseling. Only thus could we establish a reputation for honesty, which we hoped would pay off on that distant but inevitable day when we would start reporting our own invasions and victories.[6]

Besides Houseman, other American icons of culture and journalism were asked to participate--among them: Robert Sherwood (three-time Pulitzer Prize winner); radio personality Elmer Davis; *New York Times* Washington Bureau Chief Wallace Carroll; author Dorothy Van Doren; and Joe Barnes (foreign affairs editor of the *Herald Tribune*).[7] However, despite the credible personnel put on board, VOA never achieved the world admiration enjoyed by the BBC during this time. British historian Asa Briggs, through his razor-edged candor, may provide the most understandable reason for VOA's failings. He once wrote:

In general, American propaganda to Europe throughout the war was both too distant and yet too brash, too unsophisticated and yet too contrived to challenge the propaganda forces already at work on the continent."[8]

Briggs's assessment of the Voice of America during World War II, though seemingly abrasive, describes the "hidden" mission of the service as the United States became more deeply enmeshed in the global conflict at hand. Led by the philosophy of Colonel William J. Donovan, VOA was used primarily for psychological warfare[9] during the early war years, a strategy similar to the "divide and conquer" tactics already employed by the BBC and Japanese radio. By June 1942, VOA was broadcasting 24 hours each day, in 27 languages. In

Colonel Donovan's own words, the radio service had become "an instrument of war--a judicious mixture of rumor and deception with truth as bait, to foster disunity and confusion in support of military operations."[10]

One of the most illuminating examples of radio "psychwar" was General Eisenhower's Torch plan, initiated during his campaign to squelch German occupation in North Africa. Author Lawrence C. Soley, in *Radio Warfare*, describes the plan thusly:

Torch plans called for President Roosevelt to make a "live" broadcast in French to Europe and North Africa. Eisenhower was to make similar broadcasts, assuring the French that the US had "no designs either on North Africa or any part of French Africa." The broadcasts were to be carried by the BBC, but relayed over the powerful Aspidistra transmitter. . . . Voice of America was to carry the Roosevelt and Eisenhower speeches, and additional commentaries on shortwave from US-based stations.[11]

The Torch plan was not without its faults. Soley recounts a series of misinterpretations, ill-conceived moves, and, quite simply, glaring mistakes. However, it did succeed in its mission to provide a surprise element for the Nazis in North Africa, one of the contributing factors to the war's end.

Another example of the American government's clandestine radio strategy with complicity from the VOA occurred with Operation Muzak (later changed to "Operation Pancake"). This mission was portrayed as the creation of an entertainment program, to be filled with musical hits sung by well-known singers like Marlena Dietrich. In fact, the show was actually a "cover" set up by the OSS (Office of Strategic Studies) for its actual plan of recruiting musical artists to record songs for a fake German radio station. The guise went something like this: Entertainers (who were usually German exiles living in the U.S.) were enlisted to sing songs that, they were told, would be broadcast over VOA. To be on the program, it was important to have accents that would be heard as "clearly German." The reason for this last requirement soon became clear: The songs sung for this "station" were actually rewrites of familiar pop music, with the lyrics changed somewhat slightly to create an antiwar theme and, thus, some demoralization. The lyric changes actually violated U.S. copyright laws, but singers (such as Dietrich) were told to keep these "minor" infractions to themselves. After the War, although results were not empirically testable, Operation Muzak was generally seen as a successful propagandistic attempt to "wear down" the German population from within.[12]

VOA'S NEW MISSION: THE COLD WAR

For a short time after World War II, the future of VOA was uncertain. The Office of War Information clearly was no longer needed; and some media critics wondered aloud whether American transnational radio might also be eliminated. Unable to resolve this issue as quickly as that of the OWI, however, the Voice of America was directed to report to the Department of State temporarily, while Congress discussed its fate.

VOA's future was highly controversial and debatable. For example, some of President Franklin Delano Roosevelt's detractors noted how he had manipulated the service in the past, and suggested that it could happen again if placed in the wrong hands. They brought up the fact that VOA had been highly involved in promoting FDR's candidacy for an unprecedented fourth term. What other fate might befall the country if a media system were allowed to have as much unbridled control? In the face of some rather convincing arguments, Congress ultimately decided to continue funding for the Voice of America, albeit on a contingency basis.

In 1947, however, Senator H. Alexander Smith (N.J.) and Representative Karl Mundt (S.D.) provided more economic security for VOA with the introduction of the Smith-Mundt Bill. This piece of legislation was among the first to fund U.S.'s peacetime propaganda efforts,[13] and was passed in both Houses as well as signed into law by President Harry Truman. Truman followed the Smith-Mundt Bill with another pledge for congressional support billed as the International Campaign of Truth (1950-1953). Its purpose was much more directed than that of Smith-Mundt; through the Campaign of Truth, the Voice of America would be funded to help fight the "Soviet-run Cold War."[14]

This time, though, Congress wanted more "hard" data to support Truman's claim that the peacetime propaganda campaign was working . . . and would be even more effective with more money. Scholar Shawn J. Parry-Giles writes that in the absence of more quantitative "proof," "propaganda officials all seemed to agree that the most conclusive evidence of the program's effectiveness was the Soviet Union's attempt to jam VOA transmissions."[15] In addition, the Advisory Commission presented estimates of the numbers of radio receivers in the Soviet Bloc (4-5 percent).[16] Their report implied that that very same number had access to VOA broadcasts; and it put forth the idea of a "grapevine effect,"[17] suggesting that the 4-5 percent went much further than it looked.[18]

These arguments were strong enough to bolster the necessity of an American transnational radio service; it also redefined VOA's mission with respect to post-war Eastern and Central Europe. Media historian Natalie Doyle-Hennin describes the subsequent new "face" of the Voice of America:

The arrival of the Cold War injected new life and purpose into the station, and it is during this period that news and commentary with an emphasis on life in the United States became dominant in VOA programming. This period also coincided with an increase in funding, largely dedicated to the expansion of transmitter facilities to "ring around the Soviet Union," one of VOA's prime targets.[19]

In a 1951 House Subcommittee hearing (ironically, during the same year Radio Free Europe was born), then VOA Director Foy D. Kohler listed his three criteria of evaluation for the redefined service. Parry-Giles describes them in this way:

The first question pertained to whether VOA was delivering a good, strong radio signal, with good listening quality. The second criterion involved determining whether an actual audience existed, "whether they [possessed] radio sets." Finally, according to Kohler, propaganda officials had to establish "as best you can the question of the influence your . . . programs can actually exert on that audience."[20]

Despite some controversy, VOA received adequate Congressional funding that year as well as the two that followed, although radio service's efficacy continued to be open to debate, as witnessed by this exchange between VOA Director Foy D. Kohler and Senator Kenneth McKellar (D-Tenn.):

M : "What does it [VOA] do? What does it accomplish? What does the document [a collection of statistical data on receiver ownership, listenership, etc.] do? What do you accomplish by it?"

K : "We are reaching a message to the Russian people that maintains their skepticism and their disbelief . . .which puts a break on the Kremlin."

M : "How do you know you are doing that? . . . Just tell us one way."

K : "We interrogate defectors who come out of the Soviet Union."

M : "Name a single soul that you have heard say he was influenced . . . just name one."

K : (pause)

M : "I don't believe you have ever influenced a single person."[21]

Kohler provided more "proof" later, which allowed VOA to continue its operation, albeit amid doubt. In fact, simple logic should have revealed that VOA *would have* to lose some of its postwar overseas listenership. Its staunch anticommunist stance against former ally Joseph Stalin would have hardly received support from his government officials.[22] Still, the service survived.

In 1953, VOA was reinstalled as part of the U.S. Information Agency,[23] a newly formed division, separate from the State Department. Once again, however, controversy over the organization ran rampant. In the mid-1950s, because of its connection to the USIA as well as its interactions in communist countries, some VOA personnel fell immediately under a cloud of credibility with Sen. Joseph McCarthy's House Committee on Unamerican Activities. Further, because of VOA's indirect relationship to the State Department, people both within and outside of the government raised the issue of "journalism" versus "propagandistic ideology." The mere word, "propaganda," has always been distasteful to most Americans because of its association with Nazis and Communists. The image of a democratic nation spreading ideological dogma to the rest of the world was hardly well-received. As a result, the Cold War for America was often an iceberg for VOA support. Perhaps VOA employee Edward W. Barrett characterized the situation best when he wrote,

America's information-program budgets have gone up and down like a yo-yo. When Congress is frightened, personnel is hastily recruited, screened for loyalty and security, and laboriously trained. Then a lull descends, funds are cut, and much of the trained personnel returns to private industry. A few months later, the Kremlin growls again--and up goes the yo-yo.[24]

The changes of leadership within the Voice of America and USIA have often reflected the instability of their funding system as well. In the early 1960s, the Voice enjoyed its greatest amount of credibility with President John F. Kennedy's appointment of journalism icon Edward R. Murrow as USIA director. Unfortunately, Murrow was soon forced to resign because of ill health. His immediate successors, Carl Rowan and Leonard Marks, often clashed with VOA executives (such as Henry Loomis, John Chancellor, and John Daley). By the 1970s, USIA directors Frank Shakespeare (former NBC president) and James Keogh experienced even less credibility with Congress and the nation. One VOA correspondent during this time told author Julian Hale that what might be construed as "creative differences" could also be described as "plain muddle."[25]

One way to alleviate some of this "muddle" was to set up formal guidelines. In 1960, former VOA director George Allen began to formulate a "charter" for his broadcast service. It was drafted, then redrafted, before finally being signed into law by President Gerald Ford in 1976.

According to its Charter, VOA operates under three basic principles:

1. To be a "consistently reliable and authoritative source of news;"[26]
2. To represent America as its whole, rather than any one segment of society;
3. To present U.S. policies in a clear and effective manner.[27]

However, even a cursory glance at VOA's journalistic behavior during its years since the Charter have given even the mildest of critics a twinge of ethical cardiac arrest. Most important to remember is that this "charter" is little more than a guideline; it carries with it no legal authority.[28] With this in mind, some interesting observations emerge.

According to a mid-1970s analysis in Julian Hale's *Radio Power*, all VOA editorials were written by staff members. This practice, unlike the BBC's editorial policy that relied almost solely on outsiders,[29] revealed VOA's commitment to little more than its own, insular view of the world as approved by the State Department.[30]

Hale's observations were only underscored in the Reagan and Bush administrations of the 1980s, when VOA's mission was redefined to become even more insular. In a 1988 *Washington Journalism Review*, writer Steve Knoll notes that the restriction against "covert, manipulative, or propagandistic activities" was lifted; replaced instead with a mission "to unmask and counter hostile attempts to distort or to frustrate the objectives and policies of the United States."[31]

Knoll is not alone in his observations. Journalist Carolyn Weaver, in "When the Voice of America Ignores Its Charter: An Insider Reports on a Pattern of Abuses," details several instances where VOA was used more as a covert tool of espionage than a transnational news service.[32] There is little wonder that the other American-supported transnational radio networks at the time, Radio Free Europe and Radio Liberty (merged in the early 1980s as Radio Free Europe/Radio Liberty), balked at being confused with the Voice. In a public relations-generated flyer, RFE/RL issued its statement of differences between the services.[33] Among its distinctive features were

1. Independence from the USIA;
2. Emphasis on surrogate broadcasting--sending reports on behalf of those who cannot do so themselves;
3. Editorial autonomy;
4. A mission to exercise the highest standards of accuracy, fairness and impartiality in its programming.

The fall of the Berlin Wall was to signal even greater change within the structures of RFE/RL and the Voice of America.

RFE/RL: ORIGINS AND DEVELOPMENT

In contrast to VOA's immediate initiation into service by world war, Radio Free Europe and Radio Liberty began later--and less dramatically--as a direct reaction to the Cold War.

During World War II, both sides of the conflict had used the facilities and transmitter of Radio Luxembourg (which was seen as invaluable due to its unique ability to reach most of Europe). After capturing the station back from the Germans in 1944, the United States renamed it "Radio Free Luxembourg," or "Radio 12-12," and broadcast in German under the psychological warfare unit. The station broadcast news, information, humor, and even a live, on-air execution of German spies. Although Radio Free Luxembourg was admittedly American in origin, its on-air claims were to be underground and German. After it had gained the confidence of its German listeners, Radio 12-12 began to transmit misinformation and false reports of Allied invasions to create panic and confusion.[34]

After the war ended, however, the United States disbanded its Radio 12-12 unit and turned its attention instead to a new perceived threat--the rise of communism in Eastern Europe. Among the proposals made to stem the Soviet tide was a transnational radio service built to broadcast anticommunist propaganda to the region. Together with former OSS officers Joseph Grew and Dewitt Poole, CIA chief Allen Dulles laid the foundations for Radio Free Europe, to be operated under the auspices of the National Committee for a Free Europe. The station began broadcasting in July 1950, followed by Radio Liberty a few years later. In their early days of operation, however, neither Radio Free Europe nor Radio

Liberty had much in common, save for their ties with the CIA. RL Director Kevin Klose described the relationship as

separate organizations, separate administrations, separate everything. . . . They didn't talk to each other, really; they were separate institutions absolutely. Each had their own research services, their own staff, everything. The only things they shared were transmitters. And even at that, they were "RFE" and "RL."[35]

Although secretly funded by the U.S. government through the CIA, Radio Free Europe/Radio Liberty claimed to be supported by private donations and operated by Eastern European exiles.[36] According to Klose, it was like a "double scam." Not only was the Agency funding it, it was also raising funds for it in the United States. This ambiguity of origination was to cause much trouble in the 1960s, when the Senate Committee on Foreign Relations (led by Senator William Fulbright) almost shut down RFE/RL. In the early 1970s the association with the CIA was officially broken, and the Radios became funded directly by Congress, under the management of the Board for International Broadcasting.

The mission for RFE/RL became more clearly defined in the 1970s as surrogate broadcasters for those countries unable to enjoy press freedom. An independent commission set up to study the service's operations during that time declared that if "a precondition for world peace is international freedom of information," the Radios were an integral part of achieving success.[37] Ironically, however, "success" would ultimately spell the demise for RFE/RL, after the collapse of the Eastern European Bloc. In fact, nothing would ever be quite the same for U.S. transnational radio.

RADIO MARTI: ORIGINS AND DEVELOPMENT

While VOA and the Radios were concentrating much of their efforts in Central and Eastern Europe, Asia, and Africa during the 1970s and 1980s, another American transnational radio service began to make headlines much closer to home. As a reaction to what were perceived to be growing human rights violations in Cuba, the USIA set up an Office of Cuba Broadcasting to augment VOA's attendant programming to anti-Castro forces. Soon afterwards, on October 4, 1983, Radio Marti (RM) was established through a Radio Broadcasting to Cuba Act. The mission of this service was to promote "freedom and democracy in Cuba through offering objective, accurate, and balanced information to the Cuban audience,"[38] that is, to provide surrogate broadcasts to those who could not produce balanced programming for themselves. More specifically, Radio Marti was chartered by Congress with the following rationale:

1. That it is the policy of the United States to support the right of the people of Cuba to seek, receive, and impart information and ideas through any media and regardless of frontiers, in accordance with article 19 of [the] Universal Declaration of Human Rights;

2. That, consonant with this policy, radio broadcasting to Cuba may be effective in furthering the open communication of accurate information and ideas to the people of Cuba, in particular information about Cuba;
3. That such broadcasting to Cuba, operated in a manner not inconsistent with the broad foreign policy of the United States and in accordance with high professional standards, would be in the national interest;
4. That the Voice of America already broadcasts to Cuba information that represents America, not any single segment of American society, and includes a balanced and comprehensive projection of significant American thought and institutions but that there is a need for broadcasts to Cuba which provide news, commentary and other information about events in Cuba and elsewhere to promote the cause of freedom in Cuba.[39]

Like the Voice of America, Radio Marti emanates from Washington, D.C. with news, music, and features 24 hours each day, 7 days a week, through both short- and medium-wave. According to the USIA's research, Radio Marti has been "widely listened to and . . . perceived as highly credible"[40] since its inception, although media scholar John S. Nichols suggests strongly that RM is only one of several popular underground radio services that programs regularly to anti-Castro groups.[41]

Regardless of the debate over its perceived effectiveness, no one can deny that Radio Marti continues to be a strong broadcast presence in Cuba, holding true to the goals of its original charter. Perhaps this is due, in part, to its transnational service's relative "youth" when compared to its counterparts. However, a more compelling argument might be that Radio Marti, unlike RFE/RL and VOA, has not had to adjust to a new political landscape within the last few years. Castro's regime has continued to hold strong despite the collapse of the former Soviet Republic. In short, Radio Marti has not experienced the U.S. transnational broadcasting fallout caused by the collapse of the Berlin Wall.

AFTER THE WALL: THE VOA PERSPECTIVE

In 1993 President Clinton accepted the advice of some of his congresspeople to merge all transnational radio and television services under a single administration. Ironically, Kim Elliott, a member of VOA's Audience Analysis Division, actually started the debate through his 1989/1990 article in *Foreign Policy*, entitled, "Too Many Voices of America."[42] In a 1994 interview Elliott was asked to describe his original position. Elliott responded in this way:

My argument was that we needed to consolidate our resources because frequencies, transmitting sites, journalists who have abilities in these various languages in which we broadcast, are all scarce commodities no matter how much we spend on international broadcasting. If we split those commodities among competing bureaucracies, our chance of succeeding in international broadcasting diminishes; in fact, it falls short. That is the reason why the U.S. spends twice as much on international broadcasting as Britain. . . . They are very efficient and we are not.[43]

Obviously, Elliott's assertions coincided with those held by many Congressional representatives. They ultimately resulted in Clinton's federalization proposal. However, most congresspeople rarely visit VOA, the Radios, or the other transnational services affected by the new organizational plan. Often, the view "from the top" is not exactly the one seen from lower perches, as demonstrated by some 1994 interviews with VOA personnel in Washington, D.C.

In April 1994, the mood at the network seemed to be one of unsettlement over the potential consequences of American transnational radio's newest structural renovation. For example, Deputy Director of the VOA Office of Programs Alan Heil described the potential of the consolidation; but also warned of a long road to get there:

I think that if we had a truly integrated international broadcast organization, and a single one, on the British model, and certainly with the same protections for content integrity that they have, it is possible with the economies of scale . . . we probably could be absolutely and unquestionably the best. What we do is remarkable considering the limitations we have, considering the mixed system--partly a grantee organization and partly a federal organization, and each with entirely different rules and ways of operating, from philosophies to programming approaches. So it is going to be quite a number of years, probably, before we get this ideal station.[44]

Other VOA employees underscored Heil's vision of potential rockiness along the road to federalization by comparing themselves either to "former" rivals . . . or those who might be looming on the horizon. More specifically, when assessing RFE/RL's coverage in the former Soviet Bloc to that of VOA in the 1990s, Deputy Chief Joseph Buday (North European Division) responded in this way:

I do not see the clear-cut distinction anymore . . . but I don't think they have a magic political wand where they can say "I can impress and make better friends than you can." We both speak Hungarian, we both broadcast presumably American . . . ideals, explaining American policy. I don't think that being a Polish or Hungarian broadcast operating out of Munich [or Prague] makes me more competent to reach and impress the audience than if I am in Washington. I just don't quite understand. Now, if that means that you have people, resources, more stringers who report about the problems of lack of government support for farming permits in northeast Bohemia or whatever; if that is an issue, [it's] very specialized. We do now use more stringers in most of these areas to make up for that. . . . I do not see how RFE could do that any better. It is always just a matter of resources, of people.[45]

Betty Tseu (Chief of the Mandarin Service of VOA's China Branch), on the other hand, discussed her apprehensions about sharing hard-won monetary resources with the new Radio Free Asia:[46]

I have concerns for the new vigor and enthusiasm that we have [accomplished] in our reporting in recent years. The reason for this concern is because most of this new momentum came from our new recruits; these young, talented people that we have recruited and painstakingly trained afterwards. Now, this cutting of the budget would probably impact on their future promotion. You see, most of these people have their green card now. They are free to leave and choose another job if they want to. So if the China Branch does not get continued support for its personnel, I am afraid we are going to lose some of these most talented people that we have.[47]

Clearly, the goals for the Voice of America in the twenty-first century will not be established as quickly as those derived when the service pledged to assert "America's determination and ability to bring the war [World War II] to a successful conclusion."[48] But, as discussed in later chapters, the VOA's mission is evolving as the world adjusts to life without a USSR.

AFTER THE WALL: THE RFE/RL PERSPECTIVE

On October 18, 1993, Eugene Pell finally voiced the words his staff had been dreading for over two years: By 1996, more than 800 positions would be eliminated from the Radio Free Europe (RFE) service. As this announcement reverberated throughout the long corridors of its Munich-based headquarters, Pell's earlier warnings about RFE's ultimate demise became real--because all of Europe was now "free," there apparently would be little need for "Free Europe." For those who support the principles of surrogate broadcasting--that is, speaking for those who have no voice--the proposed elimination of this respected, transnational radio service was premature and ill-advised.

Despite having felt some pressure in 1990 during the Bush administration, the Munich-based, privately funded Radio Free Europe/Radio Liberty (also known as RFE/RL, or "the Radios") had survived intense scrutiny by a special commission for international broadcasting, the Hughes Commission, deployed by President Bush in 1991. The Commission, specifically charged with devising a plan to consolidate all international broadcasting by the United States, concluded (after six to seven months of research-gathering and public hearings) that the various international broadcasting institutions--RFE/RL, VOA (Voice of America), the Office of Cuba Broadcasting (including Radio Marti) and the proposed Radio Free Asia--should not be consolidated.[49]   Further, the Commission's findings indicated that Radio Free Europe would be needed for the next few years and that Radio Liberty should continue well into the next century. Unfortunately, according to Eugene Pell (former President of the Radios),[50] this report went largely ignored "because it didn't fit the conventional wisdom of some who thought the outcome should be different."

In fact, the goals and objectives of each of the transnational broadcast systems identified in the Hughes Commission Reports differ markedly. Radio Marti and the proposed Radio Free Asia, for example, have very specific geographic audiences, issues, and political concerns. Radio Free Europe/Radio Liberty, on the other hand, recognize regional differences but are most well-known for their unique approach to journalistic reporting. As stated in their original mission statements, the Radios strive to be "surrogate broadcasters"--providing unfettered news to nations who have little or no access to it. This programming philosophy contrasts sharply from the Voice of America, which exists to project the United States government's position, policy, and image throughout the world in English and other languages.   In the meantime, the staff at RFE/RL continued to transmit (from within each country, as opposed to relying on stringers living abroad)[51] news and features such as RFE/RL's "The Democratic Experience" and RL's Moscow-based "Face to Face," as well as an ambitious live, two-way broadcast between Munich and Moscow entitled "Liberty Live."

The management staff at the Radios during this time, including Gene Pell,[52] William Marsh (RFE/RL Executive Vice President, Programs and Policy), Kevin Klose (Director, Radio Liberty),[53] and Robert Gillette (Director, Radio Free Europe), exhibited highly charged emotion at Clinton's decision.   The overall feeling was that a comparison of the two American services through their mission statements was a bit like pitting apples against oranges.

VOA, founded in 1942, is a worldwide service, broadcasting partly in English and partly in other languages. Like CNN, VOA-Europe broadcasts in English only, and its "programming is based upon scripts centrally written by Americans." VOA's mission, according to an editorial in the *Wall Street Journal*,[54] is to "describe America to the outside world." Or, as Walter Laqueur writes in the *Wall Street Journal*,

There is no overlap [between RFE/RL and VOA]. The task of VOA is, to put it inelegantly, to "sell America." . . . VOA has many merits, but its direct political impact in Russia and Eastern Europe is almost nil, whereas that of the Munich radios is immense.[55]

VOA is not only generally perceived to be a voice of the U.S. government, it is *in fact* a voice of the U. S. government, headquartered in Washington, D.C. No one disputes that it does its job well. But there are those who, particularly in Eastern Europe and the former Soviet Union, fear and distrust the VOA as a government mouthpiece. Given the 40-70 years' history of government controlled media, small wonder that there is a distrust of any media speaking for any government. As American citizens have reason to know, in our own history, we are, from time to time, wary of the media. For the former Soviet Union and Eastern European countries, the experience is still vivid. Lech Walesa, former Solidarity leader and now president of Poland, wrote in 1993:

There are those institutions which have changed our world. Without them, the world would have been completely different. The Polish Section of Radio Free Europe is one such institution. . . . How fortunate that "the iron curtain" could not be raised so high as to block radio transmissions. Although the boundaries were impenetrable for people, they were not so for shortwaves. The truth seeped in, unseen by the border guards and their dogs, above the mine fields, between the barbed wire, alongside reconnaissance planes and patrol boats. It proved impossible to stop; impossible to silence it.[56]

From broadcast content to home base and lifestyle VOA is American, and unlike RFE/RL, it was not meant to be a surrogate facility, nor has it evolved over time and under changing conditions into a surrogate news facility. Despite the rationale developed for implementation of the proposed plan, VOA and RFE/RL do not overlap in programming. The issue is two-pronged--money and the "vision thing"--and the United States, with its traditional respect for freedom of speech and the role of the media in maintaining that tradition within democracies, seems to have lost sight of the difference between propaganda and news.

One clearly visible difference between VOA's and RFE/RL's philosophy of broadcasting could be found in their production facilities overseas. The casual visitor would have had great trouble finding the VOA in Munich because no signs illuminated one's way through the maze of offices and no flags flew to indicate the American presence. Located on Ludwigstrasse, near one of the wealthiest shopping districts in Europe, the edifice looked more ambassadorial than journalistic.

Whatever its undisputed achievements, the Voice of America is still perceived as an official mouthpiece, transmitting official material and propaganda. In an editorial, Kazimierz Woycicki (Editor-in-Chief, *Zycie Warsawy*) describes his view of the role of RFE/RL:

Modern democracy is largely predicated on the existence of a proper order and civilized relations within the media as an element of the democratic system. . . . The Munich based radio station owes its enormous influence to the fact that it has created its unique style of journalism. RFE transmits, to a far greater degree, the democratic way of thinking and attitude towards the world.[57]

GOVERNMENT RADIO VS. SURROGATE RADIO: POINT-COUNTERPOINT

How and why were the Radios perceived differently? In contrast to the VOA, RFE/RL has been responsible to the BIB or Board of International Broadcasting rather than to the USIA since 1973. When the Radios were founded (RFE in 1949; RL in 1951), they were not perceived favorably because they were funded by the U.S. government through the CIA (there were still at the Munich headquarters a few former CIA employees when we conducted our interviews). Further, their policies and promises were not always in sync with the possible as during the Hungarian uprising, during which RFE/RL reportedly encouraged the Hungarian people by saying that help would come--and it did not. Chastened by this experience, the radios began to streamline their system, though there is no question that one major goal of their program was to encourage dissent, to bring about, if possible, the dissolution of the Soviet Union and Eastern Europe.

In the 1970s, the Radios again came under fire during the Nixon administration, and in 1971 "all connections with the CIA were severed"[58] and, in 1973, the BIB was formed. The two Radios merged as RFE/RL, Inc., on October 1, 1976. The budget for RFE/RL was allocated by Congress and is approximately $220 million a year in 1993. Thus, since 1976 RFE/RL, unlike VOA, was a private entity that was not responsible to the United States government. The Radios' "corporate existence" was therefore quite different. As mentioned previously, VOA is headquartered in Washington, whereas RFE/RL were originally located in Munich (later reestablished in Prague). This situation had considerable impact upon the hierarchical structure and the tax situation of each entity and of its individual employees as well as negotiation for AM/FM space with governments of nations receiving both VOA and RFE/RL signals.

In the furor created by the Clinton administration's proposal to dissolve RFE/RL, integrating or federalizing them, *Pravda* commended the proposal, commenting bitterly on the role of RL in the dissolution of the Soviet Union. In Romania, Mircea M. Dabija, in *Europa*, wrote:

Radio Liberty had and still has as its target the current area of the former Soviet Union, and its sister, Radio Free Europe--the area of the other former socialist countries from the center and east of our continent. These radios inspired, established and actually financed by the main intelligence agency of the USA, the CIA, in close connection with the USIA, came into existence at the beginning of the hot cold war, which they ignited and kept up industriously and fanatically, being some of the most important and effective propaganda means of the capitalist West against the socialist East.[59]

Meant as a stinging indictment of the Radios, the Munich-based RFE/RL used the article as evidence of its continuing success and effectiveness--the material could be found in the packet prepared for the Congressional delegation to Munich in the spring of 1993, during the budget hearings. The article did serve, however, to illuminate the complexity and ambiguity of RFE/RL's past and future mission, raising the question of the integrity of the existing Radios (and the proposed Radio Free Asia Service) and its ability to foster the ideal, or Western, objective journalistic practices and ethics.

Relatedly, journalist Adam Michnik, an opponent of the Clinton plan, summarized the view of many:

In all these countries dictatorship has lost and freedom has won. But that does not mean that democracy has won. Democracy means the institutionalization of freedom. We don't have a democratic order, and that is why our freedom is so fragile and shaky.[60]

Michnik was making a clear distinction between freedom and democracy, illuminating the task ahead, which was more difficult in the short term than the peoples of these newly-freed countries were prepared for. As Robert Pirsig says in *Zen and the Art of Motorcycle Maintenance*, you can change the system but if you don't change the system, of the thinking underlying it, nothing changes. However much one may chafe under an authoritarian regime, the reality is that one gets used to and absorbs the prevailing way of thinking, unknowingly. Further, as in the communist hierarchy, certain people manage, others obey. The only persons who know how to manage in formerly communist countries are--the old managers! Thus, there is a practical dearth of information/expertise on democracy and management in the former Soviet Union and in Eastern Europe. This situation, argued the journalists at the Munich-based RFE/RL, necessitated that RFE/RL not be absorbed into the Voice of America (VOA) as per the plan issued by the Board for International Broadcasting. Simply put, RFE/RL claimed that merging with VOA invalidated the political, social, and linguistic credibility of RFE/RL, which is based upon news gathered and delivered by nationals in the language of the country. Secondly, RFE/RL provided the training ground for Eastern European journalists, necessary to developing Western media integrity, perceived to be essential to the development and maintenance of democratic institutions. Third, RFE/RL argued that there is still a strong need for surrogate international broadcasting, providing

the peoples of Eastern Europe and the Soviet Union with an objective, alternative view of their own societies, their neighbors and the world at large . . . encourage the understanding and spread of democratic ideas, values and practices . . . and provide a model of journalistic practices and ethics.[61]

There were two issues here. The first issue concerned the status of each Radio; the second issue concerned the incredible technical and technological changes occurring within transnational media worldwide. And, in fact, the status and technological issues are connected. That is, VOA negotiated with foreign governments on a different footing than did RFE/RL for transmitter sites and access to AM and FM channels. As part of the United States government, VOA negotiations with other governments often were more costly and restrictive than those of RFE/RL, because the latter was a private corporation. Thus, when the status of RFE/RL was altered, that is, federalized, all contracts currently in place had to be renegotiated in view of its new status. Therefore, one of the major reasons for federalization, to save money, actually vanished as new costs accrued under the newly created design for American international broadcasting.

Yet another, more serious consideration was that of perception and credibility. With RFE/RL's federalization, the perception of the Radios by other persons and governments has been altered. Senator Biden stated the dilemma well:

The issue is one of organization for this agreed purpose. In essence, can surrogate radios function effectively, with journalistic integrity and credibility, if their analysts and journalists are employees of the U. S. government?[62]

Here Senator Biden struck a nerve center of journalistic principles. For years, Americans railed against government-controlled presses, advocating the free-press approach followed in the United States. The media was conceived to be the "watchdog of Democracy." Why then did we propose to impose yet more governmental control over other nations? If we know, as we do, that most of the nations of the former Soviet Union and the Eastern European countries still have much the same archaic hierarchy--often run by former communists--and media infrastructure in place, now manned by poorly trained (by Western journalistic standards) journalists, why not continue to offer them (as RFE/RL now does) an alternative voice and rigorous training in journalistic principles, practices, and ethics? Why propose to introduce governmental control of the media--this time from the West, specifically from America? Was this akin to our policy of "dumping" America's cigarettes on second and third world countries without thought of the consequences? What of the consequences of losing a needed voice, particularly when virtually everyone but the U.S. Congress recognizes that although the Cold War may be over, democracy is not in place, and the newly freed countries are easy prey in perilous times for authoritarianism (or communism in new dress)? The view seemed shortsighted--but when have we ever done the "vision thing"? In Senator Biden's words,

It was a staple of the Cold War that Americans mocked countries that deployed "journalists" in the employee [sic] of governments. It would be a nice but unpleasant irony were we to mark the end of the Cold War by adopting this practice ourselves. Can anyone actually argue that journalism and government employment are compatible?[63]

The fates of RFE/RL and VOA have now been cast for the twenty-first century. We have yet to hear the voice--or see the effect--of a "Radio Free Asia" or "Asia Pacific Network."[64] Only future historians will be able to judge the wisdom of these moves.

NOTES

1. K. R. M. Short, ed., *Film and Radio Propaganda in World War II* (Knoxville, TN: The University of Tennessee Press, 1983), 29.
2. Sydney W. Head, *World Broadcasting Systems: A Comparative Analysis* (Belmont, CA: Wadsworth, 1985), 349-350.
3. Julian Hale, *Radio Power: Propaganda and International Broadcasting* (Philadelphia: Temple University Press, 1975), 32.
4. Walter B. Emery, *Broadcasting and Government: Responsibilities and Regulations* (East Lansing: Michigan State University Press, 1971), 165.
5. Head, 350.
6. *VOA Looking Toward Tomorrow Today* (Washington, DC: United States Information Agency, 1992), 4.
7. Geoffrey Cowan, Director of the VOA, Remarks at a Swearing-in Ceremony, 26 April 1994, Washington, D.C.
8. Asa Briggs, *A History of Broadcasting in the United Kingdom Vol. 3: The War of Words* (London: Oxford University Press, 1970), 412.
9. According to author Lawrence C. Soley in *Radio Warfare: OSS and CIA Subversive Propaganda* (New York: Praeger Publishers, 1989), 64, Donovan's radio strategy was opposed by playwright Robert Sherwood, FDR's appointed head of the Coordinator of Information's (COI) Foreign Information Service (FIS). Sherwood felt that "the truth" would outweigh Goebbel's "big lie;" but his position was later overruled in favor of Donovan's plan.
10. Allan M. Winkler, *The Politics of Propaganda* (New Haven: Yale University Press, 1971), 27-28.
11. Soley, 84.
12. Ibid., 126-129.
13. Robert William Pirsein, *The Voice of America: A History of the International Broadcasting Activities of the United States Government, 1940-1962* (New York: Arno, 1979).
14. Edward W. Barrett. *Truth Is Our Weapon* (New York: Funk & Wagnalls, 1953).
15. Shawn J. Parry-Giles, "Propaganda, Effect, and the Cold War: Gauging the Status of America's 'War of Words,'" *Political Communication* (April/June 1994): 207.

16. U.S. Subcommittee of the House Committee on Appropriations, Department of State Appropriation Bill for 1950 (Washington, D.C., 1949).

17. Parry-Giles includes activities such as student-distributed contraband pamphlets in the Soviet bloc when he defines the "grapevine" effect.

18. Ibid., 208.

19. Natalie Doyle-Hennin, *The World according to International Radio* (Ph.D. diss., State University of New York at Buffalo, 1991), 59.

20. Parry-Giles, 208.

21. Ibid., 209.

22. Doyle-Hennin, 59.

23. Sydney Head (op.cit.) notes that the USIA was called the International Communication Agency from 1977 to 1982; however, it was later changed because of its easy confusion with the CIA.

24. Barrett, 72ff.

25. Hale, 35.

26. Carolyn Weaver, "When the Voice of America Ignores Its Charter," *Columbia Journalism Review* (November/December 1988): 36.

27. Ibid.

28. Hale, 36.

29. It is important to add that BBC commentators were obviously hired and paid by the service's directors. Still, they were seen and treated as outside consultants.

30. Ibid.

31. Steve Knoll, "The Voice of America: Banned in the Land of the Free," *Washington Journalism Review* (May 1988), 44.

32. Weaver, 36-43.

33. "RFE/RL and VOA: What's the Difference?" (Munich: RFE/RL, 1993).

34. Short, 195.

35. Radio Liberty Director Kevin Klose, interview by authors, 7 August 1993, tape recording, Munich, Germany.

36. Soley, 221.

37. *The Right to Know*, Report of the Presidential Study Commission on International Radio Broadcasting (1973): 2.

38. USIA Home Page, Netscape 1996.

39. Ibid., Public Law 98-111 [S. 602]; 4 October 1983, Radio Broadcasting to Cuba Act.

40. Ibid.

41. For more specific information on other underground radio services during this time, read Nichols' case study, which can be found in Chapter 8 of this book.

42. Kim Andrew Elliott, "Too Many Voices of America," *Foreign Policy* (Winter 1989/1990): 113-131. For a more detailed script of Mr. Pell's views on the move to federalize international broadcasting, read the "Point/Counterpoint" case study in Chapter 10 of this book.

43. VOA Audience Analysis Division Officer Kim Andrew Elliott, interview by authors, 28 April 1994, tape recording, Washington, D.C. Elliott made it clear that his comments were personal opinions only and not necessarily reflective of the Voice of America.

44. Deputy Director Alan Heil, VOA Office of Programs, interview by authors, 28 April 1994, tape recording, Washington, D.C. Heil made it clear that his comments were personal opinions only and not necessarily reflective of the Voice of America.

45. Deputy Chief Joseph Buday, VOA North European Division, interview by authors, 28 April 1994, tape recording, Washington, D.C.

46. At press time, Radio Free Asia had been reformulated and renamed the Asia Pacific Network (APN) through a recommendation in the Broadcasting Board of Governors Report to Congress, 9 November 1995. Though not operational, the future plans for broadcasting on the APN included the countries of China, Burma, Cambodia, Laos, North Korea, Vietnam, and Tibet (each of which already receives VOA programming). The evolution of Radio Free Asia to the Asia Pacific Network is described more fully in the case study found in Chapter 12 of this book.

47. VOA Chinese Branch Chief Betty Tseu, Mandarin Service, interview by authors, 28 April 1994, tape recording, Washington, DC. Tseu made it clear that her comments were personal opinions only and not necessarily reflective of the Voice of America.

48. Donald R. Browne, *International Radio Broadcasting: The Limits of the Limitless Medium* (New York: Praeger, 1982), 95.

49. President of RFE/RL Gene Pell, interview by authors, 3 August 1993, tape recording, Munich, Germany. For testimony and findings, see the Hughes Commission Reports.

50. Mr. Pell announced his resignation from RFE/RL shortly after the announcement of the federalization plan. He left the Radios in October 1993.

51. Prior to 1989, RFE/RL's broadcasts did not originate within the countries that they served. News and features were suggested/provided by the stringers (often dissidents, once in a while spies) who lived abroad in such major cities as London, Vienna, and Paris. Now RFE/RL has bureaus in the countries that it serves.

52. For a more detailed script of Mr. Pell's views on the move to federalize international broadcasting, read the "Point/Counterpoint" case study in Chapter 10 of this text.

53. For more insight into Mr. Klose's views on federalization, read the case study, "In His Own Words," found in Chapter 9 of this book.

54. Editorial, "Yeltsin Should Ask," *Wall Street Journal,* 2 April 1993. It should be noted that this editorial (as well as all other incomplete cites) were taken from a Radio Free Europe/Radio Liberty Press packet given to the authors at the outset of our visit.

55. Walter Laqueur, "The Dangers of Radio Silence," *Wall Street Journal,* 4 March 1993.

56. Lech Walesa, "From the President of the Republic of Poland, Warsaw, May 1992, to the Polish Section, Radio Free Europe," *Board for International Broadcasting 1993 Annual Report on Radio Free Europe/Radio Liberty,* Malcolm S. Forbes, Chairman. Washington, D. C.: Board for International Broadcasting, 1993: 5.

57. Kazimierz Woycicki, "Eastern Europe Still Needs This Message," *Zycie Warsawy,* n.d.

58. Fact sheet, RFE/RL, July 1992, 8.

59. Mircea M. Dabija, *Europa,* 6-13 April 1993.

60. Adam Michnik, *Guardian,* 1 March 1991.

61. "Surrogate Broadcasting: An Evolving Concept," RFE/RL.

62. Foreign Relations Committe Report on the Foreign Authorization Act, Fiscal Years 1994 and 1995.

63. "Additional views of Senator Biden" are part of the Foreign Relations

Committee Report on the Foreign Relations Authorization Act, fiscal years 1994 and 1995, 74.

64. The saga of Radio Free Asia/Asia Pacific Network can be found in Chapter 12 of this book.

Part II

CASE STUDIES IN TRANSNATIONAL RADIO

4

The Scepter and the Sickle: Vatican Radio and the Solidarity Movement

Marilyn J. Matelski

Case Study One

Nineteen eighty-nine will long be remembered as "the year of independence" for most Eastern European countries--a year in which many nations, torn apart for centuries by outside political domination, were finally able to reclaim their rights to freedom and sovereignty. Poland was among the leaders in this great upheaval, receiving both religious and political support for its Solidarity movement. In fact, some of the nation's most influential backing came from the Vatican and Pope John Paul II (formerly Karol Wojtyla), who had himself lived under the yoke of communism in his earlier years.

It is important to note that even before John Paul's reign, Poland was unique from most other Soviet Bloc nations in its freedom to practice religion. This was most likely due to the country's overwhelmingly Catholic population and the threat of rebellion, should "the faithful" be denied access to Church rites. More specifically, it was directly related to the earlier work of Cardinal Stefan Wyszynski shortly after the war.

Cardinal Wyszynski had been the driving force behind the creation of a permanent "Mixed Commission" between Polish church and the Soviet state in 1950. The key phrase in this Polish accord was that

the principle that the Pope is the competent and highest Church authority applies to matters of faith, morality and Church jurisdiction; in other areas, the Episcopate will be guided by the Polish *raison d'état* [national interest].[1]

In other words, in exchange for a "permanent" Polish Church, clergy would agree to include, as part of their pastoral mission, a respect for the laws of the state. This allowed Catholic churches and universities to operate with little interference in Poland.

Even after Wyszynski was arrested in 1953, the agreement still continued to hold. In short, Polish peasants, because of their strong belief in and support from Roman Catholicism, had perhaps been better able than their neighbors to withstand communist rule for a long time. Unlike the cases in Yugoslavia, Hungary, and Czechoslovakia, where hundreds of nuns and priests (including Cardinal Josef Mindszenty, Primate of Hungary) were tortured and murdered for their faith, the Poles were allowed some religious freedom even under periods of great duress.

Pope John Paul, in his early days as a protégé of Cardinal Wyszynski, had made no secret of his personal commitment to free Poland. Shortly after his election in 1978, he announced plans to revisit his homeland; and for the next decade, he used any means possible--either public or underground--to influence Poland's political future. Soviet leaders were highly aware of the Pontiff's potential clout. For example, author Tad Szulc recaps this conversation between President Leonid Brezhnev and Poland's First Secretary Edward Gierek upon hearing about his impending visit:

Brezhnev said, "I advise you not to receive him because it will cause you much trouble." I replied: "How can I not receive the Polish pope since the majority of our compatriots are of Catholic faith, and for them the election was a great feast. Besides, what do you imagine I can tell the people? Why are we closing the barrier to him?" Brezhnev said: "Tell the pope--he is a wise man--that he could announce publicly that he cannot come because he has been taken ill." I answered: "Comrade Leonid, I cannot do that. I must receive John Paul II."[2]

As it happened, Brezhnev was most prophetic in his fears.

John Paul II was perhaps the most likely candidate to initiate social change in Poland in the 1980s. He understood the "reality" of living as a Catholic within an atheistic world. He also understood the unique relationship between the Church and Polish nationalism--an intricately woven identity sewn from two very different cultural threads. Using his religious authority as well as the propaganda agents at hand (such as local church meetings, Vatican Radio broadcasts, and instrumental local leaders), the Pontiff could unify a country that had been divided for almost two centuries.

HISTORICAL BACKGROUND

Catholicism in Poland can be traced back to the tenth century, when Polish rulers used religion as a political tool to gain more land for their kingdoms. The Christian movement among the royalty had little initial impact upon the rest of the country, however, because Slavic tribes had worshipped in their own ways for at least two centuries and were reluctant to be converted. Gradually, as more towns and villages were built, new generations began to combine ancient rites with Christian rituals. By the thirteenth century, secular tradition became secondary to sacred rule, especially after the Church had repeatedly defended its followers from the unjust tyranny of autocratic princes.

From 1350 to 1572, Poland entered into its Golden Age,[3] nurtured by the Church in both politics and culture. King Casimir the Great (1333-1370), a brilliant ruler and staunch Catholic, drafted Poland's first Constitution and rebuilt Krakow into a magnificent world capital. Then, in 1385, the Grand Duke of Lithuania married the Polish Princess Jadwiga, creating a commonwealth of two nations (with one parliament) that was to last over two hundred years.[4] By the sixteenth century, the Polish aristocracy had grown in wealth and power, enjoying great prosperity from this political alliance. The lower classes were less content. As a result, Poland suffered great internal strife from 1572 to 1795. Unfortunately, the constant upheaval weakened the nation considerably, leaving it vulnerable for conquest by the Prussians in 1795. Poland ceased to exist as an independent state for the next 124 years.

During this "dark" period in Polish political history, however, the spirit of nationalism was still alive, along with a strong commitment to the Catholic faith. Most historians agree that Prussia's occupation of Poland actually served to galvanize the latter's cultural identity with the Church. To be Polish was also to be Catholic--a metaphorical connection that served to bolster people's hopes for social justice and religious freedom during long periods of political strife.

Prussian rule was succeeded by Nazi occupation and (after World War II) Soviet domination. Still, the Poles stood firmly in their godless world, due in part to a rich religious heritage. Author Eric O. Hanson provides a detailed description of what it meant to be a Catholic during the Cold War years:

Over the centuries religion has become an integral part of the Polish peasants' practical interests and folk customs. Farmers pray in the morning upon rising and again at midday, kneeling in the fields when they hear the sound of the church bells. They stop at roadside shrines which cover the countryside to cross themselves or kiss the feet of a statue of Jesus. Hail Marys are said to ward off evil spirits, and throughout the day the customary peasant greeting can be heard, "Praised be Jesus Christ," and the reply, "World without end." Sundays bring rest and prayer and an opportunity to socialize with one's neighbor at church. For the peasant, regular attendance at mass, receiving communion, and going to confession are all part of being a "good" Catholic. The church building itself represents God, Christ, and the saint to whom it is dedicated. For this reason construction of churches is a vital point of contention with the government. Pilgrimages also remain a very important part of life for the Catholic peasantry. Each year the entire community travels as a group to the shrine of the Black Madonna at Czestochowa. Poland defers only to Italy in the number of ecclesiastical holidays. Epiphany, Lent, Easter Week, and Mary's Assumption are observed with mass peasant pilgrimages. The pilgrimages and their destinations are not announced outside the village. The peasants board up their farms and follow their parish priest into the countryside for up to a week. Thus, the entire life of the Polish peasant centers around his religion.[5]

With this in mind, it is not hard to imagine the enormous impact a Polish pope would have on a heavily Catholic population suppressed by Communist rule. Even before John Paul II's election, Poland had been treated differently from most other Soviet satellite nations because of its strong ties with the Church. The new Pope, armed with a local cadre of religious leaders, messages of peace and social justice, and an electronic medium to display Poland's plight to the rest of the world, was well equipped to further weaken an already fractured system of control.

THE SOLIDARITY POPE

Before the Pope's plane ever touched down at the Warsaw airport on June 2, 1979, Vatican Radio had already begun its campaign to disseminate news of his impending visit. According to a BBC broadcast,[6] the Polish section director, Father Stefan Filipowicz, toured throughout the country in 1978, giving at least 35 seminars on the accessibility of Vatican Radio as well as updates on the Holy Father's latest international travels. By early 1979, parish bulletin boards in front of nearly every church in Poland posted the hours, wavelengths, and means of locating VR stations for every potential listener. Thus, the masses were well-prepared to receive the new Pontiff, as well as his pleas for courage and strength in the quest for religious freedom.

To some outsiders, the 1979 Polish tour was seen as little more than a nine-day exercise in papal public relations. However, to those who followed Pope John Paul at each stage of his sacred mission, the Pontiff's diplomatic and emotional commitment for Polish independence was unquestioned. As a result, the initial euphoria at Warsaw airport never diminished throughout his tour--at each stop, both Catholics and non-Catholics[7] cheered his every word. Certain reporters wondered aloud as to whether or not the crowds could actually *hear* the Pontiff's words; in fact, most of the faithful were able to receive his message through transistor radio. Via Vatican Radio shortwave and local state radio AM broadcasts,[8] Pope John Paul was able to comment on such subjects as the intrinsic bond between Catholics and Poland:

The millenium [sic] of Christianity in Poland is the main reason for my pilgrimage here and for my prayers--together with all of you, my beloved countrymen, whom Jesus Christ never ceases to teach the great cause of man, with you for whom Christ does not cease to be an open book of teaching about man, about his rights, and at the same time about the dignity and rights of nations. . . . It is impossible without Christ to understand and appraise the contribution of the Polish nation to the development of man and his humanity.[9]

With words such as these, John Paul II's 1979 visit to Poland--the first ever by a Roman Catholic pope to a socialist country--became a more powerful symbolic gesture than a substantive event.

One of the most significant aspects of the Poland trip, however, was the diplomatic meeting between the Pontiff and the First Secretary of the Polish Party at that time, Edward Gierek. As the sacred and secular Polish leaders began to converse, the respective agendas of each man were revealed. Gierek, in his welcoming speech, voiced the hope that Pope John Paul's visit would further "the causes which are most dear to us: the well-being of Poland, and the good of mankind."[10] He continued:

It is this unity of the Polish nation on all fundamental questions of national and state existence, irrespective of social position, education, or attitude toward religion, that is the main source of the . . . accomplishments and the basic premise for the nation's future.[11]

The stage was now set for more direct outside intervention. Accordingly, after the Pope's visit, both he and Vatican Radio took on a more active role in Polish politics. And, as author David Willey observes:

If anyone had asked him [Pope John Paul II] whether his motives were political or religious in trying to influence the course of modern European history, I am sure he would have found the question as absurd as if it had been asked during the Middle Ages of one of the crusading kings of France or England. For Karol Wojtyla the divisions between Polish patriotism, faith and politics [were] happily blurred.[12]

Thus, in January 1981, John Paul II formally welcomed Solidarity leader Lech Walesa to Vatican City, just a few months after the free trade union agreements had been signed in Gdansk. Further, reporter Carl Bernstein asserts that the Pontiff actually formed a secret, anticommunist alliance in the early 1980s with former U.S. president Ronald Reagan to destroy the Soviet Union:

Reagan and John Paul II refused to accept a fundamental political fact of their lifetimes: the division of Europe as mandated at Yalta and the communist dominance of Eastern Europe. A free, non-communist Poland, they were convinced, would be a dagger to the heart of the Soviet empire; and if Poland became democratic, other Eastern European states would follow.[13]

For its part, the United States promised to build its Strategic Defense Initiative, as well as its covert operations among dissidents in Hungary, Czechoslovakia, and Poland; and to provide financial help to Warsaw Pact nations, economic and technological boycotts of the Soviet Union, and increased support to Radio Free Europe, Radio Liberty, and the Voice of America. One of the key personnel in this plan was CIA Director William Casey, a staunch Catholic and Knight of Malta.[14] In return, the Vatican pledged to continue its push for human rights in Poland, to provide help for dissident groups throughout the Eastern European Bloc, and to collect and deliver intelligence on internal affairs to the U.S. government.[15] Bernstein goes on to describe the mutually covert activities led by the United States and the Vatican:

Books and pamphlets challenging the authority of the communist government were printed by the thousands. Comic books for children recast Polish fables and legends, with [Communist General] Jaruzelski pictured as the villain, communism as the red dragon and Walesa as the heroic knight. In church basements and homes, millions of viewers watched documentary videos produced and screened on the equipment smuggled into the country.[16]

In addition, Vatican Radio stood by as the "watchdog" for Polish, Czech, and Hungarian church-state activities. In April 1981, for example, VR reported governmental aggression against the priests and seminarians in Czechoslovakia.[17] Shortly afterwards, the transnational Catholic radio service (along with Radio Free Europe, the Voice of America, and the BBC) was denounced by Tamas Palos, a Hungarian Party official, of "advising Hungarian workers to make their trade unions more actively come out against state bodies"[18] through its support of the "anti-socialist activities of the extremist leaders of the Polish trade union Solidarity."[19]

The Soviets were not without a secret campaign as well. Journalist Tad Szulc reveals that some documents found in the archives of the Central Committee of the Soviet Communist Party in Moscow recently revealed a six-point "Decision to Work Against the Policies of the Vatican in Relation with Socialist States."[20] This "Decision" outlined specific propagandistic strategies involving the state media, the Foreign Affairs Ministry, and the KGB. According to Szulc's findings, the latter was directed to "publicize in the Western countries [the fact] that Vatican policies are harmful," and "to show that the leadership of the new pope . . . is dangerous to the Catholic Church."[21] Some sources have also suggested (although it has never been proven) that the KGB might also have been involved in the 1981 assassination attempt against the Pontiff. Whether it was or was not may never be known--what is clear is that a physical wound did little to impair John Paul's growing momentum.

On May 13, 1981, Pope John Paul II was temporarily incapacitated by a would-be assassin's bullet. Radio Vaticana continued its shortwave broadcast activities throughout the crisis, serving as both journalist and political activist for religious freedom. On the day of the shooting, author Paul Hofmann reports:

Vatican Radio, which had routinely been covering his general audience, went right on reporting the attack, the pontiff being rushed to the hospital, and the surgery. Networks in many countries took on the running broadcast from the Vatican in one of the greatest radio hookups ever achieved.[22]

For several weeks after the assassination attempt, Vatican Radio served as the conduit between the recovering pope and his followers through taped messages from Rome's Gemelli Hospital. In one such address, John Paul II sent hopeful greetings to his Polish countrymen:

I want to speak in my native language to pilgrims and all my countrymen. Like all of you, I worry constantly about the problems of our country and pray for an abundant and happy harvest. I share with you all the hope that no one in our country lacks bread and all that which is indispensable for life.[23]

After his recovery, the Pope returned to his summer residence in Castel Gandolfo. Once again, using Vatican Radio, John Paul continued his quest to liberate Poland--but this time, he did so more pointedly than in the past. According to BBC reports, the Holy Father used VR's Polish shortwave service to remember:

the momentous events which took place a year [before] in Gdansk, Szczecin and other parts of Poland, or the gathering [of] the congress which has just got underway, the Solidarity Congress. . . . We must always remember our great contribution to the right to independent and sovereign statehood, and that the observance of this right of our nation, just as of every nation, is a condition for international order and calm in the world.[24]

Members of the Solidarity Union, who by this time had challenged several bloody attempts to destroy their growing movement, were especially heartened by Pope John Paul's candor and support. In a telegram, the delegates asserted "that in the Holy Father, they had a special guide in their endeavor to make the principles of justice, truth, love and freedom the basis of social life."[25] They subsequently invited the Pontiff to attend ceremonies for the 600th anniversary of their most holy shrine, Our Lady of Jasna Gora, in Czestochowa, where portraits of his own likeness also hung.[26] Solidarity was now identified not only as a nationalist movement but as a religious one as well.

THE MEDIA PROFILE OF SOLIDARITY

By 1982 the secret anticommunist pact between President Ronald Reagan and Pope John Paul II had begun to solidify, especially in the area of transnational radio. As shown in Table 4.1, Vatican Radio compared very favorably to the other "propaganda voices" of the world.[27] More importantly, Vatican Radio was one of the only transnational services able to overcome Soviet jamming,[28] presenting both religious and political programming each day. As one correspondent described:

Three times a day, after the standard Vatican Radio greeting "Praised be Jesus Christ," in Latin and Polish, the Poles can hear a round-up of the Pope's activities and other religious news from Rome and the rest of the world, including Poland. On Sundays and feast days a full-length mass in Polish is broadcast in a separate transmission. The church's radio does not comment on events in Poland, but it reports the views of world leaders. So Polish listeners have been able to hear the reactions of President Reagan, Mrs. [Margaret] Thatcher and Mr. [Helmut] Schmidt as well as the Pope's critical remarks since martial law was imposed on December 13th. The service has also broadcast in full the critical sermons of Archbishop Glemp, Poland's primate, which have not been reported in Poland's censored press. In order to deal with events in Poland the station's transmissions, normally lasting for 15 minutes, have often been extended in recent weeks.[29]

Quite obviously, the "hot spot" of political controversy in Poland during this time was the Lenin shipping yards in Gdansk. In the early months of 1982, a group of foreign journalists visited the site where a little-known trade union movement had catapulted itself into international recognition the year before. They noted that the previous conditions of crisis had abated somewhat--that is, martial law had been relaxed, some telephone and telex service had been restored, and travel seemed less restrictive in most areas of the nation. Unfortunately, the citizens of Gdansk, having been identified clearly as troublemakers, were not allowed to enjoy the same new privileges as their countrymen. Their spirit was quickly rekindled by the Pontiff, however, who sent his support in an address to international trade union leaders via Vatican Radio. The BBC World Service summarized John Paul's remarks, where he said that Solidarity was still an authentic and legal representative of the workers; praised it for rejecting violence; and expressed the belief that restoration of genuine and complete respect for the rights of workers--particularly their right to a trade union which had already been formed and legalized--was the only way of emerging from the difficult situation.[30]

Table 4.1
Profile of Transnational Radio Services: 1982

	Hrs. Broadcast/Week	Languages	Employees	Annual Budget
VR	210	35	350	NA
VOA	868	39	3900*	$197 m*
RFE	554	6	see VOA	see VOA
RL	476	15	see VOA	see VOA
BBC	725	46	3240	$105m
DW/DF**	80	37	1479	$110m
RM***	2073	82	NA	$700m

*The available employee and annual budget figures for VOA, RFE, and RL were combined figures only.
**DW/DF is Deutsche Welle and Deutschlandfunk
*** is Radio Moscow

These figures were taken from *U.S. News & World Report* (Lexis/Nexis Computer Search, 11 January 1982) and *The Economist* (Lexis/Nexis Computer Search, 23 January 1982).

Solidarity workers took the Pontiff's comments (as well as those from other supportive powers) to heart--within months, they aligned themselves with radical political parties and began to demonstrate more fervently (and more violently) for their cause. This resulting chaos caused state officials to outlaw the trade union and to impose martial law on the entire nation in December 1981.[31] The Pontiff was devastated by the blow. However, John Paul, clearly aware of the delicate balancing act between church and state freedoms, decided that his best diplomatic move following the censure was to voice disapproval of the union's apparent methods of social justice. Through his Primate Council, the Holy Father chided Solidarity for its part in the growing Polish crisis, citing a lack of leadership and responsibility. The Council went on to declare that

there could be no justification for hatred or violence, which should be resolutely condemned by all Christians, and clergymen in particular. On the other hand, the struggle against hatred would be successful only if social tensions could be reduced.

Essential in this respect were a fundamental change in official propaganda, which by denying the achievements of the renewal movement was insulting and stirring up society, and the return of independent youth organizations, especially for students.[32]

In truth, the Holy Father supported fully the spirit of the Solidarity movement; however, he recognized inherent dangers in creating massive change too quickly within an environment of Communist suspicion and control. As a result, Pope John Paul often changed his rhetoric, maintaining his credibility as a world leader among the Soviets, while at the same time providing hope and support to his countrymen. For example, the Pontiff's April 22 disciplinary tone against the leaders of Solidarity changed markedly in a Church sermon less than two weeks later. In a May 3 (1982) homily, broadcast on Vatican Radio, the Holy Father called to mind the Polish Constitution and its significance to the country's future. He then suggested that the Solidarity movement paralleled this Constitution greatly, providing the foundation for a new and better Poland.[33] And, to reassert his own commitment to Polish freedoms, John Paul once again merged sacred and secular diplomacy by expressing his wish to attend the 600th anniversary of the Black Madonna of Jasna Gora. He underscored the importance of this event for the Church as well as for the Polish faithful, thereby challenging governmental officials with the task of providing financial and political support for it. Unfortunately, however, the proposed 1982 papal visit to Poland never took place. With martial law in place, John Paul was precluded from visiting his followers for the 600th anniversary celebration. Instead, he relied on local clergymen (and the power of Vatican Radio's shortwave system) to send his message on that day, as well as in the days ahead.

David Willey describes an essential role of the Polish bishops during the long months of martial law; they often persuaded government officials in Warsaw to release members of Solidarity from prison (including the nation's future president, Lech Walesa). They also served as protectors and confidantes for struggling Poles. In fact, Willey suggests that the years of martial law may have actually helped to galvanize the relationship between the Church and Polish citizens. He notes:

Perhaps the most remarkable development was the adherence to the Church of many of Poland's intellectual elite, scientists, journalists, academics and artists, who had hitherto been lukewarm Christians. Churchgoing, which had been on the decline, suddenly increased. Attendance at mass by university graduates doubled during these years.[34]

Pope John Paul's 1982 disappointment did not deter him from his ultimate vision of religious and political freedom in Poland. When he finally obtained permission to revisit his homeland, his courage and commitment were evident. David Willey characterizes the Pontiff's reaction to an unhappy General Jaruzelski as "bold" and "hopeful."[35] And when he was finally able to speak to his people (thousands of whom were squeezed together in the Warsaw soccer stadium), Willey comments:

The speech was peppered with historical references ranging over a thousand years of Poland's past. It was received by the huge crowd with cheering applause and chanting. The people of the drab city of Warsaw had identified their hero and were confident that the Pope's long view of history would eventually be vindicated.[36]

After speaking to the multitudes at the soccer stadium, the Pontiff paraded through the capital, greeting throngs of well-wishers (many of whom were carrying Solidarity banners and flashing victory signals, according to Vatican Radio reports).[37] Later, he held a memorial service for his late mentor, Cardinal Stefan Wyszynski at St. John's Cathedral. In a sermon relayed live by Vatican Radio (but covered only slightly by Polish media sources), Pope John Paul commented on his role in the modern state of Poland. According to BBC reports, the Holy Father felt that he "stood at the foot of Christ's cross alongside his compatriots, and in particular those who best knew 'the bitter taste of deception, humiliation and the sufferings of the deprivation of freedom.'"[38]

Following his historical appearance in Warsaw, John Paul toured central and southern Poland. At each stop, he was received with the same amount of warmth and enthusiasm as he had received earlier. While the Pontiff carefully coded his speeches to appear doctrinal and pastoral, he nonetheless aroused both the spirit of his followers and the ire of state officials with his message of religious freedom and national pride.

INTERNATIONAL RECOGNITION

By 1984 the combined efforts of the Vatican, the United States, and other Western European nations began to reflect some measure of success. Solidarity, through Church support and other financial benefactors, had regained its momentum. The oppressiveness of martial law was growing more ineffective each day against a growing nationalistic movement. Further, reports of cruel, "inexplicable" disappearances and subsequent murders of Polish clergy began to draw media attention from around the world. One of the most grizzly of these events was the kidnapping and death of Father Jerzy Popieluszko in Gdansk, which was broadcast to the outside world by means of a Vatican Radio relay. Because Father Popieluszko had openly fought for Solidarity principles (claiming they were derived from the Gospel), he was viewed as a true martyr for the cause.[39] At his funeral (broadcast by both Warsaw Radio and VR), Poland's Cardinal Glemp prayed "that the priest's death would be the last sacrifice and that no one else would be killed for expressing his views."[40] Lech Walesa also spoke at the funeral, but his speech was edited out by Warsaw Radio and broadcast only by Vatican Radio. Walesa confirmed Popieluszko's contribution to the Solidarity movement, asserting that his death would not be in vain.[41]

As it happened, Lech Walesa's comments at the Popieluszko funeral were more prophetic than he could have imagined. The young priest's murder ultimately became a symbol for massive human rights violations occurring in Iron Curtain countries. Similar stories from Hungary, Czechoslovakia, and Romania began to emerge, eliciting media attention--and diplomatic condemnation--from around the world. In addition to its political problems, Moscow began to feel economic pressures, and ultimately surrendered some of its powers to local authorities (including the Solidarity trade union leaders in Poland). Poland had at last broken the yoke of oppression, and as David Willey observes, "an era had come to an abrupt end. The old opposition between an oppressive State and a Church which represented true national and social identity no longer held."[42]

A POSTSCRIPT

Some Polish historians might downplay the role of the Church in the Solidarity movement to free Poland. J. B. de Weydenthal, for example, believes that the cause for freedom was strong enough to supercede any one person's contribution (including the Pope).[43] However, most would agree that John Paul II's commitment to an independent Poland, though not overtly tangible, was nonetheless invaluable to its people's spiritual strength and resolve. Andrzej Adamczyk, International Secretary for the Solidarity Union, has observed that the Pope's visit to Poland in 1979 provided "a mentality to many Poles. They finally could see that they could behave in a free and independent way."[44] And when the Pope could not be present, especially during the dark period of martial law, international broadcasting (including Vatican Radio) served to influence greatly the world's support of the Solidarity movement.[45] There is no doubt that the Cold War Soviet Bloc would have eventually eroded; but the power of the scepter arguably dominated that of the sickle--at least in Poland.

NOTES

1. Tad Szulc, *Pope John Paul II: The Biography* (New York: Lisa Drew/Scribner, 1995), 157.

2. Ibid., 299.

3. Eric O. Hanson, *The Catholic Church in World Politics* (Princeton, NJ: Princeton University Press, 1987), 202.

4. Neal Ascherson, *The Struggles for Poland* (New York: Random House, 1987), 17.

5. Hanson, 203.

6. Lexis/Nexis Computer Search, The British Broadcasting Corporation Summary of World Broadcasts, 14 February 1979.

7. In the late 1970s and early 1980s, Poland was reported to be about 97% Catholic.

8. David A.Willey, *God's Politician* (New York: St. Martin's Press, 1992), 6-7.

9. Vatican Radio, 2 June 1979.

10. de Weydenthal, "The Pope Calls for a Christian Europe," 43-44.

11. Ibid., 44.

12. Willey, 37.

13. Lexis/Nexis Computer Search, *The Washington Times*, 21 February 1992.

14. The Knights of Malta are also known as the Sovereign Military and Hospitaller Order of St. John of Rhodes and Malta (or SMOM), an elite Catholic lay

organization founded in the eleventh century as protectors of the faith. Other notables who have belonged to this association include William F. Buckley, his brother James (a former director of Radio Free Europe), former NBC President Frank Shakespeare, hotel entrepreneur Barron Hilton, and Spain's King Juan Carlos.

15. Lexis/Nexis Computer Search, *The Washington Times*, 21 February 1992. However, in Szulc's biography of the Pope, this claim is denied.

16. Ibid.

17. Lexis/Nexis Computer Search, United Press International, 16 April 1981.

18. Lexis/Nexis Computer Search, United Press International, 25 July 1981.

19. Ibid.

20. Tad Szulc, "Papal Secrets," *Newsweek*, 10 April 1995, 63-64.

21. Ibid.

22. Paul Hofmann, *O Vatican! A Slightly Wicked View of the Holy See* (New York: Congdon & Weed, 1983), 268-269.

23. Lexis/Nexis Computer Search, United Press International, 9 August 1981.

24. Lexis/Nexis Computer Search, The British Broadcasting Corporation Summary of World Broadcasts, 8 September 1981.

25. Lexis/Nexis Computer Search, The British Broadcasting Corporation Summary of World Broadcasts/The Monitoring Report, 8 September 1981.

26. Willey, 37.

27. Lexis/Nexis Computer Search, *U.S. News & World Report*, 11 January 1982.

28. According to a report in *The Economist* (Lexis/Nexis Computer Search, 23 January 1982), the USSR allowed the radio services from only two major western nations into Poland without interference--West Germany's Deutsche Welle and Deutschlandfunk and Vatican Radio.

29. Ibid.

30. Lexis/Nexis Computer Search, The British Broadcasting Corporation Summary of World Broadcasts/The Monitoring Report, 11 February 1982.

31. Willey, 38.

32. Lexis/Nexis Computer Search, The British Broadcasting Corporation Summary of World Broadcasts/The Monitoring Report, 22 April 1982.

33. Lexis/Nexis Computer Search, The British Broadcasting Corporation Summary of World Broadcasts, 5 May 1982.

34. Willey, 39.

35. Ibid.

36. Ibid.

37. The British Broadcasting Corporation Summary of World Broadcasts/ Monitoring Report, 18 June 1983.

38. Ibid.

39. The British Broadcasting Corporation Summary of World Broadcasts/ Monitoring Report, 2 November 1984.

40. The British Broadcasting Corporation Summary of World Broadcasts/ Monitoring Report, 5 November 1984.

41. Ibid.

42. Willey, 45.

43. RFE/RL Research Institute Senior Analyst J. B. de Weydenthal, interview by author, 8 August 1993, tape recording, Munich, Germany.

44. Solidarnosc NSZZ International Secretary Andrzej Adamczyk, interview by author, 28 July 1993, tape recording, Gdansk, Poland.

45. Ibid.

5

The Silence of the Shepherd: Media and Church Leadership during the Philippine "People Power" Revolution

Miguel Quiachon Rapatan

Case Study Two

Numerous stories about the 1986 People Power revolution that deposed Philippine President Ferdinand E. Marcos cite the pivotal role played by the Church-owned radio station, Radio Veritas or DZRV.[1] From its shocking report of the brutal slaying of Sen. Benigno S. Aquino, Jr., chief foe of Marcos, to its riveting broadcast of the revolution, DZRV firmly established itself before the public as a courageous and credible source of news and information. When one searches in these accounts for the reasons why and how DZRV came to be highly regarded, one often finds the following analysis. DZRV's status as a Catholic religious station in a nation where about 85 percent of the population is Catholic is usually invoked as the basis for the station's effectivity.[2] Being so, DZRV was not easily subject to government interference because the 1935 and 1973 Constitutions guaranteed separation of Church and State. However, this policy did not protect other religious stations outside Manila because some of them known for their liberal orientations were raided and shut down.[3] The most serious reprimand the station received was when it was advised by the Office of Media Affairs to downplay its follow-up series on Aquino's death.[4] A more important reason then may be that because the station was located in the Archdiocese of Manila led by Jaime Cardinal Sin, the station acquired some form of political immunity. Because Marcos sorely needed and often courted the Cardinal's endorsement to legitimize his authority (e.g., Imelda Marcos was said to have visited the Cardinal and was on her knees begging for his support), Marcos could not afford to antagonize the Cardinal by harassing the station.[5] And so, DZRV carried on with its bold programming and even escalated its criticism of Marcos's rule. About a week before the revolution, the station broadcast a stinging pastoral letter issued by the Catholic Bishops' Conference of the Philippines or CBCP, the Church hierarchy, denouncing the rampant fraud and violence unleashed by Marcos loyalists during the 1986 presidential snap elections.[6] Ultimately, this letter provided the faithful with the moral framework justifying subsequent boycotts and strikes by various religious and political coalitions.[7] Consequently, along with the pulpit, DZRV was perceived by the public as the major channel through which the Church conveyed its harsh condemnation of Marcos's authority. It was also the only station to take this risk.[8] By the time, then, when the breakaway military leaders needed civilian buffers to shield them from government troops, DZRV--known as "the station of truth, the station that cares" (as its motto goes)--was the station to call. With Cardinal Sin's impassioned exhortation to help the Enrile-Ramos camp on February 22, DZRV mobilized thousands of people to assemble in front of the army headquarters.[9] From then on, DZRV positioned itself solidly behind the revolutionary forces. DZRV thus comes across as a proactive agent of social change and not just as a mere outlet of news.

Although there is some validity to this perspective, recent reappraisals point to different, if not contradictory readings. First, journalist Bryan Johnson's interviews with June Keithley and Fr. James Reuter, S.J., prominent figures in DZRV's coverage of the revolution, contend that although DZRV's extraordinary efforts were praised and rewarded with the prestigious Ramon Magsaysay Award for Journalism, Literature and Creative Communication Arts, DZRV's bravery is "a complete fiction." Keithley and Reuter assert that DZRV abandoned their commitments. Second, Cardinal Sin's request for civilian reinforcements was not a spontaneous address but a scripted performance written by an official from the National Movement for Free Elections or NAMFREL.   Third, the CBCP sanctioned civil disobedience after witnessing widespread tampering of election returns, but the Vatican instructed key Church leaders to "stay neutral."[10]

These discrepancies can be taken as examples of Putnam's concept of organizational paradoxes. For Putnam, an organizational paradox is a situation where incongruous messages are simultaneously communicated.[11] When these messages are sent by top management to middle or lower level managers and workers, tensions result because the latter group cannot ascertain what the officers demand. People want to act but feel uneasy about doing so. The predicament is acutely felt in institutions like the Church where lower levels or extensions located far from the center are authorized to make decisions on their own without seeking the approval of top management. Moreover, conflicts emerge between the front-end delivery of the message by management and the backstage setting that produced the message. Hence, disparities surface between the external form of the message and the internal factors that shaped it. Organizational paradoxes may take three forms:[12]

1. The official record of an event does not express the reality of the unofficial version as known by observers (like in the above cases of Cardinal Sin's appeal and Radio Veritas' award);
2. A standard definition of the message is at wide variance with multiple interpretations (e.g., Vatican II's teaching on social justice and human rights versus the CBCP judgment on the elections);
3. Institutional procedures for interpreting the message produce ambivalent or irrelevant responses.[13]

One reason why such organizational paradoxes occurred in the Philippine Church is because it is a transnational institution functioning on the principles of collegiality and subsidiarity, conditions that provide fertile ground for what Bateson calls double-bind situations.[14] The hierarchical structure of the Church provides each diocese with sufficient independence to manage its own affairs, but at the same time, the diocese is expected to conform with the Vatican.[15] Hence, events may arise as they did with the Philippines where local Church decisions were not congruent with Vatican guidelines. The dilemma is not peculiar to the Philippines, as similar scenarios have been played out in other countries where the magisterium's doctrinal conservatism has been at odds with liberation theologies.[16] Be that as it may, the problematic of organizational paradoxes further raises the question why these paradoxes can go by practically unnoticed before the general public. In other words, if the contradictions are indeed present, how does one account for the invisibility of the paradox? Why does the official story persist despite contrary evidences? What factors make the front-end performance successfully conceal the bickering and hostility shown backstage?

To answer these questions, this article takes the position that the paradoxes were veiled by a rhetorical vision that naturalized the described differences. More specifically, within the framework of symbolic convergence and schema theories, this article will show that DZRV was perceived as heroic and effective because of its active appropriation, articulation, and amplification of a rhetorical vision propounded by local Church leaders. However, this vision was not consistently pursued or realized by the station, especially in the moments when access to the station's faculties became a matter of life or death. DZRV did not make its facilities completely available to key revolutionary figures because of its transnational link with the Vatican. Realizing that the day may come when he would have to defend before the curia his appeal over the airwaves for mass action, Cardinal Sin engaged in a set of complex maneuvers that communicated a mixed amount of support for and reluctance to placing the station at the disposal of the revolutionary movement. DZRV's shifting responses illustrated the Church's confusion about the moral and political repercussions of its cooperation with the revolution, exposed internal conflicts within the hierarchy, and strained its ties with the Vatican.

In order to more clearly understand how the rhetorical vision superseded other rival narratives, the article begins with a brief historical background on the establishment of DZRV (see attached chronology of events). Next, we will describe the rhetorical vision of the Church and the way DZRV reflected this in their programs within the context of the broadcast practices prevalent during the Marcos regime. Third, the discussion will show that as a transnational media group, DZRV's efforts were marked by inconsistencies and struggles with a divided hierarchy. Figuratively speaking, the faithful looked to its shepherds for guidance but instead found them factious, afraid, or silent.[17] The implications of these events and a reassessment of DZRV's contributions to the restoration of democracy are addressed in the conclusion.

HISTORICAL BACKGROUND

DZRV was founded in 1958 during the first Synod of the Catholic Bishops of Southeast Asia.[18] Recognizing the vast missionary opportunities in a predominantly non-Christian Asia, the Synod sought to widen and intensify its evangelical efforts by putting up a noncommercial shortwave radio station in the Philippines. The specific goals of the station were as follows:[19]

1. To make present to all Asians the Gospel of Christ in such a way that it can have a real impact on their lives and all their activities;
2. To support the living faith of Christians and help them to live according to the teachings of Christ, especially in countries where the Good News cannot be proclaimed by other means;
3. To help answer the needs of the people and work towards their material, cultural, and spiritual development;
4. To strengthen the bonds between people through education, information, and entertainment services;
5. To maintain close relationships with the production centers.

To make the station operable, the Archdiocese of Manila, led by Rufino Cardinal Santos established in 1961 the Philippine Radio Educational and Information Center, Inc. (PREIC).[20] In turn, PREIC owned and operated Radio Veritas and appointed several priests and religious to supervise and manage its programs.[21] For the next year, PREIC secured a land donation from the family of Jose Yulo; assumed 25 percent of the total costs for land improvements, building construction, and staff development; and solicited the remaining 75 percent of capital expenses from the Federal Republic of Germany for the purchase and installation of station equipment.[22] Instead of applying for a new radio franchise, PREIC in 1964 bought the franchise of DZST, an existing educational radio station owned by the Dominican priests in the pontifical University of Santo Tomas.[23] DZST then became DZRV or Radio Veritas, the station of the Gospel truth.

In 1967, DZRV conducted test broadcasts overseas reaching as far as Vietnam and Indonesia.[24] At around the same time, a separate department called Radio Veritas Domestic was formed. According to Fr. James Reuter, S.J., former station general manager, this department was not in the original plans. It came up in response to the goodwill of the donors who encouraged the local staff to venture into some form of domestic programming.[25] RV Domestic then received from Congress another franchise registered in the name of the Catholic Welfare Organization, later known in 1968 as the Catholic Bishops' Conference of the Philippines or CBCP.[26] Consequently, PREIC held two franchises--one for RV Asia and one for RV Domestic. Although PREIC could have opened two stations, PREIC chose to run both departments in one station. Thus, by April 11, 1969, when DZRV (840 on the AM band) was formally inaugurated with studios located in Fairview, Quezon City, the station was broadcasting both domestic and overseas programs in several languages.[27]

This brief chronology (a full chronology is presented in Table 5.1) of Radio Veritas's beginnings first establishes the fact that DZRV is a local corporation functioning with a legal personality independent from the Vatican. The Vatican neither owns nor operates the station. Although DZRV receives some donation from Radio Vatican, DZRV heavily relies on funds drawn from other sources, mostly foreign such as the Archdiocese of Cologne, MISEREOR, and Holy Child Germany. DZRV is able to raise these contributions because these groups share in the station's mandate to propagate the Christian faith and dogma in Asia.[28] By virtue of this mission then, DZRV may also be considered a transnational enterprise. From time to time, DZRV relays news about the latest encyclicals and papal messages initially released by Radio Vatican and features programs such as the papal Mass during Christmas and Holy Week and about practical matters like how to live one's faith in an increasingly secular world.[29]

Table 5.1
Chronology of Events

1958	First Synod of Catholic Bishops of Southeast Asia agrees to establish a noncommercial shortwave radio station in the Philippines.
1961	Led by Rufino Cardinal Santos, the Archdiocese of Manila establishes the Philippine Radio Educational and Information Center, Inc. (PREIC).
1962	PREIC secures land donation from family of Jose Yulo, assumes 25 percent of total costs for land improvements, building construction, and staff development.
	Remaining 75 percent of capital is shouldered by the Federal Republic of Germany for equipment purchase and installation.
1964	PREIC buys franchise of DZST from the University of Santo Tomas. DZST then becomes DZRV.
1967	Radio Veritas Overseas test broadcasts begin. Congress grants a commercial franchise for radio and television to the Catholic Welfare Organization, later to be known as the Catholic Bishops Conference of the Philippines (CBCP). DZRV opens a separate department--Radio Veritas Domestic.
1968	Catholic Welfare Organization formally changes its name to the Catholic Bishops Conference of the Philippines (CBCP).
1969	April 11: Formal inauguration of DZRV studios in Fairview, Quezon City.
1972	June: One of shortwave transmitters malfunctions disabling the other transmitters.
	September 21: President Ferdinand E. Marcos declares martial law.
1973	August: Radio Veritas Overseas temporarily closes due to transmission problems.
1974	April: Federation of Asian Bishops Conference (FABC) decides to reopen DZRV.

Table 5.1, cont.

1975   May: Overseas test broadcasts resume.

1976   March to April: Regular schedules of DZRV programs.

1979   Additional transmitter put up in Palauig, Zambale.

1981   President Marcos lifts martial law.

1983   August 21: Sen. Benigno "Ninoy" Aquino is shot upon arrival at the
                Manila International Airport.

                DZRV does a follow-up series on the government investigation of
                the Aquino murder.

1984   Archdiocese of Cologne, Germany, under Cardinal Josef Hoeffner
                donates a 250 kw transmitter and curtain antennae located in
                Malolos, Bulacan.

1985   November 3: President Marcos announces presidential "snap
                elections" on program with David Brinkley.

                Corazon C. Aquino and Salvador Laurel III file their candidacy as
                President and Vice-President.

1986   February 7: Presidential elections are held but marred by massive
                cheating and violence.

                DZRV feeds election returns as counted by NAMFREL.

                February 14: CBCP publishes and broadcasts a pastoral letter
                condemning the election results.

                February 22, 6:45 p.m.: Defense Minister Juan Ponce Enrile and
                General Ramos conduct a press conference and reveal their defection
                from Marcos.

                February 22, 9:00 p.m.: Jaime Cardinal Sin is heard on the air
                asking civilian support for the Enrile-Ramos camp.

                February 23, 5:00 a.m.: Government forces disguised as Aquino's
                supporters smash DZRV's 50 kw back-up transmitters in Malolos,
                Bulacan. DZRV continues to be on the air with the help of a 10W
                transmitter but its signal weakens.

                February 23, 7:00 p.m.: DZRV signs off the air.

                February 24, 12:05 a.m.: June Keithley is heard again on the air
                using facilities of DZRH. Station is identified as DZRB for Radyo
                Bandido, the Rebel Station.

Table 5.1, cont.

February 25, 9:05 p.m.: Marcos and family board U.S. helicopters and leave the Presidential Palace.

Cardinal Hoeffner blesses the transmitter along with a new donation of another 250 kw transmitter.

Radio Veritas receives the Ramon Magsaysay Award for Journalism, Literature, and Creative Communication Arts.

1989   DZRV retrenches 73 of its employees, 53 of whom belong to the Radio Veritas Employees' Union (RVEU).

FABC separates Domestic and Overseas/Asia departments of DZRV into two independent units with their own budgets.

1991   February 28: DZRV signs off the air.

May 1: DZRV Domestic is renamed ZNN and begins its commercial broadcasts under the management of Radio Veritas Global Broadcasting Systems, Inc. RV--Asia continues under PREIC.

BROADCAST POLICY UNDER THE MARCOS GOVERNMENT

The identity of Radio Veritas as a local corporation imbued with religious communication objectives for a transnational audience set the station apart from others. This arrangement proved to be advantageous for DZRV. For one, because the station was supported by foreign funds for the explicit task of evangelization, DZRV was unencumbered by budget problems that plagued several commercial stations. DZRV's financial profile gave it a certain independence from the dictates and demands of advertisers. The station could pursue its programming policies without fear of reprisal from vested interest groups. This may explain why DZRV was the only station that broadcast the return and assassination of Sen. Benigno "Ninoy" Aquino, Jr., at the Manila International Airport. Long regarded as one of Marcos's most caustic critics, Ninoy Aquino as a news subject was anathema to the government-controlled media. By the time Aquino was on the plane bound for Manila on August 21, 1983, the media industry was dominated by a clique of "crony capitalists" whose loyalty to Marcos was generously rewarded by acquisitions of mini-media empires. For instance, sugar baron Roberto Benedicto's media holdings were a virtual oligopoly of newspaper dailies, radio stations, and television stations spread throughout the entire archipelago.[30] Despite the formal lifting of martial law in 1981, severe restrictions were imposed in these crony corporations on the kinds of news events to be covered and issues to be presented. Any complaint about the President and his family was unthinkable. Sharp and incisive journalists were bribed for their opinions (the practice was known as "envelopmental journalism"), and those who fought to maintain their professional integrity sought refuge in the alternative press.[31]

In effect, the mainstream media was characterized by a one-way vertical information flow orchestrated by crony capitalists. Information agencies provided misinformation and distorted interpretations of significant events. Because the mainstream media could only go so far with their manipulation of the news, the public was bound to demand more accurate reporting.[32] The shameless execution of Aquino served as a litmus test case for this reading of the public pulse, and the overwhelming public response to Radio Veritas's broadcast from his arrest to his burial confirmed the boundaries of government control. From then on, DZRV urged its listeners to call them up and air their feedback, thereby creating an interactive or two-way communication flow.[33] When all the other stations had practically erased from their minds the notion of the media as the watchdog of the establishment, DZRV assumed an activist role and gave the people access to a forum for social commentary and criticism. For instance, the station sponsored "Talk-to-Cory" spots where people exploited the opportunity to converse with Aquino and vent their gripes about the government.[34] During the tabulation of electoral returns, the station in its airing of Operation Quick Count, a program by the National Movement for Free Elections (NAMFREL), fielded reports of ubiquitous irregularities and blatant intimidation.[35]

RHETORICAL VISION OF THE MARCOS-AQUINO PRESIDENTIAL RACE

As a venue for public opinion, the station also facilitated disparate factions of the opposition to come together and expound on their respective agendas for ousting Marcos. Although they differed in their strategies for toppling the dictator (e.g., electoral reform versus a bloody revolution), the overthrow of Marcos was the unanimous target.[36] In terms of symbolic convergence theory, this goal became the shared group fantasy of leftists, moderates, and disgruntled rightists. Bormann reminds us that people drawn together by a shared group fantasy are not creating a fictitious screen alienating themselves from concrete realities.[37] Fantasy here is understood as a collective mode of perception and experience, akin to a mythical worldview where a specific theme is of immense importance to many and renders seemingly senseless and chaotic events to become more meaningful and predictable. People begin to feel that together they have more control over their lives.

The shared group fantasy of Marcos's downfall fostered a common consciousness that cultivated dialogue and forged a rhetorical vision that appealed to many organizations across the political and religious spectrums and empowered them to work for radical changes. Bormann defines the rhetorical vision of an organization as a "unified putting together of the various shared fantasies that gives a participant a broader view of the organization and its relationship to the external environment, of the various subdivisions and units of the organization, and of their place in the scheme of things."[38] In a sense, the vision is a synthesis of the dreams, hopes, and anxieties of diverse groups projected in the form of archetypal figures enacting a particular saga and encapsulated in certain themes, slogans, gestures, music, and other similar paraphernalia.

Such elements of a rhetorical vision were evident in the events leading to the February revolution. The presidential contest in January between the widow Corazon C. Aquino and the strongman Ferdinand E. Marcos was an arena of clashing symbols. The CBCP cast the elections as a struggle between the forces of good and evil. It referred to the slick Marcos machinery's ploy to cheat in the elections as a "sinister plot" and a "conspiracy of evil" and cautioned the faithful to conduct themselves as the "children of light (who) should be no less wise than the children of this world."[39]   The high profile of the religious and clergy volunteers at the polling centers dressed in their robes and habits, as well as the omnipresence of goons and soldiers, further dramatized the contrast between the meek and the vicious. As for the candidates, Cardinal Sin spoke of Marcos as "the curse"[40] and likened Aquino to Joan of Arc whereas Aquino in a public address identified herself with Moses standing up to the Pharaoh Marcos.[41]   In line with the metaphor of battle, Aquino's campaign staff was known as Cory's Crusaders, and everyone else who supported her as armed with the following emblems. They wore something yellow, flashed the *Laban* (Fight) hand sign, and tossed confetti at the end of the rallies. They chanted "Tama Na! Sobra Na! Palitan Na!" ("Enough! Too much! Change it already!") and sang "Bayan Ko" ("My Homeland") or played "Tie a Yellow Ribbon Round the Old Oak Tree." Although the former tune was from a nationalistic musical and the latter was an American pop hit (and Ninoy Aquino's favorite), they were quickly adopted as protest songs.   Furthermore, Aquino followers relied on news from the alternative press such as WE Forum and Malaya and tuned in to Radio Veritas for more accurate reports of election returns.

The militant motif of the rhetorical vision had already been set in place by Radio Veritas starting from the time it covered the government investigation of Aquino's murder at the airport tarmac. During this period, the station invited its growing audience to pause at noon and night to recite the Angelus and pray for the just resolution of the case.   The Church bells that rang on the air synchronized with the toll of parish bells in many parts of the country.   This signal was particularly significant to many because it recalled a practice during Spanish colonial times when Church bells were rung to warn the people of an impending attack.   Later on, during the revolution, the station picked up this theme again. Through June Keithley, the celebrated anchorwoman who was on the air until the station's transmitters were smashed by pro-Marcos thugs, DZRV acted as a "watchtower" for the rebels and the civilians by feeding reports about troop positions.[42] Because nothing about the revolution was seen in the mainstream media, the revolutionary units were entirely dependent on DZRV's bulletins of defections, marches, and assaults. DZRV also played "Onward, Christian Soldiers" as a way of encouraging the people to man their barricades despite the onslaught of firepower from loyalist brigades.[43]

A SPLIT IN THE RANKS

Although Radio Veritas had erected on the political landscape a gateway for the opposition to channel its dissent, DZRV hemmed and hawed in maintaining this stance. In recounting their efforts to sustain DZRV's image as a freedom fighter, Keithley and Fr. Reuter revealed that the station's management had on different occasions buckled under pressure and tried to dismiss them. For example, at a rally where Aquino was to launch the boycott of crony industries, DZRV retreated from the scoop of putting her on the air and gave the pretext of encountering signal disturbances. Keithley narrates: "They wanted us to *lie* about it, tell people there was a technical problem. Imagine, a Catholic station and the priests are telling us to *lie*. I got into a huge shouting match with Bishop Buhain. He said: 'I don't care about politics. My only concern is to keep Radio Veritas on the air. We have to protect this station.'"[44] At another time when the station was off the air for about five hours close to midnight on February 23, Keithley and Reuter had to scramble for another station because technicians reported that DZRV's 10W transmitter conked out. However, they question this claim: "There's a report that Veritas' standby transmitter didn't fail. They just went off the air because they were afraid."[45] By the time Keithley was heard again at 12:05 a.m., February 24, on DZRJ, she was informed by her friend in DZRV that the station decided not to patch up with her for a simulcast. She had to handle the announcements by herself. Her partnership with DZRV was over.

DZRV's pullout was not the only baffling episode. Sin's recall of the circumstances that led to his plea for people to surround the camps diverges from a published remark made by Prof. Bolasco: "Who responded to the Cardinal's call? Who asked Cardinal Sin to speak in the first place? Christian Monsod said he wrote what the Cardinal read over the radio. So it was at the urging of the elite that the Cardinal spoke out and it was basically the middle class and the elite that responded." Monsod served as a top NAMFREL official during the 1986 presidential elections. When asked if it was solely the Cardinal's idea to ask the people to gather outside the rebel camps, Monsod said that the address was not entirely the Cardinal's brainchild. "There were three of us in his (Cardinal Sin's) office (i.e., the three being Monsod, NAMFREL head Jose Concepcion, and Cardinal Sin) and he (Cardinal Sin) also made one or two telephone calls before the decision was made. The Cardinal asked me to draft the message. Of course, he corrected it before he read it."[46]

If the Cardinal had someone else compose his speech, the Vatican for their part would have preferred that he say nothing at all. According to the Cardinal, Imelda Marcos tried to have the Papal Nuncio, Bruno Torpigliani, convince the Vatican that the February 14 release of the CBCP rebuke of the election results would trigger irreparable harm.[47] When it was clear that the Cardinal would not concede, the Nuncio wrote back to John Paul II, and in the strongest terms, advised him to block the Cardinal. But the Nuncio received far less than what he aimed for. "The Pope released a lukewarm two-sentence comment on Sunday, February 16, which pointedly ignored the explosive pastoral letter. It wasn't even addressed to the bishops, but to the church that is in the Philippines . . .

[and] all its people."[48]   The response was a masterpiece of ambiguity.   The Vatican did not want trouble, and it would not stand behind its tempestuous Filipino cardinal. Nor, however, would it stand in his way. Jaime Cardinal Sin was on his own.

REASSESSING DZRV'S CONTRIBUTIONS

Despite these complicated backstage shuffling and jumble, public opinion still tilted heavily in favor of the Church and Radio Veritas. Schema theory suggests that people will adhere to a schema, an organized set of ideas, for as long as this makes sense of their everyday reality. Because the popular consensus held that the Church and Radio Veritas were the staunchest advocates of democracy as inscribed by the prevailing rhetorical vision, this schema rationalized and foregrounded all their actions as positive and selfless thereby muting discordant and irate voices.   Hence, the public felt that DZRV deserved to win the Magsaysay Award, and correspondents hailed Cardinal Sin and the CBCP as the vanguard of the civilian resistance.

From the preceding discussion, one can see that a rhetorical vision can serve as a schema orienting people's ideas and attitudes to organizations, events, and personalities. If people act counter to the dominant rhetorical vision, their deeds may be interpreted as deviant and dubious. This is what happened to Marcos when he went on the air during the revolution. Although Marcos correctly exposed the military coup plot crafted by Minister of Defense Juan Ponce Enrile and his associates, his finding was dismissed by many because he was already portrayed by the rhetorical vision as the enemy. On the other hand, Enrile, whose presidential ambitions became more transparent after the revolution, was regarded as credible because his displays of piety and confession of cheating in the polls matched the rhetorical vision. The same can be said of General Ramos who told the Cardinal that he embraced the statue of the Blessed Virgin Mary--a surprising juxtaposition considering the fact that he was a Methodist. Rebel soldiers from RAM (Reform the Armed Forces Movement) were also seen holding the rosary as they stuck to their guns, whereas loyalist troops were not known for doing the same. Whether or not they were consciously exploiting elements of the rhetorical vision to secure their interests is open to debate. The point made here is that once people construct schemas out of the rhetorical vision, people view one's gestures and symbols within the rhetorical vision.

The rhetorical vision that propelled Cory Aquino to the presidency was potent for its time. After the revolution, it needed to grow or redefine itself. The vision had to be dynamic and adaptable to the task of economic rehabilitation. With Marcos gone, the moment was ripe to institute radical changes for the benefit of the poor and the oppressed. Instead of molding a new social order, Aquino offered nothing innovative. Her recurring discourse of moral integrity and recovery went unheeded as corruption wore new names and new faces. Her network of religious supporters became a clique of advisers who indulged in the very same patronage politics that Marcos was accused of. In disgust, the RAM soldiers who were Aquino's allies in the revolution staged seven coup attempts against her.

As for Radio Veritas, the station in 1989 formally separated its Overseas/Asia and Domestic departments. On February 28, 1991, DZRV signed off the air due to funding problems. Station ZNN took over on the same band location. The change in management became controversial because first, PREIC (where five bishops including Cardinal Sin sit as incorporators) was charged with "union busting" by the Radio Veritas Employees Union (RVEU). Secondly, the new corporation that operated ZNN, Radio Veritas Global Broadcasting System (RVGBS), had the same incorporators and subscribers as PREIC. Thirdly, some members of the new administration were affiliated with Opus Dei, already known for its rigid and conservative theology and religiosity. Programming would now be tailored to their agenda.

By 1992, when Aquino's term had expired and a new presidential race was on, the government had completely turned 360 degrees. Aquino, once raised as the Joan of Arc of the revolution, was regarded as the government's chief cause for destabilization. Cardinal Sin was lambasted by the press for his unsolicited opinions on State matters and made several embarrassing statements purportedly in behalf of the CBCP. Radio Veritas, which once was the voice of the progressives, was now a commercial outfit in the hands of conservatives. In other words, the founding rhetorical vision was dead.

In conclusion, Radio Veritas's involvement in the February revolution illustrates for us a number of things. First, a station or media entity does not merely transmit information. It can be the coauthor of an emerging rhetorical vision, a key actor in the drama of social change--like DZRV, which had a substantial participation in the early formation of the rhetorical vision. Second, the rhetorical vision can be the basis for people's schema construction. For as long as people see ongoing events match the initial data informing the schema, people will retain the schema and process social developments according to this schema. Third, the rhetorical vision tends to be hegemonic and totalizing. The vision becomes the arbiter of meaning and response, especially in situations of extreme polarization. The vision may also diminish the magnitude of an organizational paradox. People who may have accurate information counter to the vision will have difficulty persuading others to accept their position. Fourth, the rhetorical vision needs to be dynamic. New realities are signified by new symbols. Along with this, for the vision to endure, it must be supported by an effective infrastructure. Fifth, transnational ties (e.g., Philippine Church vis-à-vis the Vatican) can have either an encouraging or limiting effect on an organization's response to local realities. The direction of the constraint is both ways because foreign and national interests struggle to find a common ground. Often, national concerns are more important. This is why credit must still be given to DZRV. DZRV could have totally turned a deaf ear to the people's clamor for an alternative to the straitjacketed media. But it chose not to. DZRV generated the impact it wanted as declared in its objectives and fulfilled the evangelical task of promoting human development in the light of the Gospel. If not for its connections with the Vatican, DZRV would probably not have worried too much about the consequences of its actions. After all, the people were on DZRV's side.

And so, even if the shepherd is silent, the sheep do find their way to the promised land. The shepherd has only to show his trust.

NOTES

1. For example, see the following: Jorge R. Coquia's "The Church's Mission in a Just Political Order," *Veritas*, 6 April 1986, 19; Bert Covera's "How People Power Erupted," *WE Forum*, 25 February-3 March 1986, 3; Nestor Cuartero's "People Power Mobilized by Broadcast Power," *Manila Bulletin*, 2 March 1986, 12; Fred Reye's "The Four Longest Days in February," *Philippine Panorama Magazine*, 9 March 1986, 5-7; and Lewis Simons' *Worth Dying For* (New York: William Morrow and Co., Inc., 1987).

2. Douglas Elwood, *Philippine Revolution 1986: Model of Nonviolent Change* (Quezon City: New Day Publishers, 1986).

3. Robert Youngblood, "Structural Imperialism: An Analysis of the Catholic Bishops' Conference of the Philippines," *Comparative Political Studies 15* (1982): 29-56.

4. Bryan Johnson, *The Four Days of Courage: The Untold Story of the People Who Brought Marcos Down* (New York: The Free Press, 1987).

5. Ibid.

6. See Wilfredo Fabros, *The Church and Its Social Involvement in the Philippines, 1930-1972* (Quezon City: Ateneo de Manila University Press, 1988); and Sison and Werning, *The Philippine Revolution and the Involvement of the Church* (New York: Taylor & Francis New York, Inc., 1989).

7. Elwood, *Philippine Revolution 1986: Model of Nonviolent Change.*

8. C. Maslog, ed., *Philippine Communication: An Introduction* (Manila: James B. Reuter Foundation, 1988).

9. Simons, *Worth Dying For.*

10. Bryan Johnson, *The Four Days of Courage.*

11. Linda Putnam, "Contradictions and Paradoxes in Organizations," in *Organization Communication: Emerging Perspectives, Vol. 1*, ed. L. Thayer (Norwood, MA: Ablex, 1986).

12. Ibid. See also Peter K. Manning, *Organizational Communication* (New York: Aldine de Gruyter, 1992).

13. See Cardinal Sin's narration of his negotiations with the Papal Nuncio and the Vatican in Bryan Johnson's *The Four Days of Courage.*

14. Gregory Bateson, *Steps Toward an Ecology of Mind* (New York: Ballantine, 1972).

15. See also Dennis Shoesmith's "Church," in *The Philippines after Marcos*, eds. May and Nemenzo (New York: St. Martin's Press, 1985); and Youngblood's article, "Structural Imperialism: An Analysis of the Catholic Bishops' Conference of the Philippines."

16. Tad Szulc, *Pope John Paul II: The Biography* (New York: Scribner, 1995).

17. Unity among the bishops of the CBCP has often been questioned and scrutinized. See Pasquale Giordano, *Awakening to Mission: The Philippine Catholic Church 1965-1981* (Quezon City: New Day Publishers, 1988); Dennis Shoesmith, "Church," in *The Philippines After Marcos*, R. J. May and Francisco Nemenzo, eds., (New York: St. Martin's Press, 1985); and Robert Youngblood, "Structural Imperialism: An Analysis of the Catholic Bishops' Conference of the

Philippines, "*Comparative Political Studies 15* (1982): 29-56. Moreover, several accounts report similar tensions between the Vatican and the CBCP before and after the February revolution. See E. J. Dionne, Jr., "Cardinal Sees Pope On Manila Role," *New York Times,* 7 March 1986; Antonio Lumicao Santos and Lorna Domingo-Robes, *Power Politics in the Philippines* (Philippines: Center for Social Research, 1987).

18. Radio Veritas Asia Research Section. RVA documentation culled from the reports prepared by RVA's Program Consultants 1978-1995. According to Erlinda So, General Manager of Radio Veritas Asia, there is no existing publication that completely details the history of DZRV. The nearest comprehensive resource is a pamphlet entitled "Radio Veritas Asia: A Continuing Journey in Faith" produced by RVA's Research Section and published in 1995. The same content is also found in a compilation made by RVA Research Section referred to as "RVA (Radio Veritas Asia) documentation culled from the reports prepared by RVA's Program Consultants." These consultants were Fr. Anton Weerasinghe, S.J. (1978-1981; estimated period); Fr. Paul Brunner, S.J. (1981-mid-1980s); and Fr. Jean Desautels, S.J. (1990-95). Note that Fr. Weerasinghe published in 1979 an information primer pamphlet called "Radio Veritas Asia." This pamphlet has served as the basis for the previous mentioned materials. Because the 1995 compilation is the latest update, reference will be made to this work as RVA Compilation (RVAC). Information about these documentation sources obtained in an interview with So, January 1996.

19. RVAC.

20. Ibid.

21. Ibid.

22. Ibid.

23. Ibid.

24. Ibid.

25. James B. Reuter, "The CBCP Owns Radio Veritas," *Philippine Journalism Review* 2 (1991): 24.

26. Ibid.

27. RVAC.

28. Ibid.

29. Ibid.

30. See Jose Pavia, "Government Information as Propaganda: The Past," in Maslog's *Philippine Communication.*

31. Carolina Hernandez and Werner Pfennig, eds., *Media and Politics in Asia* (Manila: University of the Philippines Center for Integrative and Development Studies, National Institute for Policy Studies, and Friedrich Naumann Foundation, 1991).

32. Ibid.

33. Maslog, *Philippine Communication: An Introduction.*

34. Bryan Johnson, *The Four Days of Courage.*

35. See Maslog and Simons.

36. See Sison and Werning and Monina Mercado, ed., *People Power: An Eyewitness History* (Manila: James B. Reuter Foundation, 1986).

37. Ernest Bormann, "Symbolic Convergence: Organizational Communication and Culture," in *Communication and Organization: An Interpretive Approach,* Putnam and Pacanowsky, eds. (Beverly Hills, Calif.: Sage Publications, 1983).

38. Ibid., 114.

39. CBCP, 19 and 25 January 1986, in UST Social Research Center, 1986.

40. Lewis Gleeck, Jr., *President Marcos and the Philippine Political Culture*

(Manila: Loyal Printing, Inc., 1987).

41. Claude Buss, *Cory Aquino and the People of the Philippines* (Stanford, Calif.: Stanford Alumni Association, 1987).

42. Mercado, *People Power.*

43. Maslog, *Philippine Communication.*

44. Bryan Johnson, *The Four Days of Courage,* 179-180.   See also Joaquin Bernas, *Dismantling the Dictatorship* (Quezon City: Ateneo de Manila University, 1990), 206.

45. Bryan Johnson, 183.

46. Christian Monsod, interview by author, January, 1996.

47. See Santos and Domingo-Robes, *Power Politics in the Philippines.*

48. Bryan Johnson, 62.

6

Vatican Radio in the Next Millennium

An Interview with Fr. Federico Lombardi, S.J.

Case Study Three

In May 1996 the authors were given an opportunity to interview several Vatican Radio personnel at their headquarters in Vatican City. Fr. Federico Lombardi, Program Director of Radio Vaticana (now in its 65th year), was especially gracious, taking the time to speak to us for over two hours. What follows are excerpts of this interview. In it, Fr. Lombardi outlines Vatican Radio's current programming strategies as well as its future challenges and direction.

NLS/MJM: You seem to have undergone some great changes within the last five years. Could you give us a brief description of your new directions in programming and technology?

FL: In the beginning of 1993 we started to transmit via satellite in Europe; and at the beginning of 1996 we expanded transmission via satellite to the rest of the world. Through this means, we now have the capability of having all of our programs (in all languages) retransmitted by interested broadcasters. The programs which are received via satellite are then rebroadcast on FM or AM, greatly increasing our audiences in various regions, where formerly Vatican Radio could be received only by shortwave. It is noted, in fact, that in Italy, in Europe in general, or in Latin America, the majority of radio listeners use FM or AM, whereas only a minority use shortwave. Now, because of our satellite technology, many local radio stations can rebroadcast what we send to them. In Italy and France [for example], we have the majority of Catholic radio stations rebroadcasting our programs in Italian and in French. Practically all Catholic radio stations in this region are FM, so the signal can be accessible to many people.

NLS/MJM: We know that Voice of America, Radio Free Europe, Radio Liberty and the BBC are also utilizing this same type of programming strategy [re-broadcasting on local AM and FM stations within a specific country or region]. VOA has told us that they have a very specific policy that if a local AM or FM station adopted a program, they would have to adopt the program in its entirety. Does Vatican Radio have a similar policy?

FL: We are very flexible. Generally, when we give the authorization for rebroadcast, we ask that the station present the full program [usually 50 minutes], without interruption, and with proper identification. But we have to address a multiplicity of situations [throughout the world]. For example, the English program in the United States has an agreement [with us] to do separate segments [20 minutes each], with two or three very distinct parts. One part might address typical questions asked by Catholics; another part might describe the life of a saint. But the station clearly identifies [even through its music at the beginning] that these rebroadcasts are only two or three selections from the entire program.

Sometimes the stations will tell us that portions of the program might not pertain to their listeners. We are flexible about this, knowing how difficult it is to relate to the specific needs of so many countries, with so many languages.

We also try to give a certain perspective on world news. In this instance, we must demand that the program is aired in its entirety so as to maintain the accuracy of the content.

NLS/MJM: So, in other words, the stations are not required to air the entire program; they have the option to rebroadcast only the portions of the show they feel would appeal to their listeners. But if they choose only one or two selections, they are required to present each segment in its entirety.

FL: You are correct. In other lands, we have national radio services rebroadcasting our program. In Poland, Lithuania, and Bulgaria, they feel a need for a constructive moral message to their people. In Poland, of course, there is a special interest in the Pope and in the Church. Our news bulletins in Polish are very much about the Pope's activities, his journeys, his foreign correspondents--the people are very happy to hear about him. This is a very popular segment in the broadcasts. We don't know if [the interest in the Pope] will have a long future; but for now, we know [and the national radios know] that this type of programming brings in large audiences. Previously, it was difficult to ascertain how many listeners were reached by shortwave. Now, with the ability to broadcast through FM radio, we have a better idea of audience numbers.

NLS/MJM: How do you do your audience research analysis?

FL: We have always shared our audience research with other international radio services like the BBC and Radio Free Europe/Radio Liberty. We paid for this participation with the other services. They asked questions to their listeners about Vatican Radio and published the survey results. This information was very useful, especially in eastern Europe. Now, I'm not so sure whether or not the information we receive from the researchers is worth the money we pay for it. Whether 3 percent or 5 percent listen to Vatican Radio is of little consequence to our programming philosophy. We have a certain nature and personality to our programming which is not of a commercial nature [dependent upon audience changes].

Our programs were very popular during the Cold War because of the anticommunist sentiment. Now, we may not have as many listeners; but we have new reasons to reach them. People are trying to find their way in a new world. With our present technology, we can reach them via satellite and through their local FM stations. For me, the reason to broadcast our message is to address the topics of the day, not to achieve high numbers in audience research reports.

NLS/MJM: How would you characterize your "main message"--your main reason for programming?

FL: This is rather well-explained in our statutes. (*Note:* At this point in the interview, Fr. Lombardi gave the authors a copy of the statutes of Vatican Radio, updated in 1995.)[1] What, for me, is important to understand is that in certain regions we know that we can't stand alone. For example, in Latin America, we must broadcast in Spanish, relating to those issues that the people in Latin America are facing. Then, they can listen to Vatican Radio, along with local church officials and the local Catholic radio stations. We cannot provide the entire picture, although we can contribute to it through our international wire services and world news releases. In this way, we can help our Latin American listeners to understand better their problems and concerns.

It's essential that we be flexible. What is needed in Latin America is very different than that needed in China or Vietnam or Zambia. We must look at each circumstance and make the necessary adjustments.

NLS/MJM: You also seem to be extending your flexibility and technological expertise on the Internet. How has that affected Vatican Radio?

FL: Right now, like most organizations, we have a limited use of e-mail and are experimenting with the Internet at several European locations. The major problems with the Internet have to do with sound versus the written word. At Vatican Radio, our job is to produce sounds--not printed material. Our only publications are in Italian, which limits the distribution at this time. But in the near future, we must ask: Should we put information on the Internet in English and German as well? This is a new concept for us.

Also, it is important to consider the basic differences between speaking and writing. When you speak, you can adjust your message if you feel you are being misunderstood; but when something is written, it is permanent and difficult to change. Another advantage to speaking is that you can communicate in ways other than words--the tone of voice, pauses, inflections--these all make it easier for the listener to understand what you are trying to say.

The Internet is [now] based primarily on the written word, although some sound can be transmitted. Thus, at present, we have to face the issue of putting something on record, and dealing with the constant examination and reexamination of published material. If we must put written information in the Internet, it could be a big change for us in what we do and how we work. I think [in the future] we will be putting more sound on the Internet--it will be another way to broadcast our message to an audience.

NOTES

1. Portions of these statutes that address Vatican Radio's programming mission are found in Appendix A.

7

"The Dice Are on the Carpet": The BBC and the French Resistance in World War II

John J. Michalczyk

Case Study Four

With the coded messages transmitted over the British Broadcasting Corporation (BBC) on the evening of June 5, 1944, "It is hot in Suez" and "The dice are on the carpet," the French Resistance was immediately alerted to the long-awaited D-Day invasion of Normandy.[1] For several years prior to the invasion, the BBC had been a lifeline for the French Resistance and the people of France.[2] During the Nazi Occupation of France, it evolved into a most effective vehicle of information as well as a beacon of hope.

In 1922 the British Broadcasting Company was given a monopoly in commercial radio, became a corporation in 1926, then rapidly developed into one of the the most professional broadcasting systems in the world under the influence of such radio pioneers as John Reith. Very fortuitous, shortly before the Nazi invasion of Poland, the BBC felt that a war was imminent and had already taken the initiative to establish "a concerted scheme of political propaganda."[3] At the outset of World War II in September 1939, the staff numbered 4,233 with 23 transmitters. The tragic phenomenon of war, however, with the growing need for both news and propaganda, boosted the staff by 1945 to 11,417 with 138 transmitters. From 1943, it was transmitting in 47 foreign languages.[4]

During the war years, the BBC became an essential propaganda weapon at home with such programs as "Women in Wartime" and "Forces Favourites," where music linked loved ones separated by the war.[5] It also served as a major vehicle for the "Anger Campaign" begun in June 1940, which was aimed at directing the hostility of the British toward Germany and its people.[6] The BBC, despite its propaganda initiative, still maintained that its mission was the communication of truthful news.[7] Even the propaganda was to be broadcast not in a crude and "heavy" way but "in a highly subtle and sophisticated manner."[8] More dramatically, however, the BBC evolved into a very finely honed tool in the French struggle against fascism, be it that of the Nazi Occupiers or the collaborating Vichyites.[9] The more commonly known images of the wartime BBC--known as Radio London or the English radio[10]--emerge from many varied sources. In *The Diary of Anne Frank*, for example, the family's primary source of information is the BBC.[11] In the "Annex," Anne listens very attentively to the British broadcasts. Film clips often show the Gestapo arresting an agent sending or receiving coded messages to and from London.[12] The rapport of the BBC with the French Resistance, however, is a complex and multilayered narrative spiced by intrigue, deception, political rivalry, and above all, imminent danger.

On June 14, 1940, a little more than six months after Germany invaded Poland on September 1, 1939, and England and France joined their Ally in the war against fascism, the Nazi Army marched triumphantly down Paris's Champs-Elysée.[13] On that fateful morning, with stately military precision, the conquerors paraded through Paris on foot and horseback and in impressive motor vehicles. For the French, the dark years of Occupation would bring down the curtain on daily life as it was known before the war, as well as on all expression of "Liberté, Egalité, and Fraternité." Resistance to the Nazi presence was soon expressed in many creative ways, from boycotting the Nazi propaganda newsreels in the popular cinema houses to painting grafitti on Nazi posters. True political resistance emerged as Charles de Gaulle, the little known 50-year-old WWI Provisional General working for Prime Minister Paul Reynaud, with his small entourage, escaped to London where they eventually became representatives of the Free French (La France Libre).

On June 18, 1940, just a few days after the Nazi occupation of Paris, de Gaulle, as a response to Marshall Pétain's broadcast of June 17, began utilizing the BBC as a propaganda vehicle against the Germans. This would be a day that would continue to live in the hearts and minds of many French through their long night of Nazi Occupation. In the studio of the French Service at the BBC, de Gaulle appeared "calm but tense" as he issued his famous "Appel."[14] It was an appeal to resist and refuse the control of the occupying force. It was both a call to action and a messsage of hope that the battle had been lost, but not the war:

Is the last word said? Has all hope gone? Is the defeat definitive? No, believe me, I tell you that nothing is lost for France. . . . This war is not limited to the unfortunate territory of our country. This war is a world war.[15]

Above all, de Gaulle made his direct appeal for support of direct resistance against the Nazis:

I invite all French officers and soldiers who are in Britain or who may find themselves there, with their arms or without, to get in touch with me. Whatever happens, the flame of French resistance must not die and will not die.[16]

The radio waves carried this bold invitation to resistance to France at 10 p.m. It was a communiqué, however, primarily aimed not at French civilians to rise up in resistance but to the professional soldier who could help organize resistance in a military fashion and maintain a rapport with the Allies. Unfortunately, few French heard this broadcast or others on June 19, 22, and 23 by this little-known general, for they were not yet accustomed to tuning in to Radio London. For Charles de Gaulle, however, this radio broadcast made a national appeal an international cause. Starting with the publishing of the text the next day on the front page of *Le Petit Provençal*, the message was sent out widely by both press and word of mouth.[17] Resistance leader Georges Bidault, then a POW prisoner in Germany, learned of it by rumor, as described in Frida Knight's account:

The fact that de Gaulle was isolated in London did not bother me. . . . One man was talking about victory. He was saying that France was not enslaved, that it had a whole empire which could help win the war. That was enough for me; although I knew almost nothing about the man, I was on his side.[18]

On June 26, a week later, de Gaulle made a stronger response to Marshall Pétain's call for Armistice:

A day will come when our weapons, forged again from afar, but well sharpened, will join those which will be of our allies, and perhaps still others, and they will return triumphantly on national soil.[19]

Winston Churchill reinforced de Gaulle's message of resistance, aiming more directly at the French population at large. On Bastille Day, July 14, 1940, Churchill alluded to the larger sector of resistance, by speaking over the BBC: "This is the war of the unknown soldiers."[20]

The repercussions to de Gaulle's resistance were serious. On July 4, he was first sentenced to four years in prison for leaving France without orders. Then on July 12, General Colson ordered him tried for desertion, and on August 2 de Gaulle was sentenced to death *in absentia*. The next four years would be a brilliant propaganda battle between the General and the Marshall, between Free France and the collaborating Vichy government. In the meantime, according to a 1973-74 questionnaire distributed to 1620 French men born between 1898 and 1922, more than 50 percent had seen in de Gaulle hope and encouragement, while approximately 15 percent of the respondents had viewed him with skepticism.[21] Early on, he would be the lone radio voice crying out in the French wilderness.

World War II radio propaganda was integrated into a larger sphere of dissemination of information. World War II historians J.-L. Crémieux-Brilhac and G. Bensimhon discuss the power of the radio in these military terms:

From 1940 to 1944, France provided both the theatre and the stakes of a propaganda confrontation without precedent in history. From the Allied perspective, just as in Vichy and in the German camp, the political and military leaders engaged in brutal "psychological warfare," in which they invested enormous means, and whose weapon *par excellence* was the radio.[22]

In the case of the BBC, this psychological warfare was carefully orchestrated in conjunction with both political and intellectual resistance. Wilkinson, in *The Intellectual Resistance in Europe*, comments upon this connection that has strong literary parallels, often connected with the names of Jean-Paul Sartre, Albert Camus, and Simone de Beauvoir:

Like other underground papers such as *Combat* and *L'Humanité, Les Lettres Françaises* countered the powerful propaganda machines of Berlin and Vichy by giving its readers news suppressed by government censors. Its mission, Edith Thomas [key contributor] proclaimed in the second issue, was to "cry out the truth." In an effort to lift morale and to encourage the faint-hearted, it reported the successes of the Allies in Russia and North Africa, as well as many acts of Resistance sabotage at home, relying on French-language broadcasts from the BBC and contacts in the underground for news.[23]

More than ever, radio began to play a vital role in the gradual dismantling of the control of the Nazis. The French had their choice of radio stations, depending on their interests and their political persuasions. Radio Vichy was immediately popular following the Armistice and thrived on the early support of Pétain and his followers. Its first overt propaganda campaign did not sit well with the more cultured and intellectual listeners, but the controllers of the station gradually toned down the blatant propaganda--without eliminating it--in order to include other aspects of French life, for example, issues about the youth.[24] French citizens under the Occupation could also listen to Radio-Paris in the hands of the Germans and collaborating talent who sold their souls in a Mephistophelian manner to gain prestige and solid earnings in harsh economic times.[25] The two stars of the radio propaganda station were Philippe Henriot and Jean-Hérold Paquis. Henriot was the more aggressive of the two, and was later named Minister of Propaganda, a Goebbels-like position that he unofficially held throughout the earlier phases of the Occupation. Former Resistance leader Jean Planchais, long-time journalist of *Le Monde*, notes, "In denouncing Radio London everyday in competition with it, Philippe Henriot recognized that it was listened to clandestinely by a considerable number of French."[26] In return, one of the BBC's broadcasted refrains was "Radio-Paris ment, Radio-Paris ment. Radio-Paris est allemande" (Radio-Paris lies, Radio Paris lies. Radio-Paris is German). "With this daily refrain, the BBC stigmatized radio broadcasting from the occupied zone. It was the opinion shared by the vast majority of the French."[27]

Although it was also possible for the French to receive the Swiss Radio-Sottens (Suisse romande), which gave more objective news, it was the BBC, however, that was considered most significant and most popular in obtaining concrete information about the Allied moves to defeat the occupying forces.[28] Jean Planchais discusses the political effect of the BBC: "Thanks to it [BBC], the radio propaganda of Vichy and Paris had a counterpart: a different version of the news that it gave, and in numerous cases, the broadcast of news that had been withheld [by Vichy and Paris]."[29]

The questionnaire distributed in 1973-74 revealed that during the war almost 50 percent of the 1620 French who responded preferred the BBC, and slightly more than 36 percent of them the Swiss Radio-Sottens (Suisse romande). Only 1 percent acknowledged that they preferred Radio-Paris and Radio-Vichy to other stations, and less than .50 percent said they listened to the Voice of America. Although this inquiry was designed almost three decades after the Occupation, strong feelings and memories still remained among the French for the BBC, considered an important port in a political storm, especially with its news and encouragement.[30]

Ehrlich describes the general program for Radio London:

The news broadcasts came on the air at fixed intervals, twelve times a day. [In spring 1944, there were 17 daily broadcasts]. The nine-thirty evening programs were followed by five minutes of Gaullist propaganda, and a half-hour variety program, "Frenchmen Speaking to Frenchmen."[31]

A typical broadcast might begin with the noting of the precise day of the fight against fascism, for example, "The 250th day of the struggle of the French people for its Liberation," as Frida Knight describes it. Knight further recalls, "after which came the words of encourgement, the latest news and the coded messages."[32] The news was directed to the general populace, most often the working class, documenting specific events of the war against fascism, as in the case of the Stalingrad campaign and the French support of the Russians.[33]

Ehrlich offers a few details about the type of messages that were sent as "Personal Messages" during a 16-minute period of the broadcast:

These were signal phrases for parachute drops of agents and supplies, for airplane landings, for submarine or surface craft arrivals, for specific Resistance actions. They were not coded sentences, but arbitrary password phrases which meant, "The plane you were expecting tonight cannot come" or "Okay to set fire to the two barges by the bridge." They were such phrases as "Marianne detests oysters," or "My wife has sharp eyes." [34]

The most popular program was "Les Français Parlent aux Français." Maurice Schumann, the "Porte Parole de la France Libre," or Free French spokesman, was most often heard on this program. Schumann, a former Cabinet Member in Léon Blum's government, was the organizer of the Gaullist radio service and provided a strong nationalist voice to the resistance. On September 29, 1942, and rebroadcast the next day, Schumann's voice called out for unity on "Honneur et Patrie," as he intoned "Une France unie est une France forte" ("A united France is a strong France").[35] He made even a stronger, more rhetorical appeal for unity in his May 18, 1944 discourse on the BBC, "Pauvre Maréchal," or "Poor Marshall" (Pétain) where he recalled the valiant efforts of the Resistance in the Glières plateau region.[36]

Although the French primarily listened to the news on these BBC programs, and then the daily editorials, often the slogans or songs remained fixed in the hearts and minds of the listeners, as confirmed by the 1973-74 questionnaire mentioned earlier. Most impressive by order of the number of respondents' recollections was Radio-Paris ment (Radio-Paris lies), Le Chant des Partisans (The Partisans' Song), Aujourd'hui Ne jour de la lutte (Today, the x day of the struggle), La chanson des V (The V Song), Lily Marlène (song), and La défense élastique (The elastic defense).[37]

In July 1940 the Special Operations Executive (SOE) was established in France. These secret agents, bearing colorful code names such as Ventriloquist, Clergyman, or Rover, were equipped with radios and codes to assist communication between the Resistance and London. Approximately 400 agents worked for SOE/F (France) and later SOE/RF (Resistance France). Fifty were women, 13 of whom died in the field. One of these women trained in radio transmission was Jacqueline Nearne who worked with the circuit Stationer. At one point she received a specific message, for example, through the BBC: "Assemble a group to pass out weapons at 0300 hours."[38]

In *The SOE in France,* M. R. D. Foot discusses SOE's contribution to radio commmunication by Georges Begué, an engineer, the first agent parachuted into France on the night of May 5-6, 1941:

But it was Georges Begué who originally proposed in the summer of 1941 what became the most conspicuous thing SOE ever did: the nightly broadcasting on the BBC's foreign programme, through some of the most powerful transmitters in the world, of scores of sentences which sounded like family greetings or like Carrollian nonsense. "Romeo embrasse Juliette," "la chienne de Barbara aura trois chiots," just might mean what they purported to mean to somebody.[39]

Foot notes that only the agents and the staff would know that the Romeo-Juliet allusion was to mark the arrival of a courier in Switzerland from Toulouse or that Barbara's dog reference was to the arrival of three passengers in Barcelona by boat. The coded system was designed both to reduce radio traffic and to carry on clandestine resistance activity without detection by Germans or Vichy sympathizers. It would be used to its maximum in the days leading up to the D-Day invasion.

Philippe Depret-Bixio offers his personal recollections from his father's Resistance work as head of a network and his own experiences as a liaison agent before he left France to join the Allied forces. He describes how the various networks utilized the resources of the BBC. These networks such as Information, Action, Maquis, SOE, etc., early on, most often worked independently of each other until coordination of the Resistance was made possible. He recalls that these groups received radio sets from London, either by parachute or directly by their liaison agents.[40] The radios, built more and more compact as the war went on, were quicker and more reliable than the SOE carrier-pigeon system.[41] It was these sets that aided in getting information back to London. Once there, the Free French and/or SOE would act on the requests, for example, of the need for arms. The BBC would then broadcast a notice that the arms were forthcoming in a message such as "les tomates sont mûres" (the tomatoes are ripe) that would be broadcast the night before the parachute drop. Another example provided by Depret-Bixio would be "les sauterelles sont rouges," (the grasshoppers are red), which would indicate a parachute drop. Repeated twice, it signified two drops.[42] Jean Planchais writes that, from 1944 on, he received "personal messages" which indicated the day and place of the parachute drop of arms. He notes that a landing site would be called "petit lapin" (a little rabbit) or "orage" (a storm). He was especially active as the BBC launched the "Plans bleu et vert" (Plan Blue and Green) in preparation for the Normandy invasion.[43]

The German and Vichy officials viewed the BBC as a major threat, especially as it aided the Resistance in the manner just described. On October 28, 1940,

Vichy made it *verboten* to listen to the foreign radio, meaning the BBC. For accurate war reports, the French listened to the London radio behind closed shutters. In most cases, the penalty for defying the ban on listening to the BBC was "six days' to six months' imprisonment, with fines varying from 16 to 1,000 francs, together with the confiscation of sets."[44] Jean Planchais, a Resistance leader in the Orne Department, approximately 100 kilometers from Caen, recalls the dangers of listening to the BBC: "Many French were arrested and imprisoned simply because they listened to the BBC. Some of them died during their deportation, even though they were not part of the Resistance."[45] Ehrlich as well suggests that any anti-Occupation activity such as listening to the BBC, "could be the first step to the concentration camp."[46] If anything, for more and more of the French population, beginning in October and November 1940, tuning in to the BBC signified the first physical act of resistance.

The constant jamming of the London radio not only interfered with the clarity of the broadcasts but gave an opportunity to the Germans to trace the noise via their roving surveillance vans. Printed fliers cautioned listeners of the repercussions of listening to the BBC. The following was one of the warning notices:

Listener of the English Radio . . .
Consider this paper as a first warning

••

Deliberately or not, by listening and promoting this propaganda, the fruit of the Jewish-Communist alliance, you are commiting a crime against your country.

Without prejudice of legal sanctions to which you are exposing yourself, know that it is the French decision that you cease your criminal action.

Try to understand wherein your duty lies. . . .

If not, we greatly regret that we will not hesitate to impose this upon you.[47]

The BBC was also carefully monitored by the Vichy collaborators who understood French and could possibly decode some of the messages, as they would later claim about the D-Day invasion in Operation Overlord on June 6, 1944. In the region of Clermont-Ferrand, near the Vichy government's headquarters, French police discovered three people tuning in to the broadcasts and investigated. When asked if he dared listen to the BBC, a severely wounded veteran of the 1914-1918 war proudly responded, "Of course I do!"[48] Vichy also monitered the radio for news about possible demonstrations, as it did on July 14, 1942, Bastille Day.

The London radio was very much aware of the political situation of France at all times through radio contacts, especially by the SOE. One of the more concrete political uses of the radio was to understand the temper of the times and urge civilian response accordingly. The BBC often urged demonstrations to show solidarity among the civilian population and to indicate to the Germans that resistance was beginning to form against their wishes. Jean Planchais recalls: "The suggested demonstrations (silent protest march in the streets, etc.) allowed some people who did not belong directly to the Resistance to show their opposition to the enemy."[49] These demonstrations often came on May Day or Bastille Day--to link them with a more nationalistic or patriotic spirit.[50]   One such demonstration was symbolically called for by the BBC on Armistice Day, November 11, 1940.   From early November, the BBC was calling for demonstrations at all war memorials. In response, several thousand high school and college students marched down the Champs-Elysée at 5:30 p.m. with flags and banners singing "La Marseillaise." They intended to lay a traditional wreath at the tomb of the Unknown Soldier at the Arc de Triomphe. The students shouted slogans such as "Long live France!," "Down with Pétain!," and "Down with Hitler!" French and German police broke up the rally. The BBC reported the demonstration and erroneously indicated that eleven students had been killed in the clash, although actual documents fail to substantiate this.[51] The reality may have been that several students were wounded and approximately 100 arrested.[52]

De Gaulle was also committed to the encouragement of public demonstrations in order to create a feeling of solidarity but also to indicate to the Germans that popular resistance was growing. Broadcasting from London, he urged the French to public demonstration by remaining in their homes on New Year's Day 1941, between 4:00 and 5:00 p.m., and between 5:00 and 6:00 p.m. in the Occupied Zone. Briggs concludes, "Broadcasting from London, it seemed, was beginning to enter *an operational stage.*"[53]

To overcome some of the danger and difficulty in listening to these broadcasts, Alsatian-born music publisher Raymond Deiss created a written information bulletin of the BBC news. His four-page bulletin *Pantagruel*--named for Rabelais' giant--was published monthly by the printers René and Robert Blanc on rue Dauphine in Paris.[54] It was distributed among sympathetic French who longed for the BBC information. The trio continued to serve as an important vehicle of developing news in the 16 issues printed from October 1940 until their arrest in October 1941. For his resistance--treason to Germany--René was beheaded in Germany in 1943, given his Alsatian birth.

Another major publication was the *Bulletin d'information et propagande*, created in February 1941 by Henri Frenay, leader of the Mouvement de Libération Nationale (M.L.N.). In this bulletin, he, Berthie Albrecht, and a former military colleague, Captain Robert Guédon, included a "factual presentation in catalogue form of events in the war in the occupied zone, taken from BBC broadcasts."[55]

A third publication, *Le Père Duchesne* utilizing material from the BBC, had its historical roots in political events of 1793, 1848, and 1871. Now, in April 1942, it took a definite anti-German stance, drawing much of its information from the BBC news. In the April 1942 issue of *Le Père Duchesne* appeared a standard anti-German joke, which can be considered anti-Semitic and in very poor taste:

A Boche [German] has made the following accusation. "I saw a Jew with my own eyes, eating a German's brains. It was exactly 9:15 PM." Now this accusation is false on three counts: 1. A German has no brains. 2. Jews do not eat pigs. 3. At 9:15 PM everyone is listening to the BBC.[56]

The BBC radio also served other purposes. In June 1940, shortly after the defeat at Dunkirk, radio announcements appealed to prewar vacationers to France for postcards. Approximately 30,000 reportedly arrived in the first mail, and eventually 10 million were received. The postcard appeal assisted significantly in the gathering of visual data for later reconnaisance, especially for the D-Day invasion.[57]

Another service provided by London radio was the broadcasting of the "Counsels." These were 33 short numbered paragraphs that first appeared in typed and then mimeographed form. "They were really a guide to the preservation of individual dignity, guide to a French conduct more icily 'correct' than the German."[58] These counsels were smuggled over to London by a Gaullist agent and then read over the BBC in September 1940. Counsel No. 30, for example, reads: "You grumble because they oblige you to get back home by exactly 11 PM. Innocent, haven't you understood this is to let you listen to the English radio?"[59]

One of the more well-appreciated messages from the BBC was the familiar Morse Code letter "V," . . . , which gave hope to the French listeners. It came to represent a "V" for Victory over the Nazi occupying forces.[60] The BBC's campaign to use this symbol of resistance grew and was taken up all over Europe, especially through the efforts of the BBC's "V" Committee of key representatives from the administration. Ehrlich comments on its symbolic power in France as well as in all of occupied Europe:

The V and the double-barred Gaullist Cross of Lorraine really irritated the Germans, the V more than the cross, because the V was universal. No sooner had the BBC begun broadcasting the Morse Code-Beethoven "V" than it began appearing on the walls of the occupied cities. Ubiquitous, ineradicable, it haunted the myth-minded Germans. They had made a fetish of the swastika, and they loathed this counter-charm. It was the handwriting on the wall.[61]

What had begun as a personal initiative of the BBC Belgian programmer Victor de Laveleye on January 14, 1941, escalated into a major international propaganda scheme and morale booster. The "V" sign became the focus of the French Service program "Les Français parlent aux Français" on March 22, 1941. The "V" campaign prospered in Europe and America until June 22, 1941, when the German Operation Barbarossa forced Russia into the war alongside the Allies. The usual graffiti seen everywhere became secondary in the new phase of the war, especially as France began to reassess its relationship with its former enemy, Russia.

Throughout the Occupation, according to Resistance member Jean Planchais, the BBC "gave the French, right from the outset, the impression that they were not alone, that the war was continuing on, and that it had not been lost."[62] This alone can be perceived by the number of hours weekly that the BBC European Service dedicated to the French language program. At the outset of the war in September 1939, it was three hours and thirty minutes; shortly after the D-Day invasion of June 6, 1944, it had been extended to forty-three hours and forty-five minutes, more than any other European country.[63] Over this period, the radio's role developed more considerably as the Resistance became more and more organized, especially in light of the formation of the Conseil National de la Resistance (C.N.R.) in May 1942.

The power of radio propaganda and military information, however, reached its apogee in the Allied preparations for Operation Overlord, scheduled for early June 1944. On May 1 and June 1, the BBC sent out scores of "messages d'alerte," warning notices that the invasion of the European mainland was imminent. The French civilian population as well as the Resistance had anxiously been awaiting the inevitable Allied landing. D-Day (or "Jour J") had finally arrived.

Historian Stephen Ambrose describes how Operation Overlord would utilize the BBC in coordinating the landing:

As the Germans were regularly picking up Resistance members and torturing them to get information, the Resistance could not be told in advance the date of D-Day. Therefore arrangements had to be made to order the execution of sabotage plans by code messages broadcast over the BBC. Leaders were told to listen to the BBC broadcasts on the 1st, 2nd, 15th, and 16th of each month. If the invasion was imminent, they would hear a preparatory code message. They would then remain on alert to listen for a confirmatory message "B," to be followed within forty-eight hours by a code launching the units into action. Each region had a different code.[64]

Meanwhile, on June 5, while relations were still chilly between the Allied leaders and de Gaulle, the head of France Libre was asked if he would broadcast news of the landing of the Allied armada on the Normandy beaches. He would be the final speaker on the BBC transmission, following the King of Norway; the Queen of Holland; the Grand Duchess of Luxembourg; the Prime Minister of Belgium; and General Dwight Eisenhower, the Supreme Commander of the Allied Forces. He proudly refused the last place position and challenged Eisenhower's recorded message. Only at 5:30 p.m., and then at 6:30 p.m., 7:30 p.m. and later into the evening of the first day of the invasion, after several harsh confrontations, de Gaulle noted in his memoirs, would he solitarily address the French. The tension was extremely high in the heated debate over content, as well as translation and editing. In his deep bass voice he intoned, "The supreme battle has been joined. . . . From behind the cloud so heavy with our blood and tears, the sun of our greatness is now appearing."[65] De Gaulle's message over the BBC also concretely affirmed: "pour les fils de France...le devoir simple et sacré est de combattre par tous les moyens dont ils deposent (for the sons of France . . . their simple and sacred duty is to fight with all the means at hand)."[66] The BBC announced that France was now mobilized under the guidance of the Provisional Government of de Gaulle.

French Resistance groups and the SOE throughout France were alerted to imminent action. When the BBC went from the *alert* broadcast to *execute,* four principal sabotage "Plans"--Blue (electricity), Green (railways), Violet (telephone cables), and Turquoise (roadways)--were in place in order to prepare for the landings on the northwest French coast.[67] By June 5, each Group had its mission and schedule in hand, for example, the cutting of telephone lines or the sabotaging of railways. That evening, while the Allied ships were almost in place for the strategic surprise landing, the BBC buzzed with hundreds of messages being transmitted to agents in the field. The usual five to ten minutes of "personal messages" took twenty. Foot offers some concrete examples of the messages intended for agent LIONEL in the Nantes SOE Clergyman circuit in order to engage in the scheduled activity:

1. For railway targets:
    A. C'ETAIT LE SERGENT QUI FUMAIT SA PIPE EN PLEINE CAMPAGNE [It was the sergeant who was smoking his pipe in the countryside]
    B. IL AVAIT MAL AU COEUR MAIS IL CONTINUAIT TOUT DE MEME [He was broken-hearted but he continued just the same]
2. For telephone targets:
    A. LA CORSE RESSEMBLE A UNE POIRE [Corsica resembles a pear]
    B. L'ITALIE EST UNE BOTTE [Italy is a boot].[68]

The BBC signal to region C (French/German border) for Plan Violet to sabotage the underground long-distance telephone cables was "Je n'entends plus ta voix" ("I no longer hear your voice"). There were those messages that had a religious allusion, for example, to Acolyte: "It was Father Bernard who told me this story." Some had political relevance, as the signal to Delegate: "Foch guards the Place Vendôme." Other messages were whimsical and quasi-surrealist, as the one to Jacques/Robin: "The moon is full of green elephants."

The most signficant and well remembered code for the Allied landing was the first two lines of 19th-century French poet Paul Verlaine's "Chanson d'Autumne" ("Autumn Song"). The *warning* message of Resistance leader Philippe de Vomécourt in preparation for action was the first line, misquoted "Les sanglots longs des violons d'automne (for *de l'*automne)" ("The long sobs of the Autumn violins"). The call to *execute* was the second line, again misquoted: "Bercent (for *blessent*) mon coeur d'une langueur monotone" ("Cradle (for wound) my heart with a tedious listlessness"). After great anxiety, the line finally came shortly before 9:30 p.m. on June 5.[69] It told, for example, the SOE'S VENTRILOQUIST circuit to stand by and then act--to cut the designated railway lines. Ironically, it was detected by the Germans, but its full implications went unheeded. The message was sent to the High Command in the area of the landings, but in the absence of General Rommel--in Germany for the birthday of his wife Lucie--the warning was not acted upon by the German Army.[70] After many false alarms in May, the Germans gave little credence to these calls to action. They believed that the most likely focus of an invasion would be the Pas de Calais. Poor weather and bad tides in the Strait of Dover, however, would deter any possible landing in the first few days of June. To German Intelligence, furthermore, it seemed absurd that the Allies would announce a surprise attack over the BBC. No special action was taken therefore to pursue the possibility of an Allied invasion.

The bicycle shop owner and Resistance leader Guillaume Mercader heard his call to action in the northern Bayeux region at 6:30 PM on June 5. He recalled the experience of being stunned by the following transmission: "'It is hot in Suez. It is hot in Suez.' Twice. Then a definite silence. Then 'The dice are on the carpet. The dice are on the carpet.' Twice again, as well as other messages which didn't concern us."[71] He immediately left his home to meet with other Resistance members and prepare for the landings.

The efficacy of the BBC's call to action was remarkable, according to Ehrlich:

It was as if trails of powder had been laid crisscross over the map of France. The railroad lines were blown apart, tunnels were blocked, bridges were broken. The lights went out, factory machines were stilled, the telephone was dead. [72]

Since September 1941, the BBC had also helped the French on a local level. Its broadcasts had prophetically looked forward to the day of the Allied embarkation. On September 15 and 27, 1941, Henri Hauck urged his French listeners of the 6:00 p.m. broadcast to prepare to take the responsibility of organizing their cities and villages in the aftermath of the landing. Hauch urged his listening audience:

(It is) to all of you, in your city or in your village, that will belong the task of taking charge of the levers of local control, to create democratic committees, to pursue agents of the enemy, and to insure food supplies and communications.[73]

The forward-looking de Gaulle in his famous "Appeal" of June 18, 1940, had already predicted the Allied defeat of the enemy:

This war is not limited to the battle of France. This war is a world war. All the faults, delays, and sufferings do not impede the fact, that there are in the universe all means to one day wipe out our enemies.[74]

In 1942, on the second anniversary of the "Appeal," de Gaulle radioed from London that the duty of all French is to utilize fully all possible means in their fight against the enemy and the Vichy agents who are their accomplices. In this radio discourse he noted, "National liberation cannot be separated from a national insurrection."[75] On his D-Day broadcast he tactfully did not broach the subject of civilian insurrection. Pierre Brossolette, Resistance coordinator of the northern region and radio broadcaster, would also make a prophetic announcement on the BBC on September 22, 1942. With great hope and vision, he predicted to the French, that on the day of victory, this man of June 18, 1940, "will be carried all along the Champs-Elysée, amid the stifled murmurs of long sobs of joy-filled women, and the endless volley of your cries."[76] The prophecy was fulfilled on August 26, 1944, as de Gaulle paraded along the Champs-Elysée following the surrender of the Germans to Colonel Rol Tanguy and General Jacques Philippe Leclerc on the preceding day.

One of the more dramatic insurrections was that of the Paris uprising on Saturday, August 19, more than two months after the D-Day landing. For four days, street by street, Paris was being liberated. On Wednesday, August 23, the

BBC erroneously announced on its 12:30 broadcast, "Paris is liberated." Despite General Eisenhower's SHAEF correction that this was premature, the BBC continued to broadcast the jubilant news.[77]

In the period following the Allied landings, the BBC was efficient in creating a New Order. It proclaimed that France is now mobilized under the Provisional Government. English radio also enjoined clerical helpers to destroy orders of the Vichy and the police and to pass to the side of the resisters. Concretely, it announced the successful actions of the FFI (Forces Françaises de l'Intérieure) and thus helped build growing local resistance in the national uprising.

CONCLUSIONS

A half-century after the Liberation, Radio London can be seen historically as having played an integral role in creating the vehicle of communication that led to final victory over the Nazi occupiers of France. As can be witnessed by documents and eyewitness accounts, the BBC fulfilled several principal roles in a larger propaganda scene. In general, it provided a strong support to the theory that the June 22, 1940, Armistice had not ended the war against fascism. Through the voices of the Free French in London, the French people would be lead in the continued, organized, and Allied-supported struggle against the Germans. In this manner, anti-Nazi and anti-Vichy French citizens were given daily encouragement and hope that their country would be soon liberated.[78] For many civilians, the London radio broadcasts had helped make them "armchair resisters." Jean Baumel, a member of the Resistance and AN Auschwitz survivor, recalls "The radio was also important [as was the Press], and many people who were not Resisters were nevertheless made sympathetic by listening to the BBC."[79] Resistance leader Georges Bidault symbolically reflects the power of the BBC to influence the lives of the French:

"Ici Londres, les Français parlent aux Français." These were the words which, in the silence of occupation, when every mouth was gagged, helped the French to surmount and overcome the lies of the enemy. Like a compass to the sailor, the wireless was to them the guide and assurance which, at the height of the tempest, saved them from despair. It is partly, indeed largely, thanks to you, dear familiar voices, that our minds stayed free while our limbs were bound.[80]

For those who acted upon the constant BBC directives, especially after 1942, they became a fraternity of resisters on whom the radio propaganda was most effective. The BBC, from that point on, was responsible for having turned an unsure, ambivalent minority of civilians into a visible active group of resisters involved in either demonstrations or military action.

Secondly, the BBC provided valuable news and information that kept the French abreast of the world at war. Outside of the national and patriotic broadcasts of reassurance, these were, for the most part, honest and balanced in the assessment of the various campaigns and the challenging task ahead. Less propagandistic than Radio-Paris and Radio-Vichy, the English radio served as a much needed antidote to the pro-Nazi stations.

Lastly, in the final days of the Liberation of France, the BBC was an indispensable instrument of *action*. In essence, it helped pilot and orchestrate the Liberation.[81] If national liberation was the goal, then the BBC would be the *guide* in this insurrection. From 1944 on, it became a necessary vehicle for directing patriotic opinion that would be essential in post-Liberation political and civilian life. At the dawn of the Occupation, London Radio had indeed helped shape de Gaulle as a pioneer of protest, resistance, as well as hope. As Liberation was becoming a reality, it aided the General in becoming a symbol of political power.

In the apocalyptic upheaval of World War II, the BBC had developed into one of the most political and creative tools for overthrowing a superior, oppressive government. In a subtle play of complex forces, influences, and pressure by both the English and the Free French under de Gaulle's direction, the radio war underlined the power of the media to help change the course of world events.[82]

NOTES

1. Stephen E. Ambrose, *D-Day* (New York: Simon & Schuster, 1994), 104. These codes and other BBC transmissions are gathered together in *Ici Londres: La Voix de la Liberté* (5 Vols.), provided through the courtesy of Maria Luniw at the BBC office in London.

2. Throughout this chapter, the word Resistance in uppercase specifically indicates the French Resistance movement; the lower-case form refers to the general anti-Nazi and anti-Vichy spirit of protest and demonstration.

3. Paddy Scannell and David Cardiff, *A Social History of British Broadcasting, Vol. One 1922-1939* (Oxford: Basil Blackwell, Ltd., 1991), 97.

4. Angus Calder, *The People's War: Britain, 1939-1945* (New York: Pantheon Books, 1969), 359.

5. Ibid., 362-363.

6. Asa Briggs, *A History of Broadcasting in the United Kingdom, Vol. 3, 1939-1945: The War of Words* (Oxford: Oxford University Press, 1970), 191.

7. Ibid., 381.

8. Ibid., 227.

9. See especially Briggs, "Britain and France," 219-234.

10. Resistance member Jean Planchais, January 8, 1996: personal communication.

11. See *Diary of Anne Frank* entries for June 15, 1943, August 5, 1943; March 27, 1944; and June 6, 1944.

12. *Spies*, television series, data not available.

13. See Milton Dank, *The French Against the French: Collaboration and Resistance* (London: Cassell, Ltd., 1978), 61, for a view of the Nazi conquest of Paris.

14. Briggs, 221.

15. For a description of the recording session of the famous "Appeal," read David Schoenbrun, *Soldiers of the Night* (New York: E. P. Dutton, 1980), p. 40. Unfortunately the historic moment was never recorded; the technician failed to make a recording of this momentous speech.

16. Schoenbrun, 40.

17. H. R. Kedward, *Resistance in Vichy France: A Study of Ideas and Motivation in the Southern Zone 1940-1942* (Oxford: Oxford University Press, 1978), 210.

18. Frida Knight, *The French Resistance 1940 to 1944* (London: Lawrence and Wishart, 1975), 55.

19. René Brouillet, "Le Général de Gaulle et la Libération de la France," in *La Libération de la France* (Paris: Centre National de la Recherche Scientifique, 1976), p. 57. All translations from the French, especially in brackets throughout the chapter are the author's, unless otherwise noted.

20. Blake Ehrlich, *Resistance: France 1940-1945* (Boston: Little, Brown and Co., 1965), 31.

21. J.-L. Crémieux-Brilhac and G. Bensimhon, "Les Propagandes Radiophoniques et l'Opinion Publique en France de 1940 à 1944," *Revue d'Histoire de la Deuxième Guerre Mondiale*, (No. 101, Jan. 1976), 13. I am grateful to M. Henry Russo of the Institut d'Histoire du Temps Présent of the Centre National de la Recherche Scientifique (C.N.R.S.) for having forwarded a copy of the results of this questionnaire.

22. Ibid., 3.

23. James D. Wilkinson, *The Intellectual Resistance in Europe* (Cambridge, Mass.: Harvard University Press, 1981), 43-44.

24. Briggs, 229.

25. Dank, 184-185.

26. Jean Planchais, January 8, 1996: personal communication.

27. Dank, 184.

28. To contrast the power of the BBC to Radio Algiers in 1943, Charles de Gaulle said that the Algiers frequencies were less well known and heard in France. Although he realized that his voice from Northern Africa was still reaching the French, he remarked that he felt "it was in a muffled manner." In *The War Memoirs of Charles de Gaulle: Unity 1942-1944*, trans. by Richard Howard (New York: Simon and Schuster, 1959), 187.

29. Jean Planchais, January 8, 1996: personal communication.

30. Crémieux-Brilhac and Bensimhon, 6.

31. Ehrlich, 30. See also Jean-Louis Crémieux-Brilhac, "La Libération de la France vue de Londres: L'Arme Radiophonique et l'Insurrection Nationale," in *La Libération de la France*, 118, where he notes that the BBC tried to use different frequencies to prevent the constant jamming of the broadcasts by the Nazis.

32. Knight, 91.

33. Ibid., 99.

34. Ehrlich, 30.

35. Charles-Louis Foulon, "Le Général de Gaulle et la Libération de la France," in *La Libération de la France*, 37.

36. Ibid., 32.

37. Crémieux-Brilhac and Bensimhon, 12.

38. Nearne is featured in the documentary television series *Spies* and discussed occasionally in M. R. D. Foot, *SOE in France* (London: Her Majesty's Stationery Office, 1976), one of the best accounts to date of British Intelligence's work with the French Resistance.

39. Foot, 110. For a description of Begué's link with the SOE, consult Patrick Howarth, *Undercover: The Men and Women of the Special Operations Executive*, 129-131.

40. Philippe Depret-Bixio, January 19, 1996: personal communication.

41. Ambrose, 101.

42. Philippe Depret-Bixio, January 19, 1996: personal communication.

43. Jean Planchais, January 8, 1996: personal correspondence.

44. Quoted in Briggs, 233.

45. Jean Planchais, January 8, 1996: personal communication.

46. Ehrlich, 91.

47. Gilles Perreault, *Paris under the Occupation* (New York: Vendome Press, 1989), 128.

48. John F. Sweets, *Vichy France: The French under Nazi Occupation* (New York: Oxford University Press, 1986), 74.

49. Jean Planchais, January 8, 1996: personal communication.

50. Crémieux-Brilhac and Bensimhon, 12. From the triumphal march of the Nazis along the Champs-Elysée in June 1940 until 1942, public demonstrations were few and far between. This changed in 1942-43 especially through the incentives of the BBC.

51. Dank, 77.

52. H. R. Kedward, *Occupied France: Collaboration and Resistance 1940-1944* (Oxford: Basil Blackwell Ltd., 1985), 46.

53. Briggs; 234, italics mine.

54. For an illustration of the first issue of *Pantagruel* in October 1940, see Perreault, 166.

55. Kedward, *Resistance in Vichy France*, 121.

56. Ibid., 153-154.

57. Ambrose, 73.

58. Ehrlich, 22.

59. Ibid., 22-23.

60. For a more extensive treatment of the "V Campaign," see Briggs, 333 ff.

61. Ehrlich, 91-92.

62. Jean Planchais, January 8, 1996: personal communication.

63. For a comparison with other European countries, consult Briggs, 440.

64. Ambrose, 103-104.

65. *The War Memoirs of Charles de Gaulle: Unity 1942-43*, 256. See also Schoenbrun, *Soldiers of the Night*, 364, for a description of the D-Day broadcast.

66. Crémieux-Brilhac, 122.

67. Jean-Marie d'Hoop, "Réponse à la Communication de M. Blumeson," in *La Libération de la France*, 232.

68. Foot, 500.

69. Howarth, p. 131. For a discussion of Philippe de Vomécourt's wartime Resistance activity, read his book *Who Lived to See the Day*.

70. Foot, 388.

71. Ambrose, 104.

72. Ehrlich, 190.

73. Charles-Louis Foulon, "Prise et Exercise du Pouvoir en Province à la Libération," in *La Libération de la France*, 504.

74. Général Jiline, "La Coopération Franco-Soviétique durant la Seconde Guerre Mondiale," in *La Libération de la France*," 210.

75. Colonel Jean Delmas, "Conceptions et Préparation de l'Insurrection Nationale," in *La Libération de la France*, 433.

76. Brouillet, p. 62. For a discussion of Brosselette's Resistance activity and suicide in Gestapo headquarters in Paris, see Ehrlich, 58-60.

77. Ehrlich, 245.

78. Crémieux-Brilhac and Bensimhon, 5.

79. Kedward, *Resistance in Vichy France,* 268.

80. Quoted in Briggs, 611.

81. Crémieux-Brilhac, 117.

82. I am grateful to M. Christian Delacampagne for his extensive contacts in gathering information for this chapter, especially from M. Henry Russo of the Institut d'Histoire du Temps Présent in Paris. I also extend my gratitude to M. Jean Planchais, M. Philippe Depret-Bixio, and M. Maurice Schumann for their firsthand experiences that they shared with me. Lastly, the archival material from the BBC gathered by Maria Luniw of the BBC proved invaluable.

8

Institutionalization of Anti-Castro Radio Broadcasting

John Spicer Nichols

Case Study Five

Clandestine radio broadcasting has always been a staple in the long-standing conflict between the United States and Cuba. For 35 years, the U.S. government and Cuban exile groups have conducted an intense campaign of political broadcasting -- much of it clandestine broadcasting -- at the Caribbean island in hopes of contributing to the overthrow of the government of Fidel Castro. During the early 1990s, after the demise of other Cold War adversaries of the United States and the commensurate decline of clandestine broadcasting worldwide, Cuba was firmly established as the number one target of underground broadcasts. As late as 1993, underground stations broadcast at least 100 hours per week more to Cuba than to other top targets in the world, such as Iraq and Iran.[1] However, by 1995, clandestine broadcasts directed at Cuba had virtually disappeared.

The broadcast war against Cuba has long been the subject of great curiosity among radio hobbyists and, more recently, of scholarly and journalistic attention and an intense policy debate in Washington. Despite the recent decline in clandestine activity, U.S. broadcasting to Cuba arguably is the most important ongoing case of cross-national political propaganda and, therefore, has larger significance for understanding international broadcasting.

Clandestine Radio Broadcasting[2] inventoried all known Cuban clandestine stations from the first one reported on the air in 1933 to those operating in the five-year period ending in 1985 and described them in their historical and political context. The purpose of this chapter is to update those listings and to analyze the significance of the marked changes in political broadcasting to Cuba during the past decade.

This analysis is predicated on the assumption that the existence of a clandestine or other station broadcasting political propaganda, the type and location of the station, and the political circumstances within which it operates are more important than any content it may broadcast. Many researchers and most policymakers focus on the manifest content of clandestine and other political stations, and their broadcasts are usually viewed as the independent variable, that is, a potential cause or contributory cause of political change in the target country. However, clandestine and other political broadcasting are treated here as the dependent variable, that is, the outcome of changing political circumstances. Significant changes that have taken place in anti-Castro broadcasting during the past decade, therefore, are a strong indication of the shifting political landscape in and between the United States and Cuba.

TYPES OF CLANDESTINE STATIONS

Soley and Nichols describe clandestine broadcasting as "illegal, political, and frequently misleading."[3] Clandestine stations are neither licensed by the appropriate government authorities in the country from which they operate nor registered with the International Frequency Registration Board, the telecommunications regulatory body of the United Nations. They usually are sponsored by a revolutionary, dissident, or other underground group or by an adversary government purporting to be one of those opposition groups. In any case, the purpose of the station is to encourage the overthrow of or other political change in the adversary regime.

Clandestine stations are distinguished from so-called "white" stations, which broadcast legally[4] and openly from known locations and with an acknowledged purpose. White stations are usually operated by foreign governments (e.g., the U.S. government's Voice of America); however, in the case of Cuba, white anti-Castro propaganda is increasingly carried over commercial shortwave stations.

Clandestine stations are categorized as either "gray" or "black." According to Elliott et al.,[5] black stations "purport to be something other than what they really are."[6] For example, a station secretly operated by a foreign intelligence agency but claiming to be that of an indigenous opposition group is classified as black. Gray stations, notwithstanding their illegal operation and hidden location, usually acknowledge their real sponsorship and purpose.

The location of the station is extremely important. While many clandestine stations claim to be operating from a transmitter inside the target country, few actually are. Because of the nature of broadcasting technology, indigenous clandestine stations can be easily located and, if the government is in control of its own national territory, can be easily closed. However, in some cases, guerrilla forces are able to establish "liberated" zones from which they broadcast antigovernment propaganda. The mere existence of an indigenous station for an extended period of time is strong evidence of the guerrillas' strength and the government's weakness and can contribute to the fall of the regime.

For example, in 1957 and 1958, Castro's guerrilla army operated Radio Rebelde, which broadcast against the U.S.-backed dictatorship of Fulgencio Batista from the Eastern mountains of Cuba.[7] Its continuation on the air was an embarrassment to the regime, and Batista ordered his army to silence it. However, despite having superior numbers, the Batista army was soundly defeated by Castro's guerrillas in its attempt to capture the Radio Rebelde transmitter, signaling the beginning of the end for the regime. In the 1980s, during the civil war in nearby El Salvador, the whereabouts of Radio

Venceremos, a clandestine station of the guerrillas fighting to unseat the government, was hotly debated. The Salvadoran government and its U.S. patron claimed that the station was actually based in another Central American country, and when a correspondent for the *New York Times* reported seeing the station inside El Salvador, he was labeled a dupe of the communist guerrillas. Acknowledging that Radio Venceremos was an indigenous clandestine station would be an admission of the government's weakness.[8]

Operating an indigenous clandestine station usually is a demonstration of the political or military viability of the sponsoring organization. It requires a reasonably sophisticated organization, technical expertise, and military or political protection of the transmitter. However, the relationship between the length of time that an indigenous station is on the air and the political success of its sponsor, especially when defined as gaining control of the government, is probably curvilinear. The fact that Radio Rebelde was on the air for more than a year, despite the Cuban army's efforts to destroy it, was a predictor of the fall of the Batista dictatorship. But, the continued operation of Radio Venceremos for more than a decade indicated that the Salvadoran civil war was grinding toward a stalemate.[9]

Exogenous stations--those that broadcast from outside the target country-- usually have the support of (or, at least, are tolerated by) the host government and do not entail the same risk as their indigenous counterparts. On one hand, because they are not based in "liberated" zones within their own countries, exogenous stations cannot claim the same degree of domestic political viability. For example, Cuban exile groups broadcasting from transmitters outside of the island do not have the same legitimacy as would the sponsor of an indigenous station. On the other hand, exogenous broadcasting usually means the existence of an external threat. Only rarely do exogenous clandestine stations operate for an extended period of time without the financial, organizational, and political support of a hostile foreign power. In some cases, the hostile foreign government will arrange for exogenous stations to be located in third countries -- usually client states -- in order to plausibly deny complicity or to avoid directly violating national and international broadcasting regulations. In other words, exogenous stations tend to represent a greater foreign threat, and indigenous stations tend to represent a greater domestic threat.

The relationship between the length of time that an exogenous station is on the air and the sponsoring exile organization's political success in its home country also is probably curvilinear, although the point of inflection arrives much sooner. Soley and Nichols conclude:

Exile imposes a geographic separation between the organization and the country to which the station broadcasts. As broadcasts continue, the geographic separation combines with temporal separation; that is, the organization becomes separated from the changes and conditions in the country that occurred since the exile was imposed. Separated by geography and time from the domestic political situation, the political party and its clandestine station become increasingly unable to formulate or articulate relevant political messages. In effect, the political party stagnates rather than changes.[10]

That appears to be the case with Cuban exile groups who, with the frequent support of the U.S. government, have directed clandestine and white broadcasts to their home country for over three decades. This trend has become particularly pronounced during the 10-year period covered in this research.

BACKGROUND

Shortly after Castro came to power in 1959, President Eisenhower ordered the U.S. Central Intelligence Agency to undertake clandestine radio broadcasts to Cuba as part of a covert plan to overthrow the new regime. Eisenhower's plan, which was carried out largely by his successor, President Kennedy, was an unambiguous disaster as a CIA-trained exile army was decisively defeated at the Bay of Pigs in the spring of 1961. This failure did not, however, end the U.S. government's appetite for hostile political broadcasting to Cuba. U.S.-sponsored clandestine and white broadcasts were beamed across the Straits of Florida for most of the next three-and-a-half decades. Radio Swan, the CIA's clandestine station for the Bay of Pigs operation, was renamed Radio Americas and moved from Swan Island in the Caribbean to the Florida Keys, and in 1962 during the Cuban Missile Crisis, the Voice of America began specially tailored white propaganda from another Florida transmitter to Cuba.[11]

In the 1970s, as the United States directed its attention to conflicts elsewhere in the world, clandestine and white broadcasts to Cuba were phased out. In 1970 the CIA's Radio Americas went off the air, and in 1974 VOA ended its Cuba-specific programming. A few low-power clandestine stations broadcast sporadically from South Florida, but for the most part, anti-Castro radio virtually disappeared for several years.[12]

A more confrontational U.S. foreign policy toward Cuba in the early 1980s fostered a revival of anti-Castro broadcasting. During the last five-year period (1981-1985) inventoried by Soley and Nichols,[13] a dozen clandestine stations were on the air. Some of them, such as La Voz de Alpha 66, a gray station sponsored by the exile paramilitary organization Alpha 66, were operated without the overt or covert approval of the U.S. government, and the Federal Communications Commission often attempted to locate and close them down. Others, such as La Voz de CID, received the encouragement and perhaps the financial support of the US government. Operated by Cuba Independiente y Democratica, an exile organization headed by Huber Matos, a former commander in Castro's rebel army who was jailed in Cuba for 20 years for counterrevolutionary activities, La Voz de CID was a network of gray stations located in the United States and both gray and white stations located in third countries in the Caribbean Basin. In terms of number of transmitters and frequencies used and number of hours of programming aired, La Voz de CID was the largest gray broadcaster in the Cuban campaign. Although the FCC required CID to close its U.S.-based transmitters in the early 1980s, the exile organization received strong encouragement from the Reagan White House for its foreign operations and was extraordinarily well financed. The source of its funds has been the subject of considerable speculation but has never been publicly documented.[14] At least one station, Radio Caiman (alligator), the only black station on the air during the period of study, was operated by the CIA. The station, which aired unusually slick programming with anti-Castro messages imbedded in heavy doses of popular music directed at "the new generation" of Cuba, claimed to be sponsored by the Comite Pro Libertad de Cuba. However, U.S. journalists,[15] the Cuban government, and the author's own off-the-record sources have established that Radio Caiman was a CIA station.[16] Caiman's transmitter was in Central America.

The greatly increased clandestine activity was supplemented by an even greater increase in U.S. government white broadcasting. In 1985 President Reagan established Radio Marti, a multimillion dollar project named for the nineteenth century Cuban patriot Jose Marti. In 1990 President Bush added Television Marti, which transmits from a U.S. military blimp floating over the Florida Keys.[17]

TEN-YEAR UPDATE

Methodology

Table 8.1 is a listing of all clandestine and white stations broadcasting to Cuba during the last five-year period (1981-85) recorded by Soley and Nichols[18] and an original inventory of such stations for the two subsequent five-year periods (1986-1990 and 1991-1995). Anti-Castro stations or programs were included in the table if they were monitored on the air any time during the five-year period and if they were primarily directed at Cuban audiences. The many commercial stations in South Florida and throughout the Caribbean Basin that have anti-Castro sentiments were not included. The lists also do not include a small number of clandestine stations believed to have operated primarily from the Miami area but not with sufficient power or for sufficient duration to be monitored. For the 1991-1995 time period, in which more complete statistics were available, the hours of programming[19] and number of frequencies and transmitters used were also recorded.

The primary sources of the updated listings were: British Broadcasting Corporation Monitoring Service; Foreign Broadcast Information Service (declassified monitoring service of the CIA); Federal Communications Commission; Cuban Ministry of Communications; and various magazines, newsletters, and other publications for radio hobbyists.[20] The Cuban Ministry of Communications, which has a special unit to monitor foreign broadcasts directed at Cuba, has made available to the author the most consistently complete and accurate data; however, no one source is comprehensive or entirely accurate. In those cases in which the sources contradict one another, the author used his best judgment. There is no claim of scientific reliability in the data reported.

Table 8.1
Anti-Castro Stations and Programs by Year and Type
(White = W, Gray = G, Black = B)

Name (Organization)	81-85	86-90	91-95	Comments
La Voz de CID (Cuba Independiente y Democratica)	G	G	G	started 1981
Radio Libertad Cubana (Commander David)	G			closed by FCC
La Voz Democratica Cristiana de Cuba/formerly Radio Cuba Libre (Partido Democratica Cristiana de Cuba)	G		W	white on WRNO
Radio Antorcha Martiana (Movimiento Insurreccion Martiana)	G	G		
Pueblo Libre - La Voz de La Junta Patriotica Cubana/ formerly Radio Mambi	G	G	W	white on WWCR, HRJA, WRNO; off air in 1994
Radio Abdala	G			
Radio Trinchera	G			
Cuba al Dia	G			
Radio Caiman (CIA)	B	B	B	off air in 1994
La Voz de la Resistencia Interna	G			
Esperanza - La Voz de los Municipios de Cuba en Exilo/ formerly Voz de la Esperanza	G		W	white on WWCR; off air in 1994
Radio Marti (USIA)	W	W	W	
Radio Libertad Cubana y Radio Felipe de la Cruz		G		
La Voz del Combatiente Cubano		G		
La Voz de Tribuna Libre (Alianza Cubana)			W	
La Voz de la Federacion Mundial de Ex-Presos a Politico de Cubanos			G&W	gray closed by FCC in 1994
Radio Nacional Cubana (Frente Nacional Cubano)			G	closed by FCC in 1994
Voz de la Fundacion (Cuban American National Foundation)			W	on WHRI, WRMI
Voz de Cuba 21 (Movimeiento Cuba-21)			W	on WRNO

Table 8.1 (continued)

Name (Organization)	81-85	86-90	91-95	Comments
Voz de Directoria de Revolucionario Democratico Cubano			W	on WWCR; off air in 1994
Radio Voluntal Democratica (Partido Revolucionario Cubano Autentico)			W	on WWCR; orr air in 1994
TV Marti (USIA)		W	W	
Radio Periodico Panamericano (Estudios Cubanos)			W	on WRNO
La Voz del Educador Cubano Libre			W	on HRJA
Radio Conciencia (National Cuban Commission)			W	on WRNO; off air in 1994
Rumbo a la Libertad (Brigade 2506)			W	on WRNO
Un Solo Pueblo - Voz de Radio Periodico Semanal (Coordinadora Social Democratica de Cuba)			W	on WRNO, HRJA
Movimiento 30 de Noviembre			W	on WRNO
Radio Roquero (Victor Garcia-Riveria)			W	on HRJA
La Voz del Veterano			W	on HRJA
Voz de la Unidad Cubana (CANF y Junta Patriotica Cubana)			W	on WRNO
Radio General Ochoa (Partido Cubano Independiente)			W	off air in 1994
Voz de Medicos Cubanos Libres			W	on WRNO; off air in 1994
Movimiento de Recuperacion Revolucionario			W	on WRNO

Findings

Using the 1981-1985 time period as a base line, changes in the number and proportion of white, gray, and black stations that were broadcasting to Cuba during the past decade are reported in Table 8.2. In addition, Table 8.3 compares the hours of programming and number of frequencies used by these stations in 1991 and 1994. Three significant trends are apparent from these data: an increase in anti-Castro broadcasting; the near disappearance of clandestine stations; and a greater proportion of U.S. government broadcasts.

Table 8.2
Number of Organizations Broadcasting Anti-Castro Content to Cuba (by Station Type and Year)

	1981-1985	1986-1990	1991-1995	Total
White	1 (8%)	2 (22%)	24* (86%)	27**
Gray	11 (84%)	6 (66%)	3** (11%)	20
Black	1 (8%)	1 (11%)	1*** (3%)	3
Total	13	9	28	

*The programs of these 24 organizations were transmitted over seven stations, mostly commercial shortwave stations that sell airtime. All other programs listed in this table are believed to be broadcast from their own (or at least a separate) transmitter. If the figures in the 1991-95 period were re-calculated to indicate percent of stations (rather than percent of programs), the trend remains essentially the same: white (64%), gray (27%), black (9%).

** La Voz de la Federacion Mundial de Ex-Presos a Political de Cubanos broadcast as both a white and a gray station during this time period and is double counted here.

*** Radio Caiman, which is counted here, went off the air in November 1994.

Table 8.3
Broadcast Hours and Frequencies Used by White and Dark Anti-Castro Stations, 1991 and 1994

	Total Broadcast Hours		Number of Frequencies	
	1991	1994	1991	1994
White (U.S. Govt)	189 (28%)	261 (37%)	6 (40%)	12 (50%)
White (Non-Govt.)	104 (15%)	83 (12%)	5 (33%)	6 (25%)
Dark (Gray/Black)	389 (57%)	362* (51%)	4 (27%)	6* (25%)
Total	682	706	15	24

*Of the three dark stations included in the 1994 data, only La Voz de CID was still on the air in 1995, although it had drastically reduced its hours of programming. Radio Caiman, which broadcast 53 hours of programming on two frequencies, went off the air in 1994, and Radio Nacional Cubana was closed by the FCC in the same year.

Increase in anti-Castro broadcasting

With the disintegration of the Soviet Union, Cuba's economic and military patron for three decades, and the subsequent collapse of the Cuban economy, the Castro regime seemed particularly vulnerable in the early 1990s. As many of the United States' traditional adversaries disappeared from the world stage and as well-financed Cuban exile organizations became powerful political forces in Washington, Cuba moved higher on the U.S. foreign policy agenda. Key policymakers argued that the timing was propitious to increase pressure on Cuba, including expanded political broadcasting to the island, and bring down one of the last socialist governments left in the post-Cold War world.[21]

During this period, the total number of organizations broadcasting to Cuba roughly doubled, and the total hours of anti-Castro programming aired also increased. Even though the number of separate stations used to broadcast to Cuba has not increased since the 1981-1985 time period, the number of frequencies used has increased significantly.[22]

The largest single increase was in the U.S. government's Radio Marti. In the summer of 1994, thousands of Cubans seeking to escape the economic hardships in Cuba set out for Florida in small boats and makeshift rafts. As part of its efforts to stem the tide of illegal immigration, the Clinton administration greatly expanded Radio Marti's shortwave broadcast schedule, leased air time on a mediumwave station located in the Turk and Caicos Islands, and doubled the power of its regular medium-wave transmitter in Florida.[23]

Near disappearance of clandestine stations

Although the amount of broadcasting to Cuba increased and the tone of the programming was consistently hostile to the Castro regime throughout the decade, the type of stations changed markedly. Since the 1981-1985 time period, anti-Castro broadcasting has moved almost entirely to the white side of the radio spectrum. In late 1994 the CIA's Radio Caiman, the only black station broadcasting to Cuba, went off the air; in 1995, only one gray station, La Voz de CID, was still in operation, although it too had drastically cut back to only one transmitter and reduced hours of programming due to funding problems.

Gone from the airwaves were the classic clandestine stations that were run by shadowy exile groups from hidden transmitters in Florida. They have been replaced by professionally produced programs played during airtime purchased by many of the same groups from commercial shortwave stations in the United States, namely WRNO (New Orleans), WWCR (Nashville), WHRI (Noblesville, Indiana), and WRMI (Miami), or elsewhere in the region, such as HRJA in Honduras. Typical is the case of La Voz de la Federacion Mundial de Ex-Presos a Politico de Cubanos, a gray station run by a group of former political prisoners in Cuba and that broadcasts sporadically from an unlicensed transmitter in Tampa. In 1992 the FCC located and closed the station and fined the operator (a Bay of Pigs veteran) $8,000 for the violation. The organization then began buying commercial airtime on a licensed U.S. shortwave station in order to broadcast its programming to Cuba.

The migration of exile stations from the dark side to the white side of the spectrum was the product of at least two factors: the gradual transformation of Cuban exile groups from the political fringe to the political mainstream, and the FCC's ambivalent efforts to silence the clandestine transmitters on U.S. soil. Prior to the mid-1980s, most sponsors of anti-Castro clandestine stations were paramilitary groups, such as Alpha 66, or largely inconsequential exile political organizations. However, in the past decade, many Cuban exile groups have been assimilated into the U.S. political system. Foremost among them, the Cuban American National Foundation and its wealthy and politically connected head, Jorge Mas Canosa, have become important members of the Washington establishment. Presidential and congressional candidates of both political parties court Mas in hopes of winning exile votes, and his organization's political action committee lavishly funds those candidates who support a hardline policy toward Cuba. A former broadcaster on the clandestine Radio Swan, Mas took on positions more consistent with his newly found establishment role, such as the chair of the U.S. government advisory board for Radio and TV Marti, and CANF produced La Voz de la Fundacion, which broadcasts over licensed stations.[24]

Throughout the decade, the FCC was caught in a cross current. Created to enforce national communications law and international treaties, it was obligated to close down unlicensed stations located within US national territory. However, the anti-Castro clandestines shared the goal of US foreign policy to bring down the socialist government in Cuba, and many of the individual and organizational sponsors of these stations had growing political influence in the White House and the halls of Congress. But, as a regulatory agency somewhat insulated from political pressure, the FCC haltingly moved against the most blatant offenders. During the period of study, the FCC closed several clandestine stations in Florida and fined the operators, including some linked to politically powerful exile groups.[25]

Greater proportion of U.S. government broadcasts

The U.S. government dropped its limited amount of white broadcasting to Cuba in the mid-1970s. However, a decade later, with Cuban exile leaders becoming part of the Washington power structure instead of political renegades and with Cuba moving up the foreign policy agenda, the U.S. government increasingly took over the burden of broadcasting to Cuba. Radio and TV Marti[26] were established with the zealous support of Cuban exiles and a broad coalition of non-Cuban conservatives. The white broadcasting of Radio and TV Marti has grown as a percent of total broadcasting to Cuba over the decade and became the largest portion by far when their programming was expanded during the 1994 immigration crisis and when all but one clandestine station went off the air. In effect, the virulent grass-roots opposition to the Castro regime heard on clandestine stations was largely replaced by the bureaucratic propaganda of the U.S. government.

DISCUSSION

The virtual disappearance of clandestine radio stations directed at Cuba and the rise of white broadcasts sponsored by newly respectable Cuban exile groups and the US government strongly indicate a process of institutionalization and ossification of anti-Castro broadcasting. Separated by 90 miles of water and 35 years from their homeland, the Cuban-American leadership is becoming decreasingly relevant in Havana despite its increasing relevance in Washington. The broadcasts that Cuban exile groups produce and air on licensed commercial stations or that are aired on Radio and TV Marti at the exiles' behest are similarly rooted more in the U.S. political reality than in the Cuban political reality. Operating a clandestine station audible in Cuba for a sustained period is risky and usually means that its sponsor has technical expertise; financial support; a sophisticated political organization, and most important, a passionate commitment to the cause. In contrast, purchasing airtime to broadcast white propaganda on a legal station or arm-twisting the U.S. government to take over the broadcasting crusade on its own stations are not strong indications of a dynamic and vital exile group closely in touch with the problems and portents of the Cuban people.

If Soley and Nichols[27] are correct in their views on the relationship between exogenous stations and political success, the changes in broadcasting to Cuba over the past ten years are signs of stagnation in the anti-Castro exile movement and institutionalization of U.S. policy toward Cuba. Like many other governmental institutions created to fight the Cold War, Radio and TV Marti are seeking to justify their continued existence. Though these institutionalized voices of the U.S. government may still sound loud and threatening in Cuba, they are largely alien to the contemporary Cuban experience and useless in the resolution of the U.S.-Cuban conflict.

NOTES

1. Mathias Kropf, *The Clandestine Broadcasting Directory* (Lake Geneva, Wis.: Tiare Publications, 1994), 44.

2. Soley, Lawrence C., and John S. Nichols, *Clandestine Radio Broadcasting* (New York: Praeger, 1987), 163-189, 323-324, 331-332.

3. Ibid., 10.

4. Although TV Marti, a "white" U.S. government station directed at Cuba, is licensed with the appropriate national authority and registered with international bodies, it is doubtful that the station is in full compliance with international radio regulations. See S. D. Bayer ("The Legal Aspects of TV Marti in Relation to the Law of Direct Broadcast Satellites"), Laurien Alexandre ("Television Marti: Electronic Invasion in the Post-Cold War"), and U.S. General Accounting Office (*TV Marti: Costs and Compliance with Broadcast Standards and International Agreements*).

5. Kim Andrew Elliott, J. A. Campbell, Gerard Hauser, and J. Marks, "Unofficial Broadcasting for Politics, Profits, and Pleasure," *Gazette* 30 (1982): 109.

6. This definition is more general than that of Soley and Nichols, which classifies as "black" those "broadcasts by one side that are disguised as broadcasts by another" (*Clandestine Radio Broadcasting*), 10-11.

7. Soley and Nichols, 163-76.

8. Raymond Bonner. *Weakness and Deceit: U.S. Policy and El Salvador* (New York: Times Books, 1984), 124-26.

9. In 1992, after a UN-broker peace accord ended the civil war, Radio Venceremos became a legal, aboveground station. See A. Arana ("Down from the Hills: El Salvador's Guerrilla Radio Faces Peace"), A. Cabrera ("En Frecuencia Modulada: Radios ex Guerrilla bajan de las Montanas de El Salvador"), and J. I. Lopez Vigil (*Rebel Radio: The Story of El Salvador's Radio Venceremos*).

10. Soley and Nichols, 313.

11. John S. Nichols, "When Nobody Listens: Assessing the Political Success of Radio Marti," *Communication Research* 11 (1984): 296. Also see Soley and Nichols, 176-184.

12. Nichols, 296.

13. Soley and Nichols, 332.

14. Ibid., 187-188.

15. See, for example, G. A. Geyer, "It's Foolish to Fiddle with Fidel," *Cincinnati Enquirer*, 9 November 1994.

16. *New York Times* (8 May 1987) reported that some of the proceeds of Oliver North's Iran-Contra operation were used for a radio station broadcasting to Cuba. Although Radio Caiman went on the air at roughly the same time, leading to much speculation among radio hobbyists, no firm connection has been established between the two.

17. K. Edlund, J. Elliston, and P. Kornbluh, *U.S. Broadcasting to Cuba: Radio and TV Marti, A Historical Chronology* (Washington: National Security Archive, 1994). See also K. H. Youm, "The Radio and TV Marti Controversy: A Re-Examination," *Gazette* 48 (1991): 95-103; and Laurien Alexandre, "Television Marti: Electronic Invasion in the Post-Cold War."

18. Soley and Nichols, 332.

19. The total hours of programming include replays or simulcasts on different frequencies.

20. Among the most widely consulted were *Popular Communications* (especially the "Clandestine Communique" column by Gerry L. Dexter), *Monitoring Times* (especially the "Outer Limits" column by George Zeller), *The ACE* (published by the Association of Clandestine Radio Enthusiasts), *Clandestine Confidential* (now defunct), and *The Clandestine Broadcasting Directory* (an annual survey by Mathias Kropf). These publications typically rely on monitoring reports of radio hobbyists around the world. Also, see Jessup ("Monitoring Cuba--To and Fro"), Van Horn ("War of Words: The United States-Cuba Broadcast War Heats Up") and Dexter ("The Anti-Castro Broadcasters: Fidel Taking Hits across the Bands").

21. G. Gunn, "In Search of a Modern Cuba Policy," in D.E. Schulz's *Cuba and the Future* (Westport, Conn.: Greenwood Press, 1994). See also C. Mesa-Lago, *Cuba after the Cold War* (Pittsburgh: University of Pittsburgh Press, 1993).

22. There were no Cuban clandestine broadcasts to the United States or other Latin American countries during this period, and Cuban government white broadcasting, including the English language service of Radio Havana Cuba, was greatly reduced, in part, because of the scarcity of electrical energy on the island.

23. C. S. Manegold, "U.S. Government Broadcasts to Cuba, and Wonders If Anyone Is Listening," *New York Times* (24 August 1994). See also L. Van Horn ("War of Words: The United States-Cuba Broadcast War Heats Up").

24. L. Rohter, "Wielding the Power of the Exiles, A Would-Be Successor to Castro," *New York Times* (8 May 1995).

25. G. Zeller. "FOIA Reveals Cuban Clandestine Busted Twice," *Monitoring Times* (January 1995): 92.

26. Although TV Marti broadcasts three-and-a-half hours of programming to Cuba, its signal is effectively jammed by the Cuban government and, therefore, not seen on the island. Radio Marti and some other white stations are also jammed but not as effectively.

27. Soley and Nichols, 313.

9

Radio Liberty during the Cold War . . . and after the Thaw

An Interview with Kevin Klose

Case Study Six

In 1993 the authors visited Radio Free Europe/Radio Liberty personnel at their Munich Headquarters. At this time, the organization had been shaken by the news of President Clinton's plans for federalization, and, understandably, emotions were running high. We were able to spend seven days with RFE/RL; and despite their obvious unsettlement, their hospitality and willingness to answer our questions was most impressive. What follows is an excerpted interview with Kevin Klose in August 1993. In it, the Director of Radio Liberty traces the Service's history as well as its future challenges and direction. Rather than paraphrase this important interview, we felt it best to present Mr. Klose . . . in his own words.

NLS/MJM: Could you give us some information on the relationship between Radio Free Europe and Radio Liberty? How did they merge into one entity? What are their similarities and differences?

KK: [First of all, it is important to note that both Radios] were founded separately, in different years. RFE was founded first, and then the CIA founded RL a few years later. They were for many years separate organizations. Separate administrations, separate everything. And they existed in separate buildings in Munich, separate sights. They didn't talk to each other. They had their own research services, their own everything. The only thing they shared were transmitters, but even then [they were identified separately as] RL and RFE. It was very interesting.

NLS/MJM: When were they put together?

KK: They merged in the 1970s when the CIA's funding of the two organizations became a political issue in the U.S. [Before that,] it was largely unknown by the U.S. public that the agency funded them, and what's interesting about that was that it was a double scam. That was the problem. Not only was the agency funding it, [but] it was [also] called [by a different name] . . . the Committee for Liberation. I think it was the original permutation of Radio Liberty's. They were taking money covertly and also raising funds in the United States. You and I are both the same age. . . . You would remember the crusade in Europe? The crusade for freedom? You used to . . . put your dimes in a can in school. It was typical of the 1940s and 1950s. So they were collecting money from the public--completely covertly funded by the U.S. Congress through a series of cutouts and secret agreements. It was the fundraising aspect of it that I think infuriated people, when it became public.

Anyway, [the Radios] existed either separately . . . or they were separate but very similar organizations until the 1970s. Then, right around the time of the Watergate break-in, [a] series of revelations about the CIA's [domestic] involvement [became public knowledge]. In the process, [the public discovered] that the Radios were funded by [the Central Intelligence Agency] as well. Boom. Big political issue. Jay William Focart, Chairman of the Senate Foreign Relations committee, led an attempt to kill off the radio stations in the early 1970s on the basis that these weren't needed anymore; they were Cold War inventions. . . . However, instead of killing them off and having them funded covertly, a public funding committee, the BIB (Board of International Broadcasting) was founded.

[The BIB] is a presidentially appointed nine member board, [and] a separate organization. [It's] not under the control of state or the USIA . . . or anybody. Completely independent. It receives money from the Congress, has federal employees and so on and so forth. It then contracts with us as a private corporation chartered in the state of Delaware. We are a private, non-profit organization. So we are in effect the grantee of the BIB. We have no specific direct relationship to the federal government in a legal sense. And that was all done to continue in these Radios the idea of independence.

Initially [the Radios] were set up independently. The smart guys who set these up in the '50s set them up as private organizations. They were always private organizations; but that was to give the government deniability. In other words, the Radios did surrogate broadcasting. They used Soviet immigrants and others [as their reporters and translators]. These people [would] come here, they [would] read whatever newspapers they could get. They would listen as best they could to Soviet broadcasts or broadcasts from the Soviet empire, sit and write down some thoughts for a while, go into a studio and record 15 minutes on their thoughts on the latest perfidies of the Soviet Empire.

NLS/MJM: So the Radios provided the facilities for them to come in. Is that what is meant by surrogate broadcasting?

KK: That's right. I mean, the idea from the beginning was to do something that the media inside the empire could not do--the attempt to give accurate reportage of what was going on inside the countries themselves. Not so much what was going on in the West or what NATO was doing, but what was happening inside Russia and the rest of the empire. A lot of it was politically charged and Soviet

Cold War stuff. But some of it was very good, and a lot of it was culture. This went on [in the] early 1950s.

Fifteen years later, the self-publishing movement start[ed] in Russia. Well, actually it started in Lithuania. [It] spread very quickly; and pretty soon things were getting smuggled out. And we put them on the air here. . . . The Soviets were jamming like mad. They used [their transmitters] against us to put up . . . noise basically, on the same wavelengths. So the Radio's idea was that if you got their hearts and minds, maybe you [could] have an effect on how people think. If nothing else, you [could] end the tremendous isolation.

You must remember what this place (the USSR) was like. It had eleven time zones; and this was just Russia. [Since] the Radios used shortwave, they bounced [their signals] off the islands here. (*At this point, Mr. Klose shows us the location on the map.*) It's a science, but it's also an art. [The Radios] had lots of transmitters to broadcast on different frequencies at the same time, because they never knew which one was going to propagate; which one would "bounce off" exactly. And those conditions changed between day and night. There are [usually] more charged particles on the sunlit side than on the night side, so you use different frequencies. [As a result,] you have to build a lot of transmitters. The idea was that you could get in over the wall. Over the curtain. [And] if that border was 10,000 miles long, look what it covers. (*Mr. Klose shows us the location on the map.*) I mean every civilization in the Northern Hemishphere is there. Half of the border is with China, the rest of it comes through Northern Asia, the Middle East, the Black Sea, Central Europe, and up to Northern Europe.

NLS/MJM: When you talked about that culture, what kinds of things could you possible do to unify [the people]?

KK: Well, you'd go to Kazakhstan; go to the intellectuals. They all had to speak Russian.

NLS/MJM: So the major tie was the Russian?

KK: Absolutely.

NLS/MJM: And other cultural ties?

KK: They were established almost from day one, in 1951, on Radio Liberty's first Russian broadcast. Later, in the first week of March of 1953, Josef Stalin died. [Coincidentally] Svoboda went on the air at that exact moment. But they didn't know it. Just think--a man who had put 20 million people to death inside his own country in the name of eliminating opposition . . . who filled the slave labor camps with millions of victims . . . now had his death reported by an oppositional force. They also went on the air Kazak service and a Qatar service. And the next year they added Ukrainian, so we now have twelve languages.

NLS/MJM: Now, do you broadcast 24 hours a day?

KK: The Russian language is broadcast 24 hours a day. But that 24 hours is not 24 hours of brand new programming. It's like CNN, where they use the same programming over and over again. They just reformat it, repackage it. But every day we have live news 24 hours a day. That's news of Russia and the environs of Russia and the former empire principally. Seventy percent of the items we broadcast are of the indigenous countries or the region right around Russia. Another 15 percent is West European and more global affairs, and another 15-20 percent--it varies--is U.S. stuff. But that's what surrogate radio is. It is meant to talk about their news, their circumstances, in their languages. VOA (Voice of America) broadcasts American news, which is great, and the BBC World Service broadcasts kind of a British take on the world. Nobody does what the Radios do--nobody.

NLS/MJM: The new organization that Clinton has in mind--what impact will it have specifically on the RL side of radio?

KK: Well, the Clinton proposal was to eliminate the Board from the national broadcasting, which is a separate, funded agency; and to replace it with something called the Board of Governors, inside the USIA. . . . Because a lot of people in Washington don't speak the languages, they don't understand what we do, and they don't understand what the mission [for RFE/RL] is. And the rap is that the Radios are a bunch of Cold War bureaucrats who have reinvented themselves. But that's the line that many people have taken.

NLS/MJM: So what will happen???

KK: I don't know; it's still playing itself out. One of the principal issues still left is whether RFE/RL Inc. will continue [to be] in existence past FY 1995. We don't know whether that's going to happen or not. In the proposed legislation, the corporation would cease to exist and become federalized, and we would in effect become a federal office. We would [then] become the office of Radio Free Europe within the Office of Surrogate Broadcasting, [and] within the International Broadcasting bureau of the USIA.

As somebody who has spent 25 years at the *Washington Post* before coming here, I do not have a high degree of confidence that a federal bureaucracy can run things better than a private corporation, just generally speaking. In the broadcast lands, from the Polish border east, many countries are now experimenting with control of the media other than by the government. The Clinton Administration, by federalizing the radio, is going the other way. The Radios are private. They take public funds for sure -- [but] it's a completely publicly supported [private] operation.

The sense of the privacy issue plays in two ways. [First of all,] journalism, well done, is very powerful and very fragile. . . . [Our target audiences] are people who have spent 75 years struggling with the poison of government-run radio. They are very sensitive to the issue of how it sounds; if it's credible or not. There's that issue. And the other issue, [one] that the Clinton administration seems unaware of completely, [is that our current status as] a private corporation [enables us to have] tremendous latitude [when demonstrating the strength] of democratic institutions. The [best] way to do that [in my opinion] is by having the strong medicine of accurate, good, balanced, objective journalism, because that is what ties a democracy together. That's what it's all about. It depends on people sharing their ideas openly and freely. That's the most precious thing a democracy gives. Freedom of speech; that's the first right. Everything else falls after that. Well, we do that [now]. You can't put a policy guideline on [freedom of speech]. . . . You can't put it down as though it were a policy of the United States government on this or that issue. It doesn't work that way.

Here's [an example of] how the privacy thing works: We had in our studios in the late spring, Alexander Rutzcoy, the VP of Russia. Okay. Rutzcoy walks in the radio station. . . . Why? . . . 'cause we're an independent radio company; we're not part of the U.S. government; we're not part of the VOA. VOA has studios in Moscow; he (Rutzcoy) wouldn't set foot in them. Why not? Because it looks like he's kowtowing to the US government in some way. [At RL,] they ask him a lot of tough questions in our studio, and he gives a lot of answers. Well, it's US taxpayers' dollars that are being spent to put this man's views on the air in the Russian language across the empire.

The Clinton administration supports President Yeltsin, it does not support VP Rutzcoy. In fact, VP Rutzcoy is a political adversary of Mr. Yeltsin's. But we believe it is extremely important for Russian citizens who are trying to build a democracy to have access to this man's views and to have him stand up in front of a very tough press corps and be called to responsibilities for his own views, and let him explain his own views. That's what democracy is; that's how the media serves democracy.

We are tribunes. A tribune stands in for [people] who can't be there themselves. So we become the eyes, the ears, and the questioners for millions of people in Russia who might want to hear what this guy's views are and either accept them, reject them, or at least ponder them, have access to them. You can't put a policy guideline around such an interview and say whether a person like that should be allowed in the studios or not. If we become federalized, the next time Rutzcoy comes in to the studios, the possibility now lies open for members of the Yeltsin government, or whoever is in power, to complain to the U.S. Embassy, to complain to the U.S. press officer, and down it comes. Now I'm not saying that's going to happen, but it changes the nature.

NLS/MJM: It's a possibility.

KK: That's right. Now, the idea of the new legislation is that with the Board of Governors and the Director for International Broadcasting, and all of those types, you have a lot of fire walls in between. But there have been no fire walls that have helped the kind of journalism that is done in the VOA, and we don't do the kind of journalism that the VOA does. They wouldn't have Rutzcoy in the studios. We do. We stick our nose in the business of a lot of people in this region because that's what journalism does, it sticks its nose in where it's not wanted. And so it's always a kind of contentious situation. By doing that, we're not looking for controversy for controversy's sake. What we are trying to do is explore the envelope--objective, Western-style journalism--so that [the] people themselves in the broadcast lands [can] hear it, [and] know that they can have it. It doesn't destroy society; it's a nation-building operation, and they can do it themselves. We've got a lot of stringers. [If] they pass through us and out into the local media, the local media will get stronger. We think it's the way you help build democratic institutions.

NLS/MJM: It seems to us also that the fact that you are federalized would make people believe that "objective" journalism couldn't happen.

KK: That's the other part. Because journalism is a public act. And it contains with it the act of putting down what you [see] and having it printed or broadcast somewhere. Because it is so public, it contains not only the act but the perception of the act. Was it done openly? Who are these people anyway? Are they what they say they are? And if they hear the slightest hint of the voice of the government [just once], they will never turn RL on again. They'll say, "Okay, I've heard it, I don't need to hear anymore." So there's a perception issue there, and it is very powerful.

NLS/MJM: It's also very fragile, as you pointed out.

KK: Very fragile. Journalism can be powerful and fragile. And it is reality. . . . Who is out there listening to it in the darkness? Millions of people across eleven different time zones, some of them are already in the next day. It is the most illusive and unique means of human communications there is. And we are by all means the most ephemeral of all of the mass media. You can't see us, you can't smell us, all you can do is hear.

NLS/MJM: And you can't even redo it, unless it's on tape. Unlike rereading an article.

KK: Exactly, so what the ear hears and the human brain perceives is a very complicated formula. If you start messing with the chemicals inside that thing, you could very easily mess it up. That's what I worry about.

NLS/MJM: Because you could say exactly the same thing being who you are now, and say exactly the same thing being federalized, and . . .

KK: And people would say that it sounded different.

NLS/MJM: That's a possibility.

KK: Right, so I have big concerns. And Washington [the central locations of the USIA and VOA] doesn't have that kind of power, partly because, you know, we are here six time zones from Washington, and Moscow is eight time zones away. [As you know,] you get more and more removed the further east you go from the capital of the world's most powerful democracy.

Since our interview with Mr. Klose, he has become the President of Radio Free Europe/Radio Liberty. RFE/RL's home page on the World Wide Web indicates that the Radios are thriving, with 240 broadcasters and journalists reaching more than 25 million regular listeners in 21 major languages. At his new location in Prague, Mr. Klose has cut the number of time zones he must deal with in half, which hopefully has doubled his abilities to be a responsible surrogate broadcaster to his audience.

10

The Argument Over American International Broadcast Federalization: Point/Counterpoint

Interviews with Eugene Pell and Kim Andrew Elliott

Case Study Seven

In 1993-1994, the authors were able to learn firsthand about President Clinton's (then proposed) plan to federalize all American international media. During the course of nine months we met with members of the USIA, the Voice of America, Radio Free Europe and Radio Liberty. The following excerpts from our interviews with Eugene Pell and Kim Andrew Elliott best exemplify both the strengths and weaknesses of Clinton's proposal.

INTERVIEW WITH EUGENE PELL, PRESIDENT, RFE/RL IN MUNICH: AUGUST 3, 1993

NLS/MJM: We were thinking . . . about the [recent announcement of the] federalization. We knew about the furor, but we didn't realize the [ramifications of the move] as much as some people relayed to us yesterday. So we thought perhaps that you might give us your perspective on the impact of reformulating RFE and VOA. What's your perspective?

EP: First, let's talk about the [federalization] article. The time frame for the legislation now appears to be that they want to get it done by October [1993], signed by the President, and then a 20-day period following enactments, for studies on all sides on the implementation process of the bill. But I'll start by giving you a little background on where we were and how we got to where we are. Since 1990 the organization has come under pressure, first from the Bush administration and certainly more recently from the Clinton administration. And it can all be summed up in a sound bite. "Europe is free, who needs Free Europe?" Now that's a very difficult thing to combat, because there has been [a] considerable misunderstanding, ignorance, I would say, on the part of Washington politicians.

I think [their] opinion about what the reality is in the east is that communism may have collapsed. This, by no means suggests to me, at any rate, that democracy is going to be successful. And there are all kinds of traps, potholes, and other things on the way to getting a point where democratic institutions take roots, where free markets thrive, and where stability follows.

I don't think that point [of stability] has been reached in any of the countries reached by broadcast. Some are more advanced than others, obviously. Hungary comes to mind immediately. And it certainly is the case that the original rationale of this place [RFE/RL] to provide a source of unfettered, uncensored news and information to societies being deprived of that by their regimes, no longer pertains. I mean nobody can say that there is a dearth of information in Hungary. Go to any kiosk, turn on any radio station, or even to a certain extent, state television. Nevertheless, there are suggestions--I'm thinking of Budapest-- that the process of transition is by no means complete. No one that I know of, myself included, thinks that communism is going to come back. But there are a lot of other "isms" working out there. And anybody that follows that part of the world at all surely understands the ethnic tension in Monrovia and certain places. The irony is that the totalitarian regime suppressed all of that for four decades, and when it collapsed, all of these other forces began again.

NLS/MJM: Much like the civil rights movement in the States?

EP: Well, I take your analogy to a point. One major difference [between civil rights in the U.S. and the democratization of the former Soviet Bloc] obviously occurs when [the U.S. believes that a] resolution to have Magyars in Transylvania stop killing each other on a daily basis in Slovakia will mean it's all over. Only seven months ago there was a Czechoslovakia, and now there isn't, driven by budget considerations, driven by this "woolly-headed notion" that everything is now peaches and cream.

NLS/MJM: How does this "woolly-headed notion" affect your broadcast services?

EP: We began to come under pressure from the Office of Management and Budget and some people in the Bush administration as early as 1991, [or even as early as] the latter part of 1990. In fact the OMB put together a five-year proposal (to phase the place out) and the budget reflected that. In every one of these instances [during that time], we were successful in fighting them off. In spite of the fact that we don't broadcast in the West, this organization has a lot of supporters, and a lot of friends on both sides of the aisles of Congress. Certainly a lot of support from the press. And it has the number of supporters from the East, who have made their voices heard during all of this.

As we got down to the '92 election, things began to heat up, in that the U.S. Advisory Commission on Public Diplomacy issued a couple of reports. This Commission is really an in-house USIA operation. They talked to no one here-- not one person--and their first report followed closely on the heels of what was a comprehensive study on the subject, done by a Presidential Commission on International Broadcasting.

NLS/MJM: I think we have it . . .

EP: They were specifically charged with coming up with a plan to consolidate all international broadcasting aspects; that was part of the central issue. In the end, they concluded that things shouldn't be consolidated, and therefore ignored the charter in writing their final report, and in making the recommendation that they did.

That group spent six or seven months studying this (the consolidation). They came; they spent a couple of days together, almost three or four full days. They visited some of our other facilities; they visited the BBC, they visited the VOA. It was a prestigious group. I thought they did a very thorough job, and I thought they reached the right conclusions--that RFE was still going to be needed for the next few years, and RL was going to be needed into the next century.

Their report, [however], was obviously ignored. . . . In February of this year, unknown to anybody associated with the (Radios), the budget proposal was revealed. It involved the shutdown of RFE/RL by the end of September '95. We were completely blind-sided by that. He (President Clinton) had made several references during his campaign to the importance of continuing [the Radios]; he had spoken very strongly in the support of developing a new circuit video service for Asia. He had committed himself to support a radio in . . . . his campaign, and this (later directive) was a complete about-face. Now faced with a sure date for execution, Mr. Forbes (who was then chairmen of the BIB and Chairman of the Board of Directors of this company) and I . . . waged a successful media campaign again. Go back and read the articles that began appearing in March of this year--and they are all compiled here in one central place--and then take a look at the letters that began to flow from the East, to Washington.

NLS/MJM: Solidarity gave us a copy of the one which they sent.

EP: They have scores of them. . . . This went on for weeks. As the tide began to turn, the White House ordered an inner agency working group to be put together to study this thing and present options. And not surprisingly, they came up with three options--a, b, c. They had no choice except to say that b was the most acceptable of them because the other two were unacceptable, but b wasn't acceptable either.

In the meantime, in April Mr. Forbes was replaced by a former congressman (democrat), and a new USIA director had been named and was in the process of being confirmed. Six of us met for breakfast on the morning of the 20th, and then four of us were left in a conference room in a downtown law firm, which had been made available for the day. I mean the door wasn't locked or the keys thrown away, but we were told to solve the problem. Come up with a solution that saves money, that saves the structure of international broadcasting, that saves the battle on the Hill, that saves face. There was a lot of face-saving going on at this point. And we did it, I thought.

The bill that is working its way through the Senate right now, pertains to things to which I certainly did not agree to, which none of us agreed to. We spent about three days on this thing, and it wasn't easy. . . . I had written papers going back a year and a half ago. We thought that all of [international broadcasting] should be brought together eventually. I've always thought that way. Before coming to this job, I was the director of the Voice of America. So I have perspectives on both organizations nobody else has. I have always believed that VOA should be set free from USIA, and I continue to believe that. I don't think it will ever realize its true potential, so long as it remains directly as an influence of the Agency and State Department. I wanted everything put together in, what we [would] call, a corporation for international broadcasting. It would have been the international counterpart of CPB (the Corporation for Public Broadcasting), and privatized. It would operate more along the lines of BBC and its World Service.

It became apparent to me early in the game that [my concept] simply was not going to fly. This administration was not going to buy into it any more than the previous one would. And much of the reason for that is that there are too many people at the USIA who believe that getting the VOA out of there would be the beginning of the end of the agency itself. In fact there have been suggestions, made on the Hill and in other places over the last few years, that that's exactly what should happen. That the educational and exchange programs ought to be given to the Smithsonian or the Library of Congress, or whatever. The traditional public affairs side of diplomacy, VOA, etc., ought to be part of the State's problem, anyway; and the Voice ought to be sent on its own to be broadcast. I knew there wasn't going to be any chance of that being enacted, so what was the next best thing? A Board of Governors, within the USIA framework--one which had some real authority--and acting as an oversight body as well as a vehicle for policy-making. [This Board] would also have responsibility for the Voice of America.

Under this board, we agreed that there should be a Director of International Broadcasting, appointed by the board. In other words it would be professional. The Director of this board would then appoint--with the board's approval--a director of the VOA, a director of surrogate broadcasting, a director of television services, and a director of combined engineering and technical operation. Under the director of surrogate broadcasting, RFE/RL incorporated would be retained as a private corporation.

This [concept] was clearly agreed to by all parties. There was never any discussion of anything else. Surrogate broadcasting and the new Asian democracy radio all would have been placed there. The objective here, from my point of view, was to construct a series of fire walls. First the board; second, the director of international broadcasting appointed by the board; third, the director of surrogate broadcasting appointed by the director of international broadcasting; and fourth, the retention of private corporate status for the organization. And it's all still there except number four.

NLS/MJM: And you didn't know anything about it.

EP: No. And I was the principal architect when it was read.

NLS/MJM: They probably had your home phone number, don't you think?

EP: Oh yeah, they knew I was coming to Washington and they scheduled an announcement for Tuesday (June 15) with a feed to the White House. The President himself was going to make it down there.

Monday night, June 14, I can tell you I was on the phone till after midnight with the White House trying to sort this thing out, in order to support it. So anyway that's how we got to working on it.

NLS/MJM: What has been the fallout so far? What are some of your concerns vis-à-vis RFE/RL?

EP: I don't know the answer to your question. We've not dealt [with all the ramifications] yet in those terms, except in passing; but clearly we have a lot of agreements with the German government. We [also] have agreements with the Bavarian government. They involve transmitter sites about forty kilometers from here. They [also] involve this building, and they involve the status of the organization as a private company doing business in Germany. They involve selective bargaining agreements for the unions here.

Anybody in the U.S. government function who thinks that all of these various agreements must be assigned to this new broadcasting director of the U.S. government doesn't know what they are talking about. . . . I'll just give you one example: The Voice of America is now paying the German government 12 million dollars a year at least for a transmitter--12 million a year. They broadcast about 40 hours a week on those transmitters.

NLS/MJM: A week?

EP: We [RFE/RL] have three transmitting sites in this country. Two in the north, and one near here. The leases go back quite far and were negotiated on terms extremely favorable to this company. But these facilities, according to those leases, may only be used by this company for its purposes. We broadcast four hundred hours a week on those transmitters, at 12.8 million a year. Do you think that if we give those up, and the U.S. wants to keep them, that we're going to negotiate those terms ever again?

There are all kinds of international agreements here that are going to come into play,. . . one that's been operating in Portugal, where we have our largest operation [for example]. I just renegotiated it two years ago myself. A new ten year agreement with the government. Who's going to renegotiate that; and is Portugal even going to be willing to entertain the notion? I don't know. I'm going down there in two weeks to try to find out.

We operate a large (division) in Spain, where we have operated without an agreement for almost twenty years. The Spanish government, for whatever reason, may not want to renegotiate. But they have this law--we pay them a fee every year to continue to use the facilities. We finally began about six months ago, a serious discussion with them . . . about including a new agreement. That whole thing is [that] the Spanish government may possibly have no interest in negotiating agreements with our staff [under the new conditions].

NLS/MJM: Agreements for?

EP: Well, we have managed over the course of the last three years to build a (very substantial FM network) throughout much of the area we broadcast.

NLS/MJM: But that would all have to be renegotiated.

EP: Of course. And I don't think, in several instances, that there would even be a chance at renegotiation. Our agreement in Poland is with Polish national radio. We in effect took over there (the old four channel), and we've got countrywide AM distribution. Now, I would be very surprised if the Polish government is going to lease one of its national radio channels to the U.S. government. I wouldn't if I were in their position. The same thing is true in the Czech lands, and Slovakia. . . . In early 1990 I took the first steps towards trying to acquire local transmitters. Things were going reasonably well and then they became bogged down.

In May I went to Prague and met with [President] Havel. One result of that meeting was that he became involved with the subject; and the Czechoslovakian Parliament that summer passed a law exempting Radio Free Europe from the provisions of the State Medium Monopoly Act, in order to make those facilities available to us. I think it is marvelous testimony about this organization.

NLS/MJM: But things have changed . . . both with our government and theirs, though, hasn't it?

EP: Yes. As for the original agreement . . . some of those transmitters are now in the Czech Republic, some of them are in Slovakia. And we walked, at the beginning of this year, a tightrope, because the [new] Czech government doesn't have much use for us. So far they haven't interfered, but given an opportunity (when the organization ceases to exist and becomes a U.S. government entity), I think that opens the door for change. And the same thing [can happen] in every other place, where we have AM and FM now, and that includes all the (states).

NLS/MJM: This is a very personal point of view, obviously. Do you think that there is some feeling, somewhere, that these things would just simply be, easily transferable. There seems to be a . . . I hate to use the word . . . but almost a naiveté, that if you have negotiated these contracts as RFE/RL, certainly the new regime can just take them over.

EP: That may be the case, I don't know. I mean if it is, it certainly springs from supreme ignorance. . . I think there's a larger agenda to play here. I think they're determined to put this place out of business.

NLS/MJM: But why? . . . But you said it began with the Bush administration.

EP: Yes.

NLS/MJM: Who started that?

EP: Well, there is a coalition of forces in play here, not just this administration. I think it's been going on for a long time. The people of the OMB had their eye on this place. Also, there is resentment that, you know, Forbes managed to turn this thing around more than once. I mean they were convinced, even two years ago, that it was all going to go away. And then they couldn't do it. And then they were certainly convinced in February it had been done. And once more, you know, these broadcast [testimonials] emerged. . . . Now Forbes is gone, and I'm about to go, and I think that's what the larger agenda is here. And federalizing it is a major step in that direction, in my opinion. That gives them far greater control over [the Radios] than they have in dealing with them a private (grantee) corporation. And I think that's what goes.

NLS/MJM: What you said earlier that you had transmitters on both sides . . . What about Clinton's administration? Who are the people now that are in the administration, that you would talk to . . .

EP: I'll tell you quite frankly we've given up talking to them. Because, you know, after a time, you come to the realization that there is no point in going on with it. Once the administration had cast its position, why bang your head against that [wall] any longer? . . . Look--we spent forty years trying to bring about this result, in various ways. The result happens, and we say good luck. And, you know, it's off we go.

NLS/MJM: It's unbelievable.

EP: It is unbelievable; and the implications of the danger lurking out there, and what might be required later . . . I don't think are understood. I mean . . . I can't give you a better explanation than that, I don't think there is one, I don't have the faintest idea what they're doing in that area.

INTERVIEW WITH KIM ANDREW ELLIOTT, VOA AUDIENCE RESEARCH OFFICER IN WASHINGTON, D.C.: APRIL 28, 1994[1]

MJM/NLS: How do you see the federalization and consolidation?

KAE: Well, I guess that since they [RFE/RL] preserved their grantee status, they haven't been federalized that much, or they won't be federalized as much as was originally thought. I wrote an article on this, I started the whole debate, I think, in the Winter of 1989-90, Foreign Policy Magazine, if you can find that. It is called "Too Many Voices of America." When that came out, Donnie Purcell put out a press release and called for a presidential commission, and there was a lot of hemming and hawing, but finally there was a presidential commission, and it met and came up with this recommendation, and the whole Radio Free Asia commission . . .

MJM/NLS: So you sort of started this, huh?

KAE: I think I did. My argument was that we needed to do two things. First we needed to consolidate our resources because frequencies, transmitting sites, journalists who have abilities in these various languages in which we broadcast, are all scarce commodities no matter how much we spend on international broadcasting, they are scarce commodities; and if we split those commodities among competing bureaucracies, our chance of succeeding in international broadcasting diminishes, in fact it falls short. That is the reason why the U.S. spends twice as much on international broadcasting as Britain, but BBC has more listeners than VOA, twice as many as VOA, more than VOA and RFE/RL combined. There is obviously a cost/benefit effect going on. They are very efficient, and we are not. They are unitary, they have everything together in one organization, and can make the necessary adjustments for each target area, and ours are divided, we are competing among ourselves, and thus we are not competing well with other countries' international broadcasting. The consolidation really did not change it that much, though it changed it a bit. I think there will be much less redundancy in languages, VOA will have to drop some languages, RFE/RL is already in the process of dropping some of their languages. Some of that will be reduced.

MJM/NLS: One of the arguments that we heard is that the transfer negotiations [for reallocating the licenses] were private. With this proposed change in status, all those things [RFE/RL] negotiated as a surrogate broadcaster would not have been achieved by VOA. Also, the [original] agreements were, in general, much less expensive [than they will be in the renegotiation].

KAE: RFE/RL does a good thing, and provides a good model. But we need both federal consolidation and [a] corporate consolidation [based] somewhat on the RFE model. The BBC model is even more appropriate. BBC was created as an independent corporation to keep its news insulated from government control, RFE and RL were created as corporations to be . . . anti-communist propaganda; organizations that found their way into being in the independent news business. They eventually found out that that's the way to do it, that is what the audience is interested in, not propaganda. Propaganda never works anywhere, period. So yes, you are right, autonomy [is extremely important]. In fact, when were negotiating for the Israel transmitter, the company that was doing the negotiations was a subsidiary of RFE/RL, because it was so difficult for VOA to do that. It is a two-edged sword, though--RFE's corporate status helps it, and RFE/RL's reputation as the surrogate hard-hitting propaganda station hinders it, in some cases.

MJM/NLS: You should have seen the looks on their faces when we were in RFE/RL, and Nancy asked Sam Lyons what he did before he came here, and he said "CIA." We did not know what to say--we wanted his autograph! He was one of those [throwbacks] to the seventies before it (the organization) changed around.

KAE: After 1978 those links were severed; and until I hear anything otherwise, I will believe them. VOA does have that part of our charter that says we have to talk about U.S. foreign policy, and that has been interpreted as our editorial, but that is it. In fact, we could fulfill that part of the charter just from reportage; it doesn't have to be in an editorial. I think there is a lot of discussion right now about whether we should continue the editorial or not; but as far as the journalism part of VOA, the newsroom is thoroughly professional.

Probably even more important than the editorial is the fact that the director of VOA is a presidential appointee, so whenever there is a new president, there is a new director of VOA who can then change the management of the newsroom. That could result in a difference of tone, not so much the sentence level of writing of news stories, but the selection of news items. . . . But if you look at RFE/RL's senior management, it is politically well-connected also; so I don't think "insulation" holds up that well for RFE/RL. It should be stronger for both of our organizations.

MJM/NLS: What are the major ways in which the present RFE/RL VOA model differs from the British model? What are the three major things that you would like to see?

KAE: The differences are profound. The BBC is unitary, so it is all one organization. According to the theory of surrogate broadcasting--that is surrogate versus official broadcasting--if a country is, say, Stalinist, then you broadcast about the domestic affairs of that country. Then, if the country becomes more democratic, they get news about their own country, so what they want to hear from a foreign radio station is U.S. and world news. The BBC can just make the necessary changes as time goes on. As the target country changes its politics, the BBC can just make the necessary adjustments. In the case of US international broadcasting, RFE/RL would have to issue termination notices to its employees, [and] VOA would have to put ads in the *New York Times* and the *Washington Post* to get employees for its news services to serve this country. Then if the target country goes back into a Stalinist dictatorship, VOA would have to issue termination notices to its employees, and RFE/RL would put employment ads in the *Times* and the *Post* to get people . . . so it is a very clunky system. U.S. international broadcasting is sort of centrally planned, just like the Soviet economy. The VOA has predetermined that it will talk about U.S. and world affairs, and it is predetermined that RFE/RE will do target country affairs. It forces the audience, then, to tune to two different stations to get a complete newscast. I think it is just a lot of bureaucratic nonsense. BBC simply provides the mix that is appropriate for each of its target countries and goes about it. The other thing that is advantageous about BBC is that it has corporate independence; that it can make a little bit of its own money through its auxiliary enterprises, and it can conduct the business. . . . It is ruthless--it hires and fires people with impunity, but it gets the job done.

MJM/NLS: What kinds of enterprises?

KAE: Well, they sell tapes, books, and research data. They can sell all kinds of things that they have; they just can't do commercials. They can do everything but.

MJM/NLS: So they have an institute similar to RFE/RL's.

KAE: RFE/RL, to some extent, can make some money too. As far as VOA, it is very clunky for us because we are a government agency. Also, the BBC has its domestic partner, the BBC domestic services, and they can borrow a lot from their resources. VOA has no such thing. RFE/RL really doesn't either. In fact, we both have sort of pariah status among the U.S. domestic media. If we had a domestic partner such as NPR and PBS, I think we would be able to do a better job.

MJM/NLS: Relatedly, I had a question about the BBC, which was that I had heard that the BBC, and I am not sure whether it was the domestic service or the world service, had gone down in some of its credibility because it was seen as being less objective, less the old BBC.

KAE: I have not seen any hard data about that. I think that domestically they have gone through some hard times because a lot of reorganizations are going on, [there's] more of a commercial incentive, [and] the director has been involved in sort of a scandal, too.

MJM/NLS: And, of course, the BBC world service doesn't worry about that.

KAE: That is all pretty transparent to the audience overseas. The BBC usually rates highest in credibility [among] the various services. And one thing that is very obvious is that they are prohibited from doing editorials and we are required to, so the difference is very apparent between the two stations in that particular aspect. Also, the BBC management has a fixed term, so if a new government is elected in London, the BBC guys will remain in place until the term of the managing director ends.

MJM/NLS: How long is that term?

KAE: I think it is a five-year term, it is fixed by the Board of Governors. The Board of Governors also has fixed, but staggered terms; so that does not change with any one government. There is [a certain] continuity . . . BBC World Service management is able to stay around and build up expertise, whereas oftentimes VOA front office management, and RFE/RL to a large extent too, are just people with good political connections [and] without any particular expertise.

MJM/NLS: And you say that the BBC will fire you.

KAE: Lately they've gotten that way, yes.

MJM/NLS: We went to a WBUR brunch that featured some BBC reporters, and when asked how long their tenures were, they said that they could be over in a half hour. They were blatant about that. Who does that--who fires them?

KAE: Their senior managers do. A lot of the BBC employees now are just contract employees; they are not people with full benefits, they are not building up pension privileges or anything like that. [On] their big news program "News Hour," everybody is on a six-month contract. The competition is so keen in London for journalists to find work, [that] to work for the BBC is an honor. And the talent is great.

MJM/NLS: On the other hand, if you are an employee at RFE/RL, you could go on for twenty years . . .

MJM/NLS: Aren't they civil service?

KAE: Most of us are civil service.

MJM/NLS: So you cannot really be fired.

KAE: It would be really difficult. You would have to do something really pretty awful to get fired. We do have some contract employees here.

MJM/NLS: Do you think they would change that in this reorganization?

KAE: No, because we are going to remain a government agency, and RFE/RL will keep its grantee status and will be subject to whatever the Czech labor laws are.

MJM/NLS: You mean that they still might not . . .

KAE: Well, it still has to be approved by Congress; the board, the RFE/RL board has approved it; I don't know who is approving it now; there is a recommendation made from management, the Congress still has to approve that.

MJM/NLS: When we were there they were talking about the possibility of Prague or Washington, since then they have changed. How upset or not upset would you have been had it been moved to Washington?

KAE: I think that would have been better if it had been moved to Washington because I would like to see more consolidation. It looks like the move to Prague, if they do move to Prague, they will entrench themselves there as a bureaucracy and that will be in effect for an awfully long time because they are going to go to all that expense to set up a radio station in Prague, they are not going to just turn it off or phase it out it after a few years. So I think it will make the real consolidation of U.S. international broadcasting much more difficult, and it will be a longer process. By that I don't mean VOA absorbing RFE/RL, I mean the real merger.

MJM/NLS: Now what about your view of Radio Free Asia?

KAE: That I think will probably be the downfall of U.S. international broadcasting because Asia is now getting to be the most important part of the world. Asia is probably the most difficult part of the world to get a signal into because it is so huge, and there is jamming from the North Koreans and the Chinese. It is one of the most difficult parts of the world to get news out of, it is one of the most difficult parts of the world to find talent who speak languages like Tibetan and Burmese and Lao, and also have broadcasting and writing skills. So when we take these really finite resources and split them between two competing stations that will really be dedicated to each other's demise, the resources will be split to an extent that we are no longer going to be capable of providing a serious effort into Asia. We will be dividing our resources in half multiplied by two . . . bureaucratic infrastructure, because Radio Free Asia will have to have its own director, deputy director, associate directors, and special assistants and senior advisors, and staff travel budgets and carpeted office suites, along with VOA which has its own (facilities) so that equals efficiency divided by four. Really, it will be the end of U.S. international broadcasting, I think.

MJM/NLS: It seems to me that Radio Marti is different than all of these things that people have talked about, isn't it kind of a unique . . .

KAE: It is, it is sort of like a marsupial, like a platypus duckbill because it is a surrogate station, but it is under VOA. . . . Radio Marti actually makes a certain amount of sense, because in Cuba you have a country where there is really a need for information, it is a small area, we can reach it though medium wave right now which . . . and we are on for 24 hours which makes for a very convenient schedule, so Radio Marti is probably successful. We don't have any hard data, but it probably is successful because all the pieces come together. TV Marti, on the other hand, is probably not visible, and it is really pushing the limits of both physics and international law. . . . The will continue TV Marti, they will go on UHF instead of VHF, they say it will be less effected by jamming, the main reason is that the Cubans won't bother to jam because on UHF the signal will not make it to Cuba anyway (laughter).

MJM/NLS: Is there a time line for [the federalization] of all of these media?

KAE: I am not all that intimate with the legislation as it is right now, so I would have to take a look at it, and I think right now it has just come out of conference, and is very close to being voted, it is pretty much a *fait accomplit* now, but you would have to get the most recent wording of the legislation. Maybe Graham Cannon in the House Foreign Affairs Committee could help you out.

MJM/NLS: Is its mission to create enough dissent to cause . . .

KAE: That would have been like the early mission of RFE/RL, which was to push back communism, but after Hungary in 1956 they came to a much more moderate mission. VOA is proud of its role, and when you hear people like Havel and Walesa congratulate RFE/RL, they also congratulate VOA and they congratulate that two stations interchangeably. Gorbachev wasn't even sure which station he was listening to, I think, he listened to the one which put through the best signal, which happened to be the BBC, because its resources weren't split (laughter) between the two. They have a transmitter down in Cyprus, and we don't because we are up in Germany with our transmitters split.

MJM/NLS: When did you first start looking at those? When you first came here or did you look at it before you came here?

KAE: I started working here in 1985, and I was a member of many long-range planning committees. There was one after another . . . and it dawned on me that we can make all kinds of strategy within VOA, but the problem is one or two levels up. I knew the whole structure of U.S. international broadcasting and I could see that VOA and RFE/RL were competing with each other in Europe. Then we had very few resources between Africa and the Philippines, we did not have any big transmitting site between Liberia and the Philippines. So tens of millions of potential listeners were just out of the picture, we could not reach them. In the meantime RFE was building a transmitter site in Portugal, and we were building a transmitter site in Morocco just a couple of hundred miles apart to broadcast to the same countries in the same language at the same time. Meanwhile tens of millions of listeners from Burma through India, Iran, Afghanistan we could not reach because of that, so it struck me that the whole structure of U.S. international broadcasting was amiss, and there was nothing that VOA could do strategically until that problem got solved, and so I did that article in *Foreign Policy*.

MJM/NLS: How did you get anyone to listen to you when you wrote your article?

KAE: I didn't. A lot of people listened, but it had really very little effect on anything because the connections were so strong to the USIA section which wanted to keep USIA control over VOA and keep VOA going; and then there is the RFE/RL support for international broadcasting crowd, so it was the interests of those two groups that really carried the day. Probably my only legacy will be that I think we have eliminated most of the redundancy between RFE/RL and VOA, but RFE just added its Serbian-Croatian service, now competing with VOA's. One-half hour every evening both stations are actually broadcasting into Serbia at the same time.

MJM/NLS: Do you see yourself working with the RFE/RL institute?

KAE: Yes, the USIA office of research used to have a media research branch, and for budget reasons supposedly they just eliminated that and absorbed those media researchers into their various opinion research divisions, which are regional divisions--there is one for the Americas, there is one for Asia, one for Africa I guess--and by doing that I think they have pretty much abdicated any claim they have to be doing the media research for this new international broadcasting bureau. RFE/RL's media research office will be moving to Washington later this year with fifteen people, so I think they will become the researchers for the new international broadcasting bureau, that is just my prediction. They will separate then from the research institute, which gathers information about the countries of Eastern Europe and Central Europe. But the thing is, now that we can go into those countries and gather news, we do not need a research institute in Munich to do that remotely. So I think the research institute is probably out. I see it as a kind of white elephant. Soros wants to take it off our hands, and maybe that is a blessing. It is obviously a great institute and all that, but I don't think it supports our broadcasting mission. We need correspondents in the country to gather hard news. To the extent to which people in those countries want news about their own countries from a foreign radio station. It comes to a certain point where we are sending coals to Newcastle, if Hungary's media finally develops to the point where people are satisfied with the journalism they are getting from Hungarian media, then they are not going to need us, except for U.S. and world news. But that is where research comes in, we just have to keep an eye on the audience and what it needs and make the necessary adjustments. The BBC can do that, and they have a very large research office compared to VOA/USIA, which is pretty small. They are market based, and we are more of a Soviet central planning model.

MJM/NLS: Which is kind of ironic, isn't it?

NOTE

1. Mr. Elliott specified on his interview release form that he was speaking from personal opinion, not as a VOA representative.

11

From "The Goddess of Democracy" to Radio Free Asia

Nancy Lynch Street

Case Study Eight

In December of 1987 I received a visit from five deans and an interpreter at Shanxi Teacher's University in Linfen, the People's Republic of China (PRC). The purpose of the visit was to conduct a Marxist "struggle" with me with a view to encouraging constructive self-criticism. With the pervasive din from competing sound systems and strobe lights of the students' all-night disco parties, little sleep for several weeks, the lack of textbooks, and recalcitrant students who refused to come to class, I was in no mood to appreciate this unique experience. In characteristic American form in that unreceptive Chinese culture, I felt compelled to bluntly inquire as to why the Chinese academics and the Chinese CCP hierarchy within our work unit seemingly were afraid of their own students. Ignoring my Western confrontational approach (to confront is shocking, if not barbaric, behavior in the Chinese culture), the Chinese deans advised me that the students were going to strike. Seemingly, the cause of their discomfort was the fact that I had given a public speaking assignment! I was to rescind the public speaking assignment, as Chinese students could not be expected to speak openly in the classroom.

I was dumbfounded by this request because in 1985-1986, the students, despite lack of prior experience in speaking publicly, had enthusiastically participated in the assignment. The deans and I circled the issue for hours. Finally, I agreed to take the assignment out of the classroom; the students would still prep the speech and deliver it after hours in front of two or three other students in the relative privacy of my apartment, while I listened and cleaned my vegetables, paper, and bowls of boiled water spread on the floor in front of me. At the end of the term in January, the officials thanked me for my part in averting the strike. I puzzled over this and other incidents of the 1988-1989 semester until April of 1989 when Chinese students began their ill-fated demonstrations in mid-April in Tiananmen Square. The apprehensions of my Chinese colleagues were fulfilled as students spoke in public, through the media, to the entire world. Thanks to the deans at Shanxi Teacher's University students received little encouragement in freedom of expression from the *waiguoren* on our campus.

OVERVIEW AND METHOD

In this study, I describe and discuss some of the elements--internal and external--that I feel played into the devastation at Tiananmen Square leading directly (following the Fall of the Wall and the dissolution of the Soviet Union) to the rationalization of the need to redirect the transnational media resources of the United States from fomenting, aiding, and abetting dissent in Eastern Europe and the Soviet Union to undertake these same activities in Asia by adding Radio Free Asia (RFA) to the Voice of America (VOA).

Research methodologies for this paper include: historical-critical research; ethnography, including participant observation and interviewing in Poland, Germany, Taiwan, Korea, the United States and the People's Republic of China (PRC). In Germany this author interviewed at Radio Free Europe/Radio Liberty (RFE/RL). In Washington, D. C., interviews were conducted with VOA personnel. Interviews with the Chinese students and Chinese professors were conducted in the PRC (1990) and in the United States (1991-1995). Names of Chinese interviewees have been changed.

In presenting the arguments here, I have looked at two of the cultures involved, the United States and the PRC, within the umbrella framework of systems theory. Understanding of the two cultures depends upon the interplay and interdependence amongst the themes selected. Analysis through critical theory, especially fantasy theory and social movement theory, helped this critic to develop her arguments. Rybacki says,

> The goal of fantasy theme analysis is to explain how and why a fantasy became a shared reality for a group. A group's shared reality is found in its rhetorical vision, "a unified way of putting together of the scripts that gives the participants a broader view of things."[1]

Internal elements crucial to this analysis include: the Chinese student rebellion tradition; the cultural roots of discontent in post-Cultural Revolution China; and the interplay of technology, foreign culture, myth, and the media in the development of the "democracy movement." Ultimately, this rhetorical theme was buttressed by the creation of the "Goddess of Democracy" (May 30), in the last days of protest (May 30) in the Beijing Spring of 1989.[2]

External elements include myths and fantasies from another perspective--the view from the United States; differing notions of democracy; the significance of the Cold War to its warriors; and finally, the interplay of various "global village" factors that significantly affected the outcome of the student movement. From the assent/dissent implicit in the "Goddess of Democracy" to Radio Free Asia, the United States and China are engaged in a cultural/political clash that shows few signs of abating as the United States continues to upgrade its signals to escalate visions at variance with Chinese socioeconomic and political realities to a new generation of college students in China through both the VOA and the incipient Radio Free Asia. Without sufficient thought for responsibility and consequences, in the guise of enabling "freedom and democracy," intensified foreign media incursions into China may end in yet another tragedy.

THE RHETORICAL FRAMEWORK OF DISCOURSE

The American Vision and the VOA

In 1995, on this 50th anniversary of "almost everything,"[3] one can see that for at least 50 years the rhetorical framework of discourse--that which guides the development of the social, political, and economic life of individuals and at least two major nations--has been the "Cold War," or to use the "Star Wars" metaphor, the struggle between the forces of good and the forces of evil (from the American viewpoint). Within this framework, communism and capitalism are engaged in a fight to the death, perhaps even a nuclear holocaust, with the sides perceived to be somewhat evenly matched. With the recent radical changes in the Soviet Union, precipitated by Gorbachev, the United States tended to take a somewhat kindlier attitude towards the Soviet Union. However, Gorbachev's visit to China in the Spring of 1989 must have precipitated uneasiness in the West. At that time Communism had a new face but its death knell had not (and still has not) yet been sounded.

Perhaps Gorbachev's proposed visit (the first by a major Soviet leader since the break between China and the Soviet Union in 1960) signaled to the United States a possible unwelcome alliance between the two largest communist nations in the world. (At the time, if one can believe the American media, scarcely anyone could foretell the Fall of the Wall and the dissolution of the Soviet Union--events of late 1989.) This in turn may have caused difficulties with U.S. policy and diplomacy, leading to identifying a possible liaison between China and the Soviet Union that would be most unwelcome in the West. Thus, when the student demonstrations at Tiananmen coincided with Gorbachev's visit, the VOA was conceived to be (more than ever) an appropriate vehicle for creating a rift between these two communist nations. VOA is the "voice" of the American government and chartered with furthering America's policies.

Wang Fei, a former Chinese media practitioner (who received his B.A. and M.A. in the PRC) and who is also attached to the staff of VOA's Chinese Branch, Mandarin Service, is very clear in describing the levels of control at the VOA. Citing earlier research in this area, Wang notes,

The first level of control is the Central Newsroom of the VOA. . . . only news items rewritten by the Central Newsroom may be used in the Mandarin newscasts. . . . The Mandarin Service may write a particular story; however, the story must be approved by the Central Newsroom before it is aired. Among a total of 135 news items, 818 sentences and 16, 484 words examined in this study, none of the stories were written by Mandarin news staff.[4]

Wang goes on to detail the process of translation from English to Mandarin (word for word), and the prohibition against adding to the English version or making value judgments. During the Tiananmen Crisis, he asserts that all negative stories were aimed at the Chinese government, and that all positive stories reflected the United States, its culture, and policies.[5] He then explains the second level of control in use during this period of time:

The second level is within the Chinese Branch itself. The Chinese Branch has a Foreign Service officer as the Branch Chief to supervise activities of the Mandarin Service. . . . The VOA Program review process constitutes a "chilling effect." . . . It is almost impossible for the Chinese Branch staffs to do anything to balance the biased news or to change its orientation within this organizational setup. . . . causes of occasional propaganda conducted by the VOA Mandarin newscasts as the findings of this research indicated.[6]

Given the two-pronged mission of the VOA, coupled with the unusual circumstances surrounding Tiananmen in the Spring of 1989--the student demonstrations upon the death of Hu Yaobang, the anticipated visit of Gorbachev, and the prevailing mood of discontent amongst students and intellectuals--one can easily see disparate visions converging. The effect of this convergence was the creation of what Jung called "syncronicity," the coming together of seemingly unrelated events at a certain moment in time, providing involved onlookers, each with his or her own rhetorical vision, with rationales and mediums for acting. The result was what is known to some as the Tiananmen Massacre, while to others, the events at Tiananmen were a national tragedy. Still others feel (or know) that a social movement must have martyrs. In this paper, I refer to that period in Tiananmen Square as the Tiananmen Crisis.

With the apparent demise of communism in the former Soviet Union and Eastern Europe, the forces of good, having fought the good fight, had won over "godless" communism. Immersed in this Darth Vader fantasy or world view, Americans seemed to thrive and strive well on this vision, which to a great degree was dependent on a strong defense industry (the "force" is with us).

Yet the end of communism in the Soviet sphere seemed to negate the common vision or fantasy that promoted so many American anticommunism initiatives for 50 years, including the continuance of VOA (conceived during WWII in 1942) and the development of RFE/RL (RFE began in 1949 and RL in 1951). The latter Radios were conceptualized as surrogate voices "for those who cannot speak," whereas VOA's benign mission "is to describe America to the outside world."[7]

Like its sister radios, VOA targets certain sectors of the world. As Wang Fei says,

According to the statistical data released by the VOA Programming Handbook (1992, 48), about half of VOA's audience lives in the former Soviet Union, East European countries and the People's Republic of China. This is another indication that communist propaganda is taken into account while forming VOA programming policy.[8]

Wang Fei is well acquainted with VOA programming as he "was a long time VOA listener in China who learned his English through the VOA's English teaching program."[9] Further, he has been a media practitioner in China and is now a researcher in the VOA Mandarin Service. Wang clearly indicates in his findings that, though the staff of the Mandarin Service perceive themselves to be objective journalists and faithful to the VOA Charter, the events of Tiananmen significantly lessened that objectivity as the service increased its output to 24 hours a day, canceling cultural and music programs and substituting news during the Tiananmen crisis. In light of the tragic ending at Tiananmen Square on June 4, the thrust of his study seems to be two-fold: (1) to examine and define the role of the VOA at Tiananmen; (2) to determine the culpability (if any) of the VOA, its Chinese Branch and the Mandarin Service staff (many of whom are Chinese dissidents with a stake in not just a protest movement but in precipitating the fall of the present government of China) in the events at Tiananmen.[10] To this end, he determines that the VOA has "the incompatible role of serving two divergent objectives at the same time: to be the government's public diplomacy institution and, at the same time, to be an objective news outlet. . . . Tensions between diplomacy and journalism continue."[11] That journalism suffers when Chinese communism is the issue seems clear from not just Wang's analysis, but from talking with Chinese students and citizens who were in Tiananmen during the occupation of the Square by the students in the Spring of 1989.

The Chinese Vision

China's students (approximately 20 years old) who participated in the Tiananmen demonstration were born during the Cultural Revolution (CR). Those "intellectuals" (primarily journalists and professors) who participated in the movement were born prior to the CR and often were "sent down" to the countryside. Some of this latter group remained in the countryside for ten to twenty years. During the CR (1966-1976), intellectuals were badly treated, often incarcerated, sometimes killed by the Red Guard.

The Red Guard was comprised of the students of China who were originally called to revolution by Chairman Mao Zedong in Tiananmen Square in 1966. Mao Zedong and Deng Xiaoping were themselves revolutionaries in their youth, protesting the corruption and lack of democracy in China and opposing the American-backed Nationalist (Kuomintang or KMT) Party and its principles. Both were leaders of the fledgling Chinese Communist Party (CCP) as it fought the Nationalists and the Japanese for 20-odd years, prior to the victory of the CCP over the KMT in 1949.   As Ruth Cherrington says in *China's Students: The Struggle for Democracy*,

It will be seen that the students {in 1989} were following the tradition of outspokenness laid down by their Beijing University predecessors during the "May Fourth" movement of 1919. . . . Before 1919, however, scholars had an obligation to point out to the ruler any poor judgments or corruption, even at the risk of incurring punishment as a reward.[12]

The "May Fourth" movement of 1919 also began at "Beida," or Beijing University, and was spurred by the Treaty of Versailles, which transferred part of China, for example, parts of Shandong Province from one nation (Germany) to another (Japan). With this issue, added to charges of official corruption and injustice, as well as calls for, among other issues, democratization and better education, some 10,000 students marched to Tiananmen Square.[13] Following the "May Fourth" movement, some students and intellectuals joined the newly formed Chinese Communist Party (CCP, founded in 1921), hoping to implement through the CCP their vision for China. Not then, and not now, do the Chinese students want the Western powers to intervene or occupy China. I believe that in the Tiananmen Crisis the situation became so chaotic that the students were overcome with the headiness of what they had wrought, that they fused with the vision given them by others, primarily through the media--both radio and television. In retrospect, they wanted the benefits of the Western intellectual tradition and the rewards of the evolving Chinese economic system, certainly not Westerners nor even Western capitalism.[14]

Chinese students can be described as seeing themselves as in a long tradition of social movements in the twentieth century, usually beginning at "Beida," developing through protests against government corruption and injustice and demonstrations in Tiananmen Square demanding freedom and democracy. In China, throughout the twentieth century, the students have actively participated in the ongoing process of nation building or tearing down, as in the sometimes unsanctioned destruction during the Cultural Revolution.[15] A primary difference between then and now is that the students' rhetorical vision is mediated in a way impossible in 1919.

Thus we had, in 1989, convergence of rhetorical visions through radio and television never before possible. Were, or are, these visions compatible?

Cultural Context of the Beijing Spring of 1989

As I indicate in the introduction, although "China watchers" missed it, those of us in China during 1988-1989 were aware that the students were dissatisfied. In both 1985-1986 and 1988-1989, I often had Chinese students in my quarters pleading with me to get them out of China and into graduate school in the States. Because my college had an exchange program with a teaching university in Shanxi Province, this was sometimes possible, though not nearly as often as the students would have liked.[16] Disgruntled students explained:

The peasants (and sometimes the workers) and the cadres of the CCP enjoy (as perceived by my Chinese students and colleagues) being able once again to put down the intellectuals. This is a repetition of the situation during the CR, when the intellectuals, stripped of everything, were sent to the countryside . . . to learn from the peasants. In the new China with its mixed economy and free market, the peasant is still above the intellectual. The intellectual lives "at the bottom of society." The students and intellectuals feel resentment in the existing situation. They do not trust the power elite, i. e., the CCP leadership, to rectify the situation.[17]

Thus we arrive at an approximation of the Chinese student vision of the world.

Qing Zhou and a friend I shall call "Tao" were both at Tiananmen Square and agree that conditions were not good for the Chinese students and intellectuals during the eighties.[18] This was a time of gradual development of private industry and joint enterprises while maintaining the existing political system--a plan heartily disapproved of by capitalist "hard-liners" in the United States who wanted an overnight, radical change in the political and economic system in China. China, being China, decided to implement change in its own fashion, slowly developing the free market in China, coexisting with state ownership.

With the dissolution of the Soviet Union and Eastern Europe in 1989/1990, capitalist "hard-liners" in America had the opportunity to impose their radical economic solutions upon those benighted societies, promising "democracy" through free enterprise, which ultimately resulted in destitution and unemployment, with few "democratic" benefits for many in the former Soviet Union and Eastern Europe. In 1995, one can see that neither "democracy" nor "capitalism" can succeed when radically imposed on former socialist countries. What is really to the point is the slow but certain development of the Chinese economy under the leadership of the present government ("hard-liners"), which chose, against the expressed will of America's finest economists to implement economic and political change slowly.

Although many of the 1.2 billion Chinese have benefited from the economic changes, in 1989, intellectuals--unlike many peasants and workers--were not directly benefiting from the changes sweeping through China. The students and intellectuals, both mainstays of the Chinese educational system and paid by the state, could not yet privatize or enter the free market as could the peasants, the workers, and the army.[19] By 1988 the government was encouraging educational work units to develop free market enterprises.[20] At the same time, students were still assigned by the dean or party secretary to their educational work unit following graduation; thus, they had no control over their lives. The only way out was to be sent abroad.[21] From afar, America seemed "like very heaven."

THE STUDENT MOVEMENT/TIANANMEN CRISIS

Reform social movements begin in alienation. That is, the participants are alienated from the prevailing value system and wish anything from "limited change to a complete restructuring of society."[22] The rhetorical activities of the student demonstrations in the Spring of 1995 in Beijing included inception, rhetorical crisis, and consummation phases--all typical of social movements in the West--and such functions of movements apparently are common in both the East and the West. The reform social movement commitment process has seven steps:

1. Alienation (the discontent of the students with existing economic/political values);
2. Availability (students are away from home, disaffected by educational standards and conditions);[23]
3. Attraction to the group (need to affiliate with peers, "significant others");

4. Readiness to join (adopt the problem-solving orientation of the group, e.g., petition the government, hold sit-ins);
5. Initiation into the movement (indoctrination into the aims, tactics and strategies of the movement);
6. Identification (identification with the spirit, the group, the leader);
7. Enclosure (intensification of interaction and communication with members. Adoption of the dress, manners, common habitat of the group).

Regarding the first two points, I have already indicated the grievances of the students. Obviously, if students live on campus, as the Chinese students usually do (until recently, all students were sent to college by the State and received tuition, room and board, and a small allowance; now they must pay roughly $200 a year unless they become teachers and then their education is free), then there will be groups to join. Away from home, one will naturally affiliate with peers. Given the discontent, it is not surprising that students would want to band together to air grievances. Points 5, 6, and 7 then become pivotal points, for it is in these areas that issues become complex.

The students were well aware of the earlier movements in China and so understood the need for songs, emblems, banners, and chants in rallying the movement. They had consultants as they planned the movement strategies-- foreigners and older intellectuals, those who perhaps remembered or participated in demonstrations in 1959 or 1966 or 1986 or other movements. Problems with the movement emerge when one looks at points 5, 6, and 7. Aims, strategies, and tactics were not always consistent. Also, no one leader emerged as an expressive leader. Instead, it appears that there were many factions amongst the student groups, thus many students vying for leadership. Further, the confrontation began to go on too long--for the government and the students-- though not too long for the outside world, which apparently fed upon the drama as it unfolded through various channels every hour of every day for many weeks. The media and the audience were insatiable.

In 1919 there was no VOA or television to transmit the actions of the movement as they occurred. In 1989 the various shortwave services and VOA exclusively were broadcast over the Beijing University system and heard over the loudspeaker system as the students demonstrated in Tiananmen Square. Further, the students were not alone. In addition to the foreign broadcasts and the television cameras, at times there were more than 1,000 foreign journalists in Tiananmen Square, demonstrating with the students. What were they to think? What they thought was, "the whole world is watching." At times, students said, "The American government will not let anything happen to us." In short, they gained courage from the companionship of media folks perceived as friends, most of whom would be gone when the tanks rolled in, their satisfaction having been achieved via satellite--for as long as the Chinese government would permit it. They were revitalized each day by VOA broadcasts, giving them the "truth" from the American perspective. Clearly this "truth" was not the "truth" of the Chinese government. Yet it became the "truth" of the students. Ultimately, this clash of visions would bring about disaster.

The mediated version of the student demonstrations at Tiananmen became distorted through the chaos generated by the complex web of divergent visions relating to the *ethos, logos* and *pathos* of all the participants, as it incorporates the vision of the Chinese government, the competing visions of the student groups, the visions of American and Chinese scholars, the vision of the commercial media, and the vision of the VOA and other international shortwave facilities. The Tiananmen Crisis has shown us the devastation wrought by the "Global Village" concept concerned only with technology--not with the audiences whom it is meant to serve.

Everyone at Tiananmen wanted something from their version of the vision. The foreign media services and journalists each wanted and delivered their own version of the *ethos, logos,* and *pathos* of the events at Tiananmen. The US transnational shortwave service (VOA) apparently engaged in both reporting and diplomacy (a euphemism for promoting the national interests and policies of the U.S.).

The student groups had conflicting versions of *ethos, logos,* and *pathos* at Tiananmen--they ultimately sought to rally not only the audience in the West but the audience at home, two very different audiences. Too late, the students realized that without the peasants and workers solidly behind them, they could not "win." China has a long tradition of overthrowing dynasties, always with the commitment and participation of the peasants who represent approximately 80 percent of China's 1.2 billion people.

The Chinese government had its version of events and negotiations during the Tiananmen Crisis. In each case, each wanted to craft the message for its own audience, and given the nature of the available media, which included radio, television, fax machines, and cellular phones, each was able to do just that. And then, there were the many audiences: the American audience; the Asian audience; the European audience. What did each want--and what did each receive?

ANALYSIS

Understanding the chronology of events leading to the events of June 4, 1989, can aid in discovering answers to the questions raised here. In the aftermath of Tiananmen, the chronology reveals the slow but certain movement toward disaster, as demonstrating students, caught up in the rush of events, seemingly certain that if they persevered, they would "win," did not comprehend what that might mean given their uncertain backing, and the unclear leadership and goals of the movement in collision with the power of the government. Other events during this period of time--for example, Gorbachev's visit, the hidden struggles for power behind the scenes as General Secretary Zhao Ziyang is blamed for the disorder and is dismissed sometime between May 21 and May 26[24]--were beyond the students' abilities to factor into their strategies. At the same time, the foreign audiences watching the events unfold, as well as the foreign journalists reporting those events, often had little understanding of and no context for interpreting issues and events.

Phase I

15 April: Hu Yaobang, Politburo member and former general secretary of the CCP dies of a heart attack at age 73.

16 April: Four thousand Beijing and People's University students march to Tiananmen Square, call for freedom and democracy.

17 April: Students ask for dialogue with officials, lay wreaths at the Monument to the People's Heroes.

19 April: More demonstrations at university centers in Beijing. Government warns that demonstrations are illegal and that participants will be punished.

20 April: More clashes between students and police. Reports of injuries. Students in Shanghai protest.

21 April: Fifty to one hundred thousand students defy government order and stay overnight in Tiananmen Square for Hu Yaobang's state funeral. Order to clear the square ignored; government backs down.

22 April: Memorial service for Hu in the Great Hall is broadcast. Students chant for Li Peng to come and address them personally. He does not appear.

23 April: Reports of unrest in other cities--Xi'an and Changsha. Beijing students coordinate boycott of classes.

24 April: Tens of thousands of students in Beijing begin class boycott to press home demands for talks with government.

25-26 April: Chinese Television, followed by the *People's Daily*, label unrest as a conspiracy to negate Communist Party leadership.

26 April: *People's Daily* prints editorial attacking students. Anger and resentment among the student body.

*27 April: Massive march of tens of thousands of students. Police roadblocks fail to stop students. Demonstrations elsewhere. Students continue to boycott classes.[25]

*27 April: 150,000 students march through streets of Beijing in protest against editorials. Half a million people line the streets to cheer them on. The government agrees to talks.

*27 April: 200,000 students from 42 colleges march 25 miles on the city's main streets. More than a million people crowd both sides to cheer the students.[26]

From the last three entries, we see problems that emerged in the reporting on the Tiananmen Crisis. One also begins to get a sense of how long the student demonstrations created havoc in the city of Beijing and its environs. In any city of any country, regardless of political orientation, it is difficult to conceptualize how the business of everyday life could go on amidst the daily chaos. In Beijing, capital of a Third World country, everyday life is difficult enough without citizens, officials, and police coping with daily demonstrations. Food must be brought into the city from the surrounding countryside; water to drink must be boiled; ten million people must work and live. To have the police force, transportation system, communication system, and health system tied up for the two weeks indicated here would stretch the resources--and patience--of any government. The students, however, had learned the tactics of social movements--and had incorporated most--from petition to escalation by April 27.[27] On April 29, General Secretary Zhao Ziyang returned to Beijing and

at the invitation of All-China and Beijing Students' Federations, State Council spokesman Yuan Mu, Vice-Minister of the State Education Commission He Dongchang, Secretary General of the Beijing Municipal Party Yuan Liben and Vice-Mayor Lu Yuchen attend a 'dialog forum' in the afternoon and meet forty-five students from sixteen colleges in Beijing. . . . The talks last for about three hours and are televised in detail.[28]

The students, however, were not satisfied with the meeting or its results. Since the students were not elected, some felt that nothing could be gained. Student leader Wuer Kaixi refused to be present and "tells reporters that the 'forum' is not a 'dialogue' at all, but a trick of the government to destroy student solidarity."[29]

Phase 2

Phase 2 of the Student Movement in 1989 began on "1 May, International Workers' Day. Student leaders present an ultimatum to the government: proper dialogue or more demonstrations."[30] Things did not get better from there as student demonstrations escalated from marches to fasting--and the government, the students and the journalists readied for the visit from Gorbachev. The students apparently felt the government would make concessions to them, rather than lose face with Gorbachev. In this, they strategize correctly--the government does not move to clear the square--yet.

13 May: Thousands of Students march to the square with hundreds ready to go on a hunger strike. "Give me democracy or give me death" becomes the slogan.

15 May: Arrival of Mikhail Gorbachev. Escalation of protest activities, workers and citizens join protest. Hunger strike begins.

16 May: Itinerary of Gorbachev changed. Thousands of students on hunger strike.

17 May: Gorbachev leaves for Shanghai--more demonstrations.

18 May: Gorbachev leaves China.

20 May: Li Peng declares martial law. Confrontations between PLA and public.
               News blackout attempted.

               Almost daily demonstrations the next week. On the seventh day of
               martial law, American journalists--for example, NBC--are still
               reporting from Tiananmen Square.[31]

28 May: Beijing students encouraged by worldwide march of Chinese students.
               In Hong Kong, one and a half million people march in support of the
               students.[32]

In this phase of the movement, the escalation is clearly focused on disrupting
Mikhail Gorbachev's visit and destroying the Sino-Soviet summit.   But the
government is now nearly out of time and patience and the demonstrators,
encouraged by the participation of Chinese worldwide (May 21 and May 28),
push even harder.   During Gorbachev's visit, there were some 1,000 foreign
journalists in China, many of them Americans and "Give me democracy or give
me death" becomes a potent slogan of the movement. On May 30, the students
unveil the "Goddess of Democracy" in Tiananmen Square. They are warned by
the government that it is illegal to erect the statue. The government attempts,
unsuccessfully, to bring down the statue that sits facing the huge picture of
Chairman Mao in Tiananmen Square--symbolizing the confrontation.

Apparently replenishing their courage from the goddess, the students announce
on May 31 that "they will resume dialogues with the government and retreat
from the square only after the government responds to their four conditions."[33]
The conditions include: End martial law; remove the army from Beijing;
guarantee not to "settle accounts after the autumn harvest;" and finally, to grant
freedom of the press. The next day, 3,500 students receive new tents, which
they put up in the square. The tents are gifts from Hong Kong.[34] On June 1,
foreign and Chinese journalists are briefed on new press regulations. The
confrontation is entering into Phase 3; events are converging.

Phase 3 and the Aftermath

June 2:   The army surrounds the city and takes control of the major media, i. e.,
               radio, television, telegraph office, and post office. In the countryside,
               peasants demonstrate in support of Li Peng government. Hunger strike
               declaration (72 hours) by Liu Xiaobo, Zhou Tuo, Hou Derchien, and Gao
               Xin (prominent intellectuals) in protest of martial law.[35]

June 3:   "The Xinhua News agency broadcasts the full text of a 'mobilization for
               action.'" Serious confrontations arise. At 6:00 p.m., the radio and TV
               stations issue three emergency orders signaling the forthcoming
               violent repression.   The government warns the people to obey the
               martial law. Towards midnight, troops enter the city.[36]

June 4:   "The massacre: at 12:57 A.M. on June 4, fires are evident and series of gunshots are heard from the Square in the distance."[37]

*June 5:   According to VOA, "Chinese troops slaughtered demonstrators for more democracy, killing thousands of them. At least 1400 people are believed dead in the massacre perpetrated on Tiananmen Square by the People's Liberation Army early Sunday morning."[38]

*June 5:   According to *Ming Pao News:* "Li Peng was shot by a military officer at the Great Hall of the People. Deng Xiaoping has died."[39]

*June 6:   According to VOA: "Deng Xiaoping has not appeared in public since he received Gorbachev in late May. According to reports from Hong Kong, Deng has died. Li Peng was wounded in an attempted assassination. He was shot by a young military officer, who killed himself shortly afterwards."[40]

*June 6:   According to VOA, "unarmed Chinese students staged demonstrations and parades on Tiananmen Square. As a result they were run over by military vehicles and killed by gunfire. It is a shocking and horrifying massacre."[41]

*June 6:   According to VOA, "on Tuesday, troops loyal to different sections have deployed in battle array and occasional armed conflicts have occurred. The boom of cannon from a military base in the south of the city can be heard."[42]

Thus, we see that legal reports from Tiananmen Square during the Tiananmen Crisis continued until June 1st. At that time, and in the days following, the students were requested to leave the square. According to Chinese reports, on June 3 the troops ordered the last of the students out of the square and some either refused to leave or waited too long. Ultimately, no one knows how many students, citizens and soldiers died. Reports from the Chinese number the dead at 300. Reports from Hong Kong estimate the dead at 2400. Chai Ling, one of the student leaders, estimates the dead between two hundred and four thousand.[43] We shall probably never know the true number of the dead, but we can look at the Tiananmen Crisis and examine it so that such situations might be averted in the future, at least insofar as outsiders in this "Global Village" are responsible for such tragedies.

As Phase 3 of the chronology indicates, the Tiananmen Crisis escalated until many died. The chronology also suggests that foreign media may have exacerbated an already out-of-control situation by placing an uninformed and biased "spin" on events and airing what we now know were unfounded rumors. In 1995, Deng Xiaoping is not yet dead--what was the purpose in suggesting to the Chinese people that he was dead? What was the purpose in suggesting to the Chinese people that the army was in revolt? Why did VOA, along with many other foreign services, seek to incite, not calm, further turmoil in a friendly country?

CONCLUSION

There are several possible answers to these above questions. As Wang Fei notes, the pattern of American behavior and diplomacy through the Voice of America's Mandarin Service "continued to take a strikingly activist tone against communism especially during the crisis time."[44] Rationally, the behavior cannot be justified. After analysis of reports from many perspectives, it is clear that the order of events, the numbers, the "body count" (to use the United States' government's Vietnam War euphemism), all differ from report to report. It is equally clear that foreign intervention spurred the students to ever more heroic efforts.

As time went on, one sees that the students fashioned the message to the audience they though might "save" them through such slogans as "Give me democracy or give me death." The creation of the "Goddess of Democracy" near the end of the crisis was just as clearly an appeal to the Western audience. Each time the students seemed about to quit, having done all they could to make their positions known, they were spurred on to greater efforts by shows of solidarity through demonstrations throughout the world. Once the demonstrations began (perhaps before), the world media and its audience exerted incredible pressure (with little tangible support) on the students to endure, to "win." Converted to the twentieth century belief system, the Chinese students bought the myth of the power of the media and the good intentions of the Western democracies (a situation not unlike that of Hungary in 1956). When the end came, as we knew and they knew that it surely must, they had been led like lambs to the slaughter, while we were safe in our beds.

I submit that the American warrior vision coupled with the Cold War "Star Wars" fantasy, which seemingly still guides American diplomacy, needs to be examined, particularly as it impacts upon our international media policies, recently under revision. Since the Tiananmen Crisis, the Fall of the Wall, and the dissolution of the former Soviet Union, our international media policies have been scrutinized and apparently found to be good. The strategies of the Radios apparently worked in Eastern Europe and the USSR. Why not in Asia?

The strongest arguments for the point of view expressed in this paper are the "placement operation" begun in China after 1989 by the Mandarin Branch (placement means sending materials to radio stations in China, as opposed to direct broadcasting),[45] the restructuring of the international broadcasting system, and the creation of Radio Free Asia (RFA). These developments validate the need for urgency if we are to avoid implication in such crises in future.

Like RFE/RL, Radio Free Asia is meant to be a surrogate voice, a voice to create dissent, and this voice has now been added to that of VOA in China. Why? Perhaps because, in part, we are still trapped in a fantasy world that never was. A second option might be that American hegemony requires that all our friends subscribe to "free market democracy," whatever that might be--an end to be achieved by any means possible. And, not unlike our involvement in the Vietnam War (according to Robert McNamara in 1995, a war that should not have been), we may yet live to regret our inability to move on, to develop our own resources and generate a new vision of ourselves appropriate to the "new world order"--rather than attempt to make others over into our own image. As we have yet to learn, that is no longer an option.

NOTES

1. Karen Rybacki and Donald Rybacki, *Communication Criticism* (Belmont, Calif.: Wadsworth, 1991), 86. Authors are quoting, in part, E. G. Bormann, "Symbolic Convergence Theory: A Communication Formulation," *Journal of Communication 35* (1985), 434.

2. Photographers and reporters of *Ming Pao News , June 4: A Chronicle of the Chinese Democratic Uprising* , trans. Zi Jin and Zhou Qin (Fayetteville, Ark.: University of Arkansas Press, 1989), 137.

3. Cover title of *The Nation*, 15 May 1995.

4. Fei Wang, *Objective Journalism or Propaganda: A Content Analysis of the Voice of America Mandarin Service's Newscasts before, during, and after the Tian An Men Crisis*, (Ph.D. diss., Bowling Green State University, 1993), 104.

5. Ibid., 115.

6. Ibid., 116.

7. Editorial, "Yeltsin Should Ask,"*Wall Street Journal*, 2 April 1993. (*Note*: This editorial, was taken from the press packet given to the authors at RFE/RL headquarters in Munich.)

8. Fei Wang, *Objective Journalism or Propaganda: A Content Analysis*, 104.

9. Ibid., 14.

10. Ibid., see especially 108-125.

11. Ibid., 108.

12. Ruth Cherrington, *China's Students: The Struggle for Democracy* (New York: Routledge, 1991), 3.

13. Ibid., 20-23.

14. This becomes clear in an interview with Tiananmen demonstrator Qing Zhou on 14 May 1995. In an interview with John Harbaugh, Special Assistant of Voice of America, Chinese Branch, VOA and Betty Tseu, Chief, Mandarin Service, Chinese Branch, VOA, 28 April 1994, Washington, D.C., Harbaugh says "the ideas and issues that are now generating so much dissatisfaction within China are not values like democracy, not values like freedom, but rather opportunity and pretty much economic opportunity."

15. I do not argue this issue in this paper.

16. I write about the tensions within the culture in my book, *In Search of Red Buddha* (New York: Peter Lang, 1992).

17. Ibid., 218.

18. Qing Zhou, personal interview on 14 May 1995. Xiao Tao is a former colleague in the PRC.

19. For instance, the peasants could sell in the free market, the workers could produce and sell beyond the state's needs, and the army could engage in commerce, such as shipping coal from Shanxi or running hotels such as the one I stayed in near Tai Shan.

20. At Shanxi Teacher's University, our president was attempting to find joint ventures to develop on Hainan Island and elsewhere.

21. Now students are free to choose employment on their own. This may be one of the benefits from Tiananmen Square. However, this new policy could be detrimental to primary and middle school education in China's provinces.

22. A. J. Stewart, "A Functional Approach to the Rhetoric of Social Movements," *Central States Speech Journal 31* (1980), 298-305.

23. See Street, *Red Buddha.*

24. *Ming Pao News*, 118.

25. Adapted from Cherrington, 139-140, and other sources. Oddly, there are as many different chronologies as there are writers. In one chronology, Hu Yaobang dies on May 13, in another on May 15.

26. This description from *Ming Pao News*, 28. Numbers vary considerably from account to account.

27. J. W. Bowers and D. Ochs, *The Rhetoric of Agitation and Control* (Reading, Mass.: Addison-Wesley, 1971). The steps include: petition, promulgation, solidification, use of a flag issue, use of a flag individual, invention of derogatory jargon, nonviolent resistance, and escalation.

28. *Ming Pao News*, 35.

29. Ibid.

30. Cherrington, 151.

31. Ibid., 152.

32. *Ming Pao News*, 123.

33. Ibid., 128.

34. Ibid.

35. Ibid., 129-140.

36. Ibid., 140-143.

37. Ibid., 143.

38. "Rumours and the Truth," *Beijing Review*, 11-17 September 1989, 22.

39. Ibid., 23.

40. Ibid.

41. Ibid., 22.

42. Ibid., 24.

43. *Ming Pao News*, 153.

44. Fei Wang, *Objective Journalism or Propaganda: A Content Analysis*, 107.

45. I learned of the placement operation in our interview with Harbaugh and Tseu, Chief of the Mandarin Service, 28 April 1994, tape recording, Washington, D.C.

12

From Radio Free Asia to the Asia Pacific Network . . . and Back Again

Nancy Lynch Street

Case Study Nine

On 28 April 1994 the editors of this book, Matelski and Street, interviewed VOA administrators John Harbaugh and Betty Tseu at the VOA offices in Washington, D.C.[1] At this time, the bill to create Radio Free Asia (RFA) had been passed by the U.S. Senate. On 30 April 1994 President Clinton signed the bill, which contained, amongst other provisions, the removal of a cap on arms sales to Taiwan. According to the *New York Times International*, Mr. Clinton "signed the bill despite 'serious reservations' about provisions he said could interfere with his conduct of foreign policy."[2] In the pages that follow, the reader will see that the issues of RFA and Taiwan are indeed related and justify Mr. Clinton's objections as, given recent Chinese history, the Chinese government would find both provisions intrusive and offensive, if not confrontational. The excerpted interview with Harbaugh and Tseu, which follows, ranges over a broad spectrum of related issues regarding VOA, RFA (now designated the Asia Pacific Network--APN) and the evolving Chinese culture.

BT: Did you listen to the VOA in China?

NLS/MJM: Not very much--it usually didn't come in very well. I listened just enough to get a sense of what my students were listening to because many of them said that they listened to VOA [to practice their English].

JH: When were you there, Nancy?

NLS/MJM: I was there in 1985-1986 and again in 1988-1989. Not in the last three or four years, but a lot during the latter part of the eighties and in the summer of 1990. I taught English to juniors and seniors and those we called the "going aways." My college had begun an exchange program . . . in what was then a "closed" city--Linfen, Shanxi Province. I taught English, and my students had been taught, prior to 1982, by Chinese teachers only. . . . The English wasn't all that good. You know, American students will speak in class, whereas Chinese students who know everything will not say a word [thus, they learn to read and write English, but not to speak it well].[3]

In any event, that was when I became interested in VOA and listened to it. The contrast between RFE/RL and VOA interests me. . . . I do have some trouble with your tape [shown by the VOA guide prior to this interview], which asserts that 100 million Chinese listen to the program. I doubt seriously if that is true.

JH: I don't know either, I haven't heard the tape. Is that the one by Margaret Jaffe? And what is the statement, that 100 million Chinese . . . ? That might have been made in 1989 right after Tiananmen. I do think that listenership soared then, but as for right now, I'm sure we do not have any idea what the listenership might be.

BT: The fact is that there is no way to verify the number of listeners we have in China, and my personal experience has been that you find, when travelling in China, a sort of "underground." . . . That is, if there is any official connection, the number of people who admit they listen to VOA tends to be a lot smaller.

JH: Our own best guess, at least I will speak for myself here, but I have discussed it with others in the past, is that we probably have between 20 and 60 million listeners. The PRC journalist--when he arrived back in the United States after Tiananmen--said that an internal poll taken by the party on listenership had indicated that there were 60 million daily listeners to VOA in China. That would have been in the period just prior to Tiananmen.

NLS/MJM: That assumes that most everyone has access to a shortwave radio.

JH: A lot of people have shortwave radios because the China Central Radio Broadcast broadcasts shortwave and has for decades, which is why shortwave radio is spread throughout China. Only in recent years have they started to move toward AM and FM radio stations.[4]

BT: Also, the listenership fluctuates . . . depending on what is going on.

NLS/MJM: May I ask a question which occurred to me which is related to shortwave? As I understand the strategies of Radio Free Europe versus VOA, technically speaking, RFE/RL did quite a lot with shortwave, obviously pre-breakdown of the Soviet bloc, and so obviously did VOA, and it seems to me that there seemed to be separate strategies after that, meaning that I think that RFE/RL was thinking about actually getting transmitters, FM stations, FM frequencies, AM frequencies, whereas it seemed to me that VOA strategy [in Eastern Europe at least] was not so much to get the transmitters, but to negotiate with local FM stations or local AM stations to set segments of programming on. . . . Do I have a clear understanding of this?

JH: I can't speak for VOA in Europe, we are so compartmentalized.

NLS/MJM: I guess I am trying to ask you "What is the strategy?" with that as a backdrop. Shortwave is [technically] the worst service, although obviously a very, very useful mechanism, but, as things develop, not ideal for the signal strength and everything else. What is the strategy of the China Branch for strengthening signals? Are you still doing shortwave, are you planning to do anything about FM transmitters, and are you trying to gather affiliates [in China]?

JH: Right now, our only reliable vehicle [in the PRC] is shortwave. In Taiwan, in freer areas surrounding the PRC we have more options. In the PRC, shortwave will continue with ten hours of shortwave daily. We are pushing "placement" quite aggressively, placing with local radio stations around China. There is a good bit of interest in the PRC in this kind of placement, but the political reality does not permit them to be free and relaxed [the individual radio stations and the gatekeepers]--so often if our materials are used, they will be used in a disguised fashion, so that it is not obvious to authorities who do not appreciate the use of VOA materials by local radios.

NLS/MJM: Now when you say "disguised," one of the things that the tape asserted was that you clearly identify "this is it," [VOA materials]. . . . So how do you . . . ?

JH: We identify it, but they may take it out.

BT: Let me give you one example. We have a program that is distributed in China that is extremely popular which is called "American English." It is a five- or ten-minute program in English, teaching idioms, usage, and that sort of thing. It is done by a male and a female voice, the female is the Chinese announcer, and the male is American. When this program was placed in China, I found as a fact that they have edited them out, and just leave out the female announcers' voices and left the male voice in, and then they found another announcer to do it over again, and I have tapes that show me that this is our program . . . and they have done similar things to our other programs as well, in a similar fashion. In other words, where we send over the tapes, they always voice it again, and they sort of reword it.

JH: Without permission, which is OK with us, but we have to be very careful, there is a lot of interest in doing this sort of thing.

BT: It is not our intention . . .

JH: It is not our intention, no, but this is the political reality that they are working with, and so they will find ways to . . .

BT: In one case they referred to VOA as a "foreign friend". . . which supplied us with this material, so we are [become] the anonymous foreign friend.

NLS/MJM: It is an interesting policy difference. I would like to be clear what I am writing about; the policy is one thing, the fact is another.

JH: Well, right, what we provide them is the materials with the knowledge that there may have to be alterations in order to actually use the materials, and some stations will do that.

NLS/MJM: I understand that, but your published policy is that they cannot.

BT: That's right, that's right, and we are upset because of it, but the problem is that verification is very tough, because each and every station, when they broadcast, this time I just came back from a trip and found this out, and we were really upset over it, and the placement . . . but the problem is that we have admonished them, and told them that this is not the way again, but the problem is, how do we prove it? How do we prove it, because the station always comes back and says, "Oh, I am sorry, I am following your direction now." However, how do I always monitor them?

NLS/MJM: This is very interesting, because one wonders how much the VOA may have done during the Tiananmen Square uprising towards promoting [dissent]. The expressed view of RFE/RL is that [dissent] was their function in Eastern Europe and in the former Soviet Union. They were deliberately hiring exiles, living, say in Paris, like Branislaw,[5] to help put together their broadcast. They hoped that they would create from it dissent, and it sounds very much like there may have been a [similar] VOA input although that is not the expressed mission.

JH: There was no placement during Tiananmen, the placement operation did not, if you are speaking about that incident in particular, and how these materials might be reused in other ways by local radio stations. If that is what you are suggesting right now, we had no placement operation in 1989.

NLS/MJM: When did the placement operation begin?

JH: Last year. Placement is sending materials to radio stations, as opposed to direct broadcasting. What we did was to describe as well as we possibly could what was going on in China, and we reported news from here. However, Betty was in Tiananmen Square during the last week of May, and we had our English language correspondent in Beijing throughout that period. So we had a presence in Beijing during critical times, but of course, one person or two people cannot see everything that is going on, just as CNN could not see everything that was going on despite a big presence. In addition, we relied on CBS, NBC, CNN, and everyone else who was there. So what we are reporting back into China was what the foreign media were making available in Beijing at that time and to the rest of the world, plus folks like Betty and a few others who were in China to witness it themselves. So this is what we gave back to China, of what was going on. We did not go beyond that, but that is a tremendous amount of information and material. What we did prior to Tiananmen, and what we continue to do, is to try to provide insights and thoughtful information that will provoke people to think about issues [rather than] just accept what is being told to them, when everyone knows and they know too that they are only told what the Party wants them to know. So certainly we try to provoke peoples' minds. But VOA's policy and the Chinese branch policy has never been to incite rebellion. We want people to think about their lives, to think about their society, and to think about their systems. Then to have some sort of information so they can balance and measure what they are being told from their own official media. So that is our role and that is our function. But when it came to Tiananmen, our function and our role was to try to inform the Chinese people about what was going on as best we could, and to do that, we relied on very professional reporters.

NLS/MJM: Now in the future, there is Radio Free Asia, which, I understand, will have more of a surrogate function.

JH: It is designed by Joseph Biden certainly to be more of a surrogate operation, yes.

NLS/MJM: So how do you see that? Then you will still be China Branch, VOA? How is that going to work?

JH: Good question. The legislation hasn't been finalized, and until the legislation is finalized, we don't know what this is going to be.

NLS/MJM: Is it coming soon? In 1997? Are they talking about that in relation to Hong Kong, or . . . ?

JH: No, I think decisions, final decisions will be made much sooner than that, probably within the coming weeks. The legislation was first passed in the House, and then passed in the Senate, and has been in reconciliation committee for the last six weeks, approximately. I was told on Tuesday that the process has been completed. The early word . . . my understanding is that the status of Radio Free Asia as a separate grantee, such as RFE and RL, is not assured by the reconciliation compromise, so we don't know just what we are dealing with yet.

NLS/MJM: It is not assured . . . meaning?

JH: Who knows? That would depend in large part on what the appropriations committee does . . . and I know there are skeptics within the appropriations committee about the wisdom and necessity of Radio Free Asia. There is a lot more ground to cover before we know what we are dealing with.

NLS/MJM: So it would be a dissident service, as opposed to what you do.

BT: "Dissident service" depends on how you define dissidents. Do you mean dissidents within the United States, or do you mean the dissidents left in China? These are becoming two quite different groups. The Radio Free Asia project is immensely popular with the dissidents in the United States, because every one would be 120 percent for it, in fact many of them will probably take up writing or voicing, or special programs to voice their own views on democracy, and the movement.

NLS/MJM: The dissidents in exile.

BT: Yes. But meanwhile, in China, who are these people? Do people in China still recognize these people? Do they still feel in tune with these people? That is a very different question. In Beijing University there has been a vastly different atmosphere since Tiananmen. The new movement, according to some of the writings we have seen, has changed. Their tactics have changed, the goal has changed, the relationship with the labor movement and the peasants has changed.

NLS/MJM: Yes, I read just the other day. . . . It's the old Maoist strategy [take the countryside].

BT: At that time, maybe the peasants weren't ready, but now with the economic movement leaving such a huge gap in the incomes between those who have and those who have not, this condition might be more mature.

NLS/MJM: But also, so many of the dissidents tend to be the intellectuals who make 120 yuan a month, and peasant farmers can make more than that, and workers can make more than that, so the have nots [the "intellectuals," the students] need to align themselves.

BT: The workers, in particular, are the ones who are suffering, and that is a tremendous force to be reckoned with in China.

NLS/MJM: They are the individuals in China who live at the "bottom of society" and therefore they would have . . .

JH: They have been knocked out of the economic transformation, but the ideas and issues that are now generating so much dissatisfaction within China are not values like democracy, not values like freedom, but rather opportunity and pretty much economic opportunity. So the message that the dissidents in exile have carried does not have that much weight with so many of the people, the dissatisfied people. Not only that, [but] they left, and they lost, by simply leaving China, a lot of their moral authority.

NLS/MJM: And by staying out of China, I mean that most of the people whom I know who came back with me in 1986 and 1989 are still here doing a Ph.D. or postgraduate work, not knowing whether they can go back.

JH: But the leaders as well are here in the States, and by virtue of being here and safe (and we get this in our mail a lot from our listeners)--in fact I got a letter just last week which speaks exactly to this point--there is not much identification among the people in China, even those who are dissatisfied, with the leadership of the exile community here in the States, so we may be sending the wrong messages and speaking from the wrong platforms, even if it does go into operation.

NLS/MJM: How did the notion of Radio Free Asia begin? Was it begun or in some ways encouraged by these exiles in the United States?

JH: Certainly, certainly. Joseph Biden has been the driving force behind Radio Free Asia. Joseph Biden has been, of course, a strong supporter of surrogate radio [RFE/RL]. They are chartered in Delaware, there are personal connections between surrogate radio and Joseph Biden, and he has been the champion of Radio Free Asia all through the process.

NLS/MJM: The other issues that both of you raise are really significant, about what is journalism and if you have a dissident in the United States, who is safe, is that necessarily a surrogate speaking for people who can't speak? We tried to ask RFE this, and they [said only that] "we are journalists." We kept thinking, "Yes, but if you are basing this on people who clearly have a different slant, this seems like a significant question about the exiles and dissidents."

BT: We are in contact with just about everyone we can find in the exile community. We have a very good relationship with them, and we have followed their every action for the past five or six years, but not to the extent that we advocate their cause. We were very careful to screen whatever is news and whatever they would like us to tell people in China. That is very different. And also we have learned that many of these people would like us to do more. For example, Harry, when he was here, actively proposed a series of programs, ten to twenty programs that he would do himself based on his research, based on his interviews, and he would be the person who voices the whole thing. We were not quite ready for that kind of material, however you can be sure that if there is a Radio Free Asia, this will be the ideal kind of programming that Radio Free Asia will be having on the air. This is just one example.

NLS/MJM: Did the concept of Radio Free Asia begin after Tiananmen, or was it before that time?

JH: Now there is another [and this is speaking very personally].
Tape recorder is turned off here.

NLS/MJM: [recorder is running] My observation was that there were the family background disputes (intellectual backgrounds) always vying for power, and I wondered if you found that breakdown here, because based upon Chinese student observations . . .[6]

JH: What we have here is a very rigorous examination, a three-hour written translation and the standard of evaluations is very high, plus the voice test. Now this is an indirect answer to your question, but over the last four or five years we have had thousands of applicants here at VOA, and we have hired approximately 30 of them. And almost all of these applicants are graduate students from the PRC. So it is a very select group to begin with, and then it is winnowed down to a very, very few successful candidates, we have no idea who has applied until after they have successfully passed the exam, we never know who has applied, there are just numbers assigned, so it is a totally anonymous application process. The people who make it in are simply strong, highly skilled people, period. And it has nothing to do with background.

BT: We observed some of them, because we are careful in asking people's backgrounds. These people are still very sensitive. Anybody that went through the cultural revolution would not be as forthright, and others have struggled on their own and made it on their own.

JH: But very few of them, very few of the people that we have hired from the PRC began college after 1977 as that changed everything, so most of our people are post-1977. So it is not basically a political entry into the mainstream but rather an earned entry into the mainstream.

NLS/MJM: That is one aspect of the question. The other [aspect] is based upon whether some have the family, the university and the examinations. But they come from different backgrounds/families [due to the Cultural Revolution]. These quarrels don't die easily, they are part of the belief system.

JH: This is not a quarrel. They have gone through graduate programs here in the States before coming in here, and it is not a problem here. It may be a problem in China, but it is not a problem here.

NLS/MJM: That is what I am asking, because I know it is still a problem in China.

BT: When you compare this with the previous generation, the ones earlier, about ten to fifteen years earlier, when VOA had the difference that people who came from Taiwan and those who came from mainland China, the conflict between these two groups is a lot different than what you are talking about now, among PRC people themselves, because of their origin.

NLS/MJM: I am just saying that if you are in a university in China and you are working there, you soon get to know . . .

BT: Because where you come from and where you got to--where you are today-- really have no bearing as to how you get a promotion in VOA and how you work on your next report. It is irrelevant now. However, the older struggle between Taiwan and the PRC people in terminology, in ideology, in ways of living, even now may still be going on.

JH: It was sharp, very sharp, six or seven years ago it was still very sharp, but the PRC-Taiwan issue has now been pretty much decided, and the PRC side has held sway. It is not challenged any longer, it was challenged before. Our audience is in the PRC, we have to satisfy our audience, that is the guiding principle. That was hard for people from Taiwan to sign off on, but they know they lost that battle.

NLS/MJM: Let me ask a very general question, as there is not much time left. As you can imagine, we heard some great stories about what RFE/RL felt that federalization would do to them rather than for them. How has the legislation affected you? I have heard about cutbacks and such, how would you characterize the federalization?

JH: We don't know yet because we have not seen how it will impact us. The federalization actually of the Chinese broadcasting, speaking very parochially, the federalization move is really irrelevant to us. What matters to us is . . .

NLS/MJM: So you don't know what will happen in this?

JH: No, we have to see how this plays out, and we could be devastated, this operation that we have worked very, very hard to make strong could be devastated by this action. Perhaps it won't be, but we don't know.

BT: I have concerns for the new vigor and enthusiasm that we have in our reporting in recent years. The reason for this concern is because most of this new momentum came from our new recruits, these young, talented people that we have recruited and painstakingly trained afterwards. Now this continual cutting of the budget would probably impact on their future promotion. You see, most of these people have their green card now. They are free to leave and choose another job if they want to, so if the China branch does not get continued support for its personnel, then I am afraid we are going to lose some of these most talented people that we have.

JH: Now there is another aspect of federalization also, and that is that in theory, and I'm sure in fact, it will create a board of governors that will further remove us from USIA, which I think most people at VOA are very happy about. Now if we get a politically unbalanced board of governors, that could ultimately hurt our broadcasts, and I hope that does not happen. But if we have a politically well balanced board of governors, I like the fact, by virtue of this new [structure]. . . . USIA does not, in no way affects our programs, has no control over our programs, they have no idea what we are putting on the air. However, USIA does play and has played every year with the VOA budget, at viewer's expense, and I like very much that we are moving farther from USIA so that there can be less interference of this sort on our operations.

DISCUSSION: THE INTERVIEW AND RELATED ISSUES

The interview presented here, conducted in 1994, illustrates the commitment of the interviewees, Harbaugh and Tseu, and the Chinese Branch of VOA to continued shortwave broadcasts to China, in the wake of the ill-fated, VOA-named "Pro-Democracy" Movement in 1989. The ongoing debate in Congress regarding the creation of RFA/APN, in the face of China's anger over U.S. interference (if not overt agitation), particularly the reporting of VOA, demonstrates the single-minded commitment of the U.S. government to eradicate Communism from the face of the earth by any means possible. This time by forging yet another international shortwave radio service through the creation of RFA/APN to Asia, with China as a primary target audience.

Having been successful in discrediting the Chinese government in their handling of the student movement at Tiananmen, and perhaps in anticipation of yet another such movement in China, the U.S. seeks to strengthen and increase its presence amongst students and "intellectuals" in the PRC. Currently, VOA in China is once again regarded, with some reason, as an "enemy radio." Since Tiananmen, there have been several dissertation analyses of VOA's participation in the events of April, May, and June 1989, one by a staff member in VOA's Mandarin Service. Written by Chinese graduate students in the U.S. (presumably, in regard to Tiananmen, with the protesting students, rather than with the Chinese government), these dissertations nonetheless develop arguments that give weight to the view of VOA as not only an "enemy radio," but at critical times, a very erroneous voice, creating further chaos and misinformation.

At the time of the interview in Washington, D.C., the authors were not unaware of significant dissertation research utilizing textual content analysis, participant observation, interviewing, and statistical techniques designed to elicit information regarding VOA's involvement in reporting the events of Tiananmen from the inception of the movement on April 15 to its tragic conclusion on June 6. These analyses suggest that VOA's coverage of the student "pro-democracy" movement was aggressive and, at times, seriously misleading and mistaken as when, during the volatile atmosphere of the last days of the student "disturbance,"[7] VOA described the death toll as 1,400 killed, later raising it to 3,000--when in fact to this day no one knows the actual count.

Earlier in the student movement, on April 20, VOA (without known corroboration from other sources), "reported that 200 students were arrested after the clash between students and police."[8] Even more interesting is the characterization of the movement as a "democracy" movement. According to Zhou He in "The Role of the Chinese National News Media and the Voice of America in the 1989 Chinese Pro-Democracy Movement,"

the VOA basically depicted the students and their supporters as "peaceful" demonstrators who were staging a "pro-democracy" movement. They were motivated by a desire to push for reforms, democracy and freedom--ideas borrowed from the United States. As early as April 19, 1989, the VOA began to use the phrase "pro-democracy" to describe the demonstrations in Beijing.[9]

He asserts that it was VOA that characterized the movement as "pro-democracy." Later, he quotes Steve Snider (an officer with the VOA's Office of External Affairs) saying that "China saved VOA."[10] In describing the intensity of VOA's involvement in covering the Tiananmen Crisis, He says,

The VOA appeared to go all out to cover the Chinese movement. Despite the budgetary difficulties, it increased its Chinese staff from 41 to more than 70 during the movement. It expanded its Mandarin broadcasts by more than 25%, added frequencies and transmitters to counter jamming, used a one-million watt medium wave transmitter to reach the southern coast of China, opened telephone hotlines for its Chinese audience, and switched to all news programming during the peak of the movement.[11]

The information delivered was always supportive of the student demonstrators and, until martial law was declared, only mildly critical of the Chinese government. Nevertheless, at that time, VOA functioned under the influence of the USIA and its directives for public policy and diplomacy. In the late eighties, the U.S. and China were beginning to fall out after the honeymoon stage of the late seventies and early eighties, when China had begun its (very) gradual movement towards social and economic change--but not significant political change. In this stage, China did not move as quickly as the U.S. might have liked, nor did they move to dismantle Communism and adopt Western democracy. When the Soviet Union collapsed and the revolutions of the Eastern European countries had taken place, Washington apparently felt that the entire world should immediately embrace a totally free market economy and Western-style democracy.

Unlike the USSR and Eastern Europe however, China has (perhaps wisely) moved more slowly. Too slowly for the U.S. government. Thus, the issue arose in U.S. government/political circles of adding yet another incursive transnational media service into China. This time, the service was to be a surrogate service, functioning much like RFE/RL, utilizing only indigenous languages and, unlike VOA, not offering an English language service.

With the inclusion of RFA/APN in America's transnational voices, one can predict that, in the future, if Chinese students, intellectuals, workers, and some peasants should once again occupy Tiananmen Square and present a list of demands, that the combined groundwork efforts of VOA and APN might be enough (with the whole world listening and watching CNN) to seriously challenge the Chinese government, which is apparently the thrust of public diplomacy in the United States, though one does wonder which brand of authoritarianism might follow such an effort. Or, worse, the extent of the disorder, chaos, and desolation that might follow, as in the former USSR, which, due to its precipitous embrace of the free market and Western-style democracy, has been through a painful breakdown in public trust as the result of its ill-thought plunge into Western-style democracy and a "free market" economy without the necessary infrastructure to sustain such a shift, thus leading to social, economic, and political chaos in the nineties, not to mention the loss of hope for a decent life for many.

A culture must be ready for Western-style democracy--and the question must be asked, should non-Western countries be forced to adopt our form of democracy? Even in the West, there are many variations on democracy. In Scandinavia, for instance, there has been, until very recently, strict control of television programming, especially for children--because, as in other countries, among them China, the function of media in relation to the government and the culture is seen differently than in the United States. There are as many variations on "democracy" as there are countries who practice "democracy"--in the West and in the East.

Is there some legitimate rationale for forcing other countries to mimic or kowtow to the United States--and to pay dearly if they do not succumb to our threats and blandishments? Or, worse, any sane rationale for deliberately provoking and inciting others to rebellion--with no thought for our right (or not) to incite dissent and death (following a philosophy, which was deadly to the ancient Athenians of Plato's day, that "might makes right") and further forcing them to assume an ideology about which they know little or nothing?

For the Chinese students did not take to Tiananmen Square initially in pursuit of democratic freedoms, rather they were much more concerned with personal freedoms and economics (with living at the "bottom of society"),[12] which, contrary to the seemingly prevailing U.S. ideological belief system, are not synonymous with democracy. As Su Xiaokang says, "In fact, not many Chinese students and intellectuals, including me, knew much about democracy at that time."[13] Some American scholars have also written about this lack of understanding on the part of the Chinese students. As Joseph W. Esherick and Jeffrey N. Wasserstrom observe:

The Western press and Chinese dissidents abroad usually characterize the events of China's spring as a "democracy movement." There is no question that "*minzhu*" was frequently invoked in the protesters' banners and slogans, but it would be hasty to associate *minzhu* (literally: "rule of the people") with any conventional Western notion of democracy.[14]

Esherick and Wasserstrom offer the example of movement leader Wuer Kaixi in his televised dialogue with Li Peng on May 18. Explaining what it might take to remove the students from the Square, Kaixi says, "If one fasting classmate refuses to leave the square, the other thousands of fasting students on the square will not leave. . . . On the square, it is not a matter of the minority obeying the majority, but of 99.9 percent obeying 0.1 percent." Esherick and Wasserstrom comment that "this may have been good politics--and Wuer Kaixi certainly made powerful theater--but it was not democracy."[15]

RADIO FREE ASIA AND THE ASIA PACIFIC NETWORK

As we write the final draft of this book in June 1996, Radio Free Asia, now known as the Asia Pacific Network (APN), is not yet operational. Authorized by the U.S. Congress in the International Broadcasting Act of 1994, the Asia

Pacific Network was incorporated as a private corporation on March 11, 1996, after a thorough review and revision of the existing international broadcasting system of the United States. The new U.S. transnational news service's mandate "is to broadcast to China, Burma, Cambodia, Laos, North Korea and Vietnam. All programs will be in the language of the receiving country."[16] Programming to China will be in three languages: Mandarin, Cantonese, and Tibetan. Unlike VOA programming, there will be no English language programming.

Also unlike VOA, APN's purpose "is to provide accurate and timely information, news, and commentary about events in the designated countries and be a forum for a variety of opinions and voices from within Asian nations whose people lack adequate sources of information."[17] According to APN's president, Richard Richter, renaming the new voice Asia Pacific Network is "less confrontational than the Radio Free Asia name implies. We will not go out of our way to deliberately provoke these countries, nor engage in 'stick in the eye journalism.' There will be little world news, but news about each country."[18] Richter indicated that the new service "will subscribe to wire services and other publications on the fringes of these countries and will have bureaus." Bureaus will be located in Hong Kong and Bangkok with stringers throughout the area, for example, Katmandu. An attempt will be made to "follow the particular idiosyncrasies of each country [in programming decisions] and material will be couched in terms which are sensitive to the area."[19]

Richter further indicated that the transmitter sites had not yet been selected, though the Philippines is among many possibilities. The Foreign Relations Authorization Act, Fiscal Years 1994 and 1995 makes clear that "the conferees also expect that the State Department and the USIA will use their best efforts in seeking permission to use US transmission facilities overseas for Radio Free Asia Broadcasts."[20] In this report, the Committee of Conference

wishes to emphasize its expectation that Radio Free Asia will be a credible source of news and information about developments within the target countries and developments within the East Asian region. The committee of conference underscores that Radio Free Asia is not being created with the objective of broadcasting propaganda. Indeed, the committee of the conference expects Radio Free Asia to adopt appropriate editorial policies to ensure the highest professional standards.[21]

The Act also notes that cost and "technical issues" may prevent start-up of Radio Free Asia "in 1995 or thereafter."[22] There had been a considerable battle regarding RFA since the germination of the idea, most likely from Senator Biden and others who are strong supporters of surrogate radio, particularly RFE/RL, during the years described in the chapter "America's Voices," when RFE/RL and VOA had been threatened with the possiblity of extinction, due to the Fall of the Wall, the Eastern European revolutions, and the dissolution of the Soviet Union in 1989. Initially, the perception was that the Cold War was over, therefore there would be no further need of services such as RFE/RL to act as surrogate voices for "people who could not speak."

In "America's Voices" (Chapter 3) and in the interview with Radio Liberty's Director Kevin Klose, one senses that, despite the perceived triumph of the

West, post-Cold War trauma could endure. The Foreign Relations Authorization Act (FRAA) cited here, acknowledges that the initial reaction in the early 1990s was premature. Thus, Sec. 307, "International Broadcasting Bureau," creates the bureau to "carry out all nonmilitary international broadcasting activities supported by the United States Government other than those described in sections 308 and 309." The activities described in sections 308 and 309 are those of RFE/RL and RFA/APN.[23]

As originally formulated, RFE/RL and RFA/APN were linked in the new international broadcasting structure. Ultimately, the final Conference Report disengaged them, recognizing the difficulties that RFE/RL would face in developing a new site (Prague) and image in the former Soviet Union and in Eastern Europe and acknowledging that

the conference substitute removes from this section all references to Radio Free Asia. The committee of conference acknowledges the fundamental differences and challenges facing RFE/RL and Radio Free Asia. Tasking RFE/RL with the responsibility of overseeing the creation and management of a new surrogate broadcast service would be unwise since RFE/RL is undergoing a period of unprecedented consolidation and reorganization of its own operations. The committee of conference also recognizes the need for Radio Free Asia to be allowed maximum flexibility to create and implement appropriate broadcast services for the Asian continent.[24]

The committee made further restrictions on RFA's (APN's) charter, limiting its budget to $22 million each year, authorizing $8 million in start-up costs, and established RFA as an independent grantee, not tied to RFE/RL.[25] Further, the language of the committee's revisions agrees with that of Richard Richter, in its expectations of the content to be broadcast through RFA/APN, stating that

Radio Free Asia will be a credible source of news and information about developments within the target countries and developments within the East region . . . not being created with the objective of broadcasting propaganda. Indeed, the committee of conference expects Radio Free Asia to adopt appropriate editorial policies to ensure the highest professional standards."[26]

According to the APN handout provided by President Richard Richter, APN's staff "will consist overwhelmingly of native speakers of the language broadcast." Currently, the network is searching for staff, prior to its initial broadcasts to China in August 1996.

ASIA PACIFIC NETWORK PERSONNEL

At start-up of the new service, the personnel chosen thus far have impressive journalism credentials. President Richard Richter has more than 25 years' experience with CBS, ABC, and public television as a TV News producer. Vice President of Programming and Executive Editor Daniel Southerland has been a "correspondent in China and South East Asia for 18 years with the *Washington*

Post, Christian Science Monitor and UPI." Craig Perry, who has "some 20 years experience in radio, film and television administration and production," is Vice President, Management and Administration. Chief Financial Officer Patrick Taylor has "more than 20 years experience in financial management in the private sector." The Mandarin Service Chief is Liu Yuan, a free-lance television producer and a doctoral candidate in anthropology at Brandeis. "Born in Beijing, suffered permanent injury during the Cultural Revolution." Liu Yuan is producing *Red Guards*, a documenatry series in development for PBS. Tibetan Service chief Jigme Ngapo was "born in Tibet and educated in China." He "most recently worked for the International Campaign for Tibet" and is known for "even-handed objectivity." David Baden is a "veteran of 12 years service with Radio Free Europe/Radio Liberty" and was instrumental in "bringing the Prague headquarters up to broadcast capability after the move from Munich."[27]

SCHEDULE FOR APN ON-AIR

*July 15: Temporary studio operative at 1201 Connecticut Ave., N.W.

*September 1: Tentative date first broadcast. Two hours in Mandarin. From temporary studio and RFE/RL studio in same building.

*October 1: Move into permanent headquarters, 2025 M St., N.W., former home of National Public Radio. (Date dependent on prompt approval of building plans by D.C. government.)

*October 15-January 15: Start broadcasts of other language services on incremental basis. Tibetan, Burmese, Cantonese, Vietnamese, North Korean, Khmer (Cambodia), and Laos. Mandarin 5 1/2 hours, Cantonese and Vietnamese 2 hours, the others 1 hour a day.[28]

ETHICAL APPROACH TO BROADCASTING

According to the "Foreign Relations Authorization Act," Radio Free Asia will "(1) provide accurate and timely information, news and commentary about events in the respective countries of Asia and elsewhere; and (2) be a forum for a variety of opinions and voices from within Asian nations whose people do not fully enjoy freedom of expression."[29] All programming, according to the APN handout provided by Richter, will originate in Washington, D.C., "incorporating reports from correspondents and participants throughout Asia."[30] What this suggests is that, like RFE/RL, APN will use native Asian language speakers living in the United States to help create news broadcasts and commentary. As noted in the interview with Harbaugh and Tseu of VOA, there are various groups of dissidents--and each has its own agenda. Because all APN broadcasts will be in the indigenous language--for example, Mandarin for most of China--it will be difficult, if not impossible, for the interested observer (American scholar, journalist, or citizen) to ascertain just what is being broadcast into China (or on any other service) at any given point in time. The U.S. International Broadcasting Act of 1994 (PL 103-236, Title III) declares:

The continuation of existing United States international broadcasting, and the creation of a new broadcasting service to the people of the People's Republic of China and other countries of Asia which lack adequate sources of free information and ideas, would enhance the promotion of information and ideas, while advancing the goals of United States foreign policy.[31]

Despite its status as a surrogate broadcaster, forbidden to indulge in propaganda, the Asia Pacific Network is also obliged to advance "the goals of United States foreign policy." Although standing alone, APN, despite the best of journalistic intentions and ethics, may find that it's message is necessarily coupled with that of VOA, particularly in times of stress, given the current stance of the United States vis-à-vis China. The gaze (perception) of the other (the Asian audience) is just as important as the perception of the service of itself--and these perceptions may be altered by (among other elements) the presence of the VOA. In addition, one has to assume--given APN's mandate--that American ideology, the Clinton administration's policy, organizational self-interest, and American journalistic norms will further skew the message, the mandate, and journalistic ethics. However, Richter maintains that he and his staff are determined to see that this does not happen. In the world of transnational radio, by its very nature, Western journalistic integrity and "objectivity" may be difficult, if not impossible, to maintain.

Author's note: In late September 1996, RFA/APN did go on the air--as Radio Free Asia. Controversy over the name of the network and its implications continued almost up to broadcast time. Excerpts from the following news release (obtained via the Internet) describe the last few hours of the Asia Pacific Network before it reverted back to Radio Free Asia:

LAT 30/9/96

Washington--Over the weekend, America took a little-noticed but far-reaching step in its policy toward Asia--one that is likely to arouse the ire of China, Myanmar (Burma) and other repressive governments.

Radio Free Asia went on the air.

. . . In the week before its initial broadcast, the radio service suffered its way through one more bruising Washington political battle--a final reminder of how contentious the creation of Radio Free Asia has been.

The directors of the station had wanted to broadcast under a different name: the Asia Pacific Network. They figured that this name might have a less combative ring than Radio Free Asia, which evokes memories of the fiercely anti-communist role that Radio Free Europe played during the ideological struggles with the Soviet Union.

Some Republican leaders on Capitol Hill did not like the name change. "We must have the courage to confront tyranny, and to do so under the banner of freedom," thundered Rep. Christopher H. Smith (R-N.J.) at a congressional hearing.

Finally, the Republicans' heaviest hitter, Senate Foreign Relations Committee Chairman Jesse Helms (R-N.C.), insisted that the name be changed back to Radio Free Asia before the service went on the air.

. . . "It was, by statute, named Radio Free Asia for a purpose," explained Marc Thiessen, a spokesman for Helms. "It was supposed to confront totalitarian ideology in Asia, the same way Radio Free Europe and Radio Liberty combated totalitarian rule in Eastern Europe and the Soviet Union."

And so, last Wednesday, the service returned to its maiden name. Asia Pacific Network became Radio Free Asia once again. "We were instructed to change the name back," Richard Richter, president of the service, said in an interview, making it plain that this wasn't his own choice.[32]

Such are the vagaries of life in an overwrought democracy.

NOTES

1. John Harbaugh, Special Assistant of Voice of America, Chinese Branch, VOA and Betty Tseu, Chief, Mandarin Service, Chinese Branch, VOA, interview by authors, 28 April 1994, tape recording, Washington, D.C.

2. *New York Times International*, Sunday, 1 May 1994, p. 8.

3. This classroom behavior is standard in Chinese classrooms where the student is discouraged from voicing opinions or asking questions, or doing public speaking, as indicated in Chapter 11. Persons who speak up are considered "forward" and are not well-regarded by their peers. This was, at least, the case as late as 1989 in university classrooms in Shanxi Province, PRC.

4. In 1988, Chinese work units in the provinces also relied heavily on the wired speaker concept, that is, news and music via the extensive public speaker system installed throughout the unit. For instance, I had a speaker just outside my door, which, with music and news, regulated the day in the work unit.

5. We met with Bronislaw Wildstein in July of 1993 in Krakow, Poland. Prior to the end of the Cold War, Wildstein was a stringer for RFE/RL living in Paris. With the success of the Solidarity Movement, Wildstein returned to Krakow as Director of Radio Krakow, his years as a dissident-in-exile ended.

6. Here Street was alluding to the observations made by colleagues and students in China and documented in her book, *In Search of Red Buddha* (New York: Peter Lang Publishing Co., Ltd., 1992), 217-226. Without a common understanding of the tensions then existing between "good family background" and "bad family background" intellectuals, this issue, in my opinion vital to understanding Tiananmen, could not be further addressed. The subsequent discussion does not focus on this issue, but on the issue of dissidents within VOA's service, those dissidents in the U.S. and the dissidents in China--also relevant issues.

7. Chinese government's euphemism for what the world's news services, in particular, describe as the "Tiananmen Massacre."

8.   See Zhou He, "The Role of the Chinese National News Media and the Voice of America in the 1989 Chinese Pro-Democracy Movement," (Diss. Indiana University, 1992), 291.   Here Zhou He references VOA story CN-3, 1:52 p.m., 20 April 1989.

9.   Ibid., 302.

10.   Ibid., 317.

11.   Ibid., 315-316. From interviews with Hess, Carlson, and Trescott.

12.   See Street, *In Search of Red Buddha*, 205-219.

13.   Zhou He, "The Role of the Chinese National News Media," 338.

14.   Ibid., 338-339. Zhou He is quoting Joseph W. Esherick and Jeffrey N. Wasserstrom, "Acting Out Democracy: Political Theatre in Modern China," *The Journal of Asian Studies* 49 (November 1990), 834.

15.   Ibid.

16.   Handout obtained from Richard Richter, President, Asia Pacific Network, Washington, D.C., n.d.

17.   Ibid.

18.   Richard Richter, President, Asia Pacific Network, telephone interview by Street,   14 June 1996, Boston/Washington, D.C.

19.   Ibid.

20.   "The Conference Report (to accompany H.R. 2333) of the Foreign Relations Authorization Act, Fiscal Years 1994 and 1995, "25 April 1994, 208.

21.   Ibid.

22.   Ibid.

23.   Ibid., 58-63.

24.   Ibid., 206.

25.   Ibid., 207.

26.   Ibid., 208.

27.   APN Status Report, 13 June 1996.

28.   Ibid.

29.   The Conference Report, 61.

30.   Handout, Richard Richter, 2.

31.   Press Release, Broadcasting Board of Governors, 14 March 1996, citing the U.S. International Broadcasting Act of 1994, Section 302 (4).

32.   "Radio Free Asia Becoms a Reality;" sent by Kim Nguyen 1 October 1996, available from newsgroup ott.vietnamese, organization emr.

Epilogue

The Sacred and the Secular: Transnational Radio in the Twentieth Century

Marilyn J. Matelski and Nancy Lynch Street

THE MANDATE FOR TRANSNATIONAL RADIO

As noted earlier, G. K. Chesterton observed, in reference to radio, "I think it probable that centuries will pass before it is seen clearly and in its right perspective; and that then it will be seen as one of the turning-points in the whole history of England and the world."[1] Certainly Marconi's contributions to developing transnational radio and its initiation through Vatican Radio in 1931 forged a new weapon in the fierce and ongoing battle for the hearts and minds of the people on this planet in the twentieth century. Transcending space and time, international radio has been, and continues to be, instrumental in facilitating seemingly unlikely alliances, reminiscent of the medieval coalitions between Church and State.

The Russian Revolution of 1917, viewed by some scholars as the beginning of the Cold War (briefly interrupted by fighting fascism in World War II), initiated efforts on the part of the Pope and the Vatican, as well as Western heads of state, to curtail the spread of communism as the primary competing ideology to capitalism (often erroneously identified with democracy). In this century, the "world" was carved, through political and economic alliances, into what came to be known as: the First World (Western Europe and North America); the Second World (the USSR and Eastern Europe); and, the Third World (Asia, Africa, and South America).[2] Transnational radio became a tactical tool to propagate the faith (or in its negative version, propaganda)[3] which ultimately, as in its 1980s "Star Wars" and "Evil Empire" incarnations in the West, seemingly ended in an alliance between the sacred and the secular (between the Vatican, the U.S. and perhaps Great Britain), a quiet agreement between Pope and President, Church and State, to bring down communism before the twenty-first century.

As promised in the introduction to this book, the authors have focused here on (1) Vatican Radio and Radio Veritas; (2) the British Broadcasting Corporation; and (3) the United States' radios: VOA, RFE/RL, Radio Marti, and the newly created Radio Free Asia/Asia Pacific Network. Much of the broadcasting of each of these transnational services has been (and is) directed to: communist nations, such as China and Castro's Cuba; formerly communist unions, such as the USSR; and, other nations in Africa, Asia, and Latin America, where, due in part to repressive authoritarian governments (which are often supported by the United States government) revolutionaries are feared to be "easy prey" for communism. These revolutionaries might also look to the PRC for leadership.

Thus--contrary to U.S. "democratic" principles and its own revolutionary beginnings against the "tyranny" of King George--in order to suppress communism, the U.S. government often supports, through its transnational radio services and other means, repressive regimes, aiding in the suppression of revolutionary movements to preserve and extend its hegemony in the West. It appears, however, that to extend its hegemony in the East (e. g., beyond Taiwan and South Korea), the U.S. government takes the opposite tack--supporting and inciting social movements calling for radical change, perhaps in the hope of creating civil war in China, thus breaking the back of the emerging dragon.

With China emerging as a major world power in the twenty-first century, new and increased emphasis is placed on eradicating communism in Asia. The desire to accomplish this task is not, and has not been, a purely ideological one. Rather, it is a case of who shall have power--military, political, and economic power--superpower. If, for instance, it were possible to incite further incidents in the PRC, even to aid in the inception of a civil war, then China might be ripe for dividing (as in North and South Korea), thus weakening her and negating her potential as a major player in the global political arena and economy in the twenty-first century.[4]

Zhou He, in his analysis of the role of media at Tiananmen, says that on 6 June 1996 VOA broadcast the following story: "The official Chinese media indicate a hardline politburo member may have taken over the leadership of the Chinese Communist Party. . . . US officials say China's top leaders may have fled Beijing, which has been in turmoil since the army's weekend massacre in Beijing."[5] In response to Zhou He's questions concerning these and other errors in reporting by VOA during the Tiananmen crisis, one VOA staffer replied, "We never say the VOA never made a mistake. It would be pretty silly to think we never made one mistake. After all, we were some 8,000 miles away. Things were happening so fast. . . . When the shooting started, it was very easy to be carried away."[6] Zhou He attributes being "carried away" to the "fluid and chaotic nature of the 1989 Chinese movement, partly from the censorship by the Chinese government and partly from the VOA's reliance on the Western media."[7]

At Tiananmen, there were more than a thousand journalists from all over the world and many forms of media impacting an extremely volatile situation--a standoff between students and government that ended in bloodshed. If the VOA is committed to integrity and to Western journalistic ethics and yet one attributes its errors to, in part, "reliance on Western media," then what is one to think of Western media and "journalistic ethics," particularly when they are most needed-- during times of crisis? If transnational radio is to maintain integrity, it must strive to maintain objectivity. Yet, many of the case studies included in this book indicate that the focus of transnational radios (whether surrogate radio or radio that is the voice of the government) may be to encourage and invite, if not incite, the very dissent that they then report on, as seemingly happened at

Tiananmen--hardly an "objective" stance, nor consistent with Western journalistic ethics. At Tiananmen, the "errors" may have been strategic--just another dimension of public diplomacy and policy--and more protesters may have died as a result.

Further, just as the Western powers are finally leaving the last outposts of nineteenth-century Western imperialism (e.g., Hong Kong), this exit could be averted and Western hegemony--forged through a coalition of Christianity, capitalism, and Western-style democracy--could be spread not only throughout China but also throughout the rest of Asia. At first, as in previous and similar circumstances, people would be "free" and the hallowed sign of democracy--free elections--instituted. In 1996 the prime example is that of Russia and its presidential election. In this case, with the formerly communist Russia in social, political, and economic turmoil, the U.S.-supported and financed Boris Yeltsin may be president, he says, "even if he loses."[8] Ridding the world of communism is not really the point. If, for instance, China can be infiltrated and get caught up in civil war, and/or be divided into North and South,[9] she will not be able to emerge as a major player in the twenty-first century. Anything is possible. Things are not what they seem. The Cold War is heating up in the East.

Thus, Vatican Radio, the VOA, the BBC, and the RFA/APN transmitters are now trained on Asia, all have satellite capability and all agree on the mission. Success in creating dissent, as in Poland's Solidarity movement and the other Eastern European revolutions, within Asia and especially China, requires a coalition. The following discussion and analysis are developed first along those divisions and inferences drawn from the coalition--driven by both secular and sacred motivations--of the voices of three distinct sovereign entities: the Vatican, Great Britain, and the United States.

BACK TO THE PAST

The transnational radios have influenced a wide variety of crisis situations around the world since their inception. Prior to World War II, Vatican Radio provided a "lifeline" to a besieged Vatican. In the eighties, Pope John Paul forged an alliance between the Vatican and the Solidarity Movement utilizing Vatican Radio in the movement's struggle against the USSR in Poland. Radio Veritas may or may not have been instrumental in overthrowing the Marcos regime in the Phillipines. As John Michalczyk suggests ("'The Dice are on the Carpet': The BBC and the French Resistance in World War") the BBC's directives beginning in 1942 helped to create a strong resistance, a demonstrably active social movement in France during the German occupation, reliable in providing "honest and balanced" information and in the final days acted as "an indispensable instrument of *action*." Though the BBC dealt in propaganda, as did Radio-Paris and Radio-Vichy, it did so in the best interests of France. Thus, its propaganda may be characterized as for the "good," helping to "change the course of world events," or, defeat Germany and its allies, thereby ensuring the triumph of the West in what was already perceived to be a struggle between the powers of good and evil, though the vision was not yet well-articulated. If fascism could be stopped, could communism be far behind?

During World War II, the Allied and Axis forces both used transnational radio. On February 24, 1942, the VOA entered into the existing mix of the European transnational systems (e.g., the BBC, Vatican Radio, Deutsche Welle, and Radio Moscow). With the aid of the BBC and by capturing shortwave transmitters, VOA was soon broadcasting 24 hours a day in 27 languages. From its inception, however, VOA was engaged in psychological warfare and became "an instrument of war--a judicious mixture of rumor and deception with truth as bait, to foster disunity and confusion in support of military operations"--a position from which, some would argue, they have not deviated, but have carried over into other contexts.

Other contexts, such as the containment of the Soviet Union following World War II, prompted the United States in 1951 to create yet another transnational radio, RFE, and later, RL-- under the aegis of the CIA. Director Kevin Klose, in the interview in Chapter 9 points out that RFE/RL merged in the 1970s "when the CIA's funding of the two organizations became a political issue in the United States," resulting in the founding of the Board of International Broadcasting (BIB). RFE/RL were surrogate broadcasters and private organizations, unlike VOA, which was under the banner of the USIA. However, both VOA and RFE/RL, regardless of their status vis-à-vis the United States government, were meant to be weapons in the rapidly accelerating Cold War--the struggle (some had thought "to the death"--an Armageddon if you will) between "godless" communism and the Christian/capitalist coalition.

The Cold War rhetorical vision and/or fantasy captured the imagination of the West. In turn, the United States government, and its people, devoted its twentieth-century presence and resources toward the elimination of communism from the globe, often making strange alliances and supporting conservative and/or authoritarian governments in its single-minded devotion to the Cold War rhetorical vision through unfettered defense and military spending. The desire for U.S. hegemony in the political and military spheres undermined its civilian economy in the 1980's even while making Cold War Warriors of us all--the twentieth-century version of a medieval crusade. As Alex Callinicos says in *The Revenge of History: Marxism and the East European Revolutions*,

There was thus a kind of symbiosis between American politico-military hegemony and the economic rise of Japan and Western Europe. This led to a growing level of tension between the US and its allies--over trade, nuclear strategy, relations with the Eastern bloc--but at the same time tended to stabilize the situation. . . . Washington's response to the signs of its decline--most dramatically evident in the US defeat in Vietnam and the wave of Third World revolutions during the 1970s culminating in the victory of the Sandinistas in Nicaragua--was significantly to increase defence spending and more generally to assert its global political role, a process begun under the Carter administration but continued with gusto by Ronald Reagan. . . . If the world was evidently by the 1980s economically multipolar, politically it was still bipolar. But the East European revolutions looked set to change all that.[10]

"All that" meant a great deal.   With the Soviet Union virtually toothless and impoverished after years of Cold War, following the revolutions in Eastern Europe and the dissolution of the Soviet Union, an economically troubled United States emerged as the single superpower. Or, as Andre Gunder Frank observed (8 April 1990), "The Cold War is over. Japan and Germany won it," in reference to the disheveled "end state" of both the USSR and the United States and described by Callinicos as "superpowers come down in the world."[11] With the Cold War at an end, and the economy in decline, the United States government turned its attention to--more war.

In the eighties, the U.S., under the "Reagan Doctrine," had supported authoritarian governments in the Third World, containing revolutionary challenges (such as those posed by the liberation theologians in South America and discussed in Chapter 1). Callinicos notes that Washington adopted "what Fred Halliday calls 'a policy of counter-revolution on the cheap,' . . . involving especially the promotion of right-wing guerilla movements against various Moscow-aligned regimes (Nicaragua, Angola, Cambodia, Afghanistan)."[12]   In December 1989, following the East German and Czechoslovak revolutions, the Bush administration gave the nation a surprise holiday gift through the successful invasion of Panama, terminating in the deaths of an estimated 3,000 civilians, although some put the figure as high as 7,000 civilian deaths.[13] The Noriega-Panama invasion was followed by the invasion of Kuwait by Iraq in August 1990, leading to the U.S. made-for-television war--the Gulf War. Clearly, the "end" of the Cold War had ushered in a new era of war and power alignments.   Thus, when the Congress began to debate the feasibility of curtailing and/or merging the various American transnational radios, at issue was the need for public diplomacy carried out under the aegis of the USIA, through the VOA, or, the necessity of the continuance of RFE (RL would continue). Also at issue in the debate was the need for yet another radio--Radio Free Asia, ardently championed by Senator Biden (see Chapter 12) as a surrogate operation, similar to RFE/RL. In June 1996, President Richard Richter indicated that he conceptualized the Asia Pacific Network (later renamed Radio Free Asia--see Chapter 12) as similar to National Public Radio in the United States, that is, unlike VOA, a nonconfrontational source of information, news, and cultural transmission to the nations of Asia not yet perceived to be free: Burma, North Korea, Vietnam, Laos, Cambodia, and China.[14]

VATICAN RADIO AND RADIO VERITAS

Given the origins of the power basis of the Catholic Church,[15] which go back to antiquity in the oneness of church and state/Emperor and God (through the Roman and Byzantine empires to the rebellion of England's Henry VIII against the Pope's authority),[16] it is not surprising that Pope John Paul II should seek to free Poland. As Marilyn J. Matelski notes (in "The Scepter and the Sickle: Vatican Radio and the Solidarity Movement"), "Shortly after his election in 1978, he announced plans to revisit his homeland; and for the next decade, he used any means possible--either public or underground--to influence Poland's political future." The former Karol Wojtyla, born to Polish peasants, saw no contradiction in inviting the then-leader of Poland's Solidarity movement, Lech Walesa, to the Vatican to discuss strategy. The strategy, developed first by Cardinal Wyszinski and the Soviet Union in 1950, emphasized the alignment of power between the Polish Church and the Polish State. A part of John Paul II's strategy was the use of Vatican Radio for religious and political purposes. In the early 1980s, according to Carl Bernstein, John Paul II joined forces with Ronald Reagan.

Though John Paul II appears to have been totally committed to overthrowing Communist rule in Poland, he and/or the Church hierarchy apparently did not follow the same unswervingly righteous path in the case of the 1986 Philippine "People Power Revolution," discussed in Miguel Quiachon Rapatan's case study (Chapter 5). In this study, Rapatan says that despite the perception of Radio Veritas's "active appropriation, articulation, and amplification of a rhetorical vision . . . this vision was not consistently pursued or realized by the station, especially in the moments when access to the station's facilities became a matter of life or death." Rapatan attributes this lack of commitment to dissension in the Curia and to possible "moral and political repercussions of its cooperation with the revolution." Once again we have a conundrum--the Church voice and the voice of the people silenced (through transmitters going down at propitious moments, e. g., the declaration of martial law on September 21, 1972, by President Ferdinand Marcos). DZRV does not resume broadcasting until March 1976, and martial law is not lifted by Marcos until 1981. Following the lifting of martial law, DZRV signs off the air on February 23, 1986, and Marcos leaves on February 25, 1986. One day before, the facilities are used by June Keithley who is identified as DZRB for Radyo Bandido, the Rebel Station. Again, the covert interplay of the sacred with the secular--and perhaps with a Washington political scene that was also unsure which way to swing, Washington having supported Marcos for so long in the Philippines, as well as having been a strong, conservative presence there.

To Washington and the Vatican (and hence Radio Veritas) the "People's Revolution" must have been anathema, portending more communism on the Pacific Rim, to a government and a church steeped in fantastical, at times fanatical Cold War rhetoric. In the Reagan era, we perceive the alliances referred to in Bernstein's observations regarding the relationship between the Vatican and Washington. In addition, Presidents Reagan and Bush each forged strong alliances with Margaret Thatcher and England. We have reached the crux of the argument. Despite the protestations of "objectivity" of the various radios, each of them and their governments, especially in the 1980s, had, as we have shown, strong personal and political ties with one another, as well as a commitment to destroy communism and emerge victorious from the Cold War. During much of the Reagan-Bush era (RFE/RL, VOA, Radio Marti), Margaret Thatcher was Prime Minister of England (BBC). John Paul II's (Vatican Radio and Radio Veritas) tenure spans that of Reagan and Bush, into the Clinton era (VOA, RFE/RL, Radio Marti, and RFA/APN). Oddly, in the allegedly post Cold War era, the U.S. supports more, not fewer, surrogate radios.

Within the parameters of many of the themes discussed within this book, the
1980s, from the declaration of martial law in Poland in 1981, to the declaration
of Martial Law in China at Tiananmen on May 20, 1989, was a confusing
decade. Under that confusion, however, lay common purpose, and with the Fall
of the Wall, the revolutions in Eastern Europe, and the dissolution of the Soviet
Union, the world seemingly came to the end of an era. The West did not,
however, succeed in eradicating communism. The Cold War is heating up in the
East.

THE BBC

The BBC *persona* is recognized around the world. In World War II, as
described in Chapter 2, the BBC, "especially in German-occupied territory . . .
was regarded as the most dependable source of news about the war." It also
worked at bringing the then-isolationist America into the war. Some
transnational experts say that the BBC "enjoys probably the best reputation in
the world for its transnational radio service." In 1996, through National Public
Radio (NPR), Americans can listen to the World Service--unlike VOA, which
cannot be transmitted to the United States. Thus, relatively few Americans are
aware of VOA or the content of its broadcasts. However, as seen in the
interview with VOA's Elliott, the BBC has become a model for transnational
broadcasting in its organizational structure as well as for its content. It did,
however, play a large part with its colleagues (VOA, RFE/RL, and VR) in the
Cold War. As Natalie Doyle-Hennin observes,

Unlike the Voice of America, the BBC produce[d] no official editorial commentary on
behalf of the British government. Rather, commentaries [were] solicited from outside
the organization in order to conserve the BBC's self-imposed role of objective
observer and reporter of world events.[17]

Other observers tend to agree with the objectivity of BBC reports. Even so, the
BBC apparently realizes that its reporting is not apolitical. Doyle-Hennin
reports that a Director General of the BBC, Sir Charles Curran, says
"broadcasting to other countries is, primarily, about politics, and even when it
isn't directly about politics, then it is about the background to politics, the life
of the country, the way we think, the way we behave, the way we look at other
peoples."[18]

With regard to the impact of government foreign policy on programming,
Doyle-Hennin also observes that the BBC's coverage of human rights differs
qualitatively and quantitatively from that of the VOA and Radio Moscow. She
says, "Unlike VOA and RM reports, the BBC's news accounts involving human
rights have no obviously apparent foreign policy agenda. They appear as
straightforward hard news accounts."[19] Doyle-Hennin's account concludes with
the observation that whereas "human rights is a distinctly political subject in the
news texts" for VOA and RM, the BBC reports from a more "neutral stance."[20]
This also appeared to be the case in the BBC coverage of the Tiananmen crisis.
Because the BBC is distanced from government and because it speaks with one

voice rather than a tangle of voices coupled with the distinct pull of U.S. policies and foreign policy agenda(s), it at least appears to be more "objective," if it is in fact not more "objective" in its outlook than other transnational radios. In addition, the BBC has long had its own research institute; until the creation of the RFE/RL Research Institute, the BBC conducted whatever audience research was possible during the pre-Fall of the Wall Cold War era for many of the transnational radio systems, including those of the U.S.

Further, the remarks of the former Director-General of the BBC, Sir Charles Curran, seem to indicate that the BBC is under few illusions as to the nature of the BBC's mission, and within that perspective the BBC may be viewed as relatively "objective."

AMERICA'S VOICES

From the foregoing discussion, one sees that the U.S., under President Clinton, has recently added to, not reduced its voices. Under the recently crafted Foreign Relations Authorization Act, Fiscal Years 1994 and 1995, the Board of International Broadcasting has been replaced with a nine member Board of Governors, with the Director of the USIA as a constant member. No more than four members of the board may be of the same political party and the term of office for each will be "for three years, except the Director of USIA who shall remain a member for his or her term of service."[21] In addition to the Board of Governors, the Senate amendment to the House bill provides for an International Broadcasting Bureau "within USIA to include the following elements: VOA, Office of Surrogate Broadcasting, Worldnet Television and Film Service, Engineering and Technical operations and other elements established by the Director of International Broadcasting in concurrence with the Director of USIA."[22] Sections 308 and 309 of the Act explicitly refer to both RFE/RL and APN as surrogate broadcasters, not under the control of the International Broadcasting Bureau. However, the Board of Directors for RFE/RL "shall consist of the members of the Broadcasting Board of Governors . . . and no other members."[23]

The creation of Radio Free Asia/Asia Pacific Network is in the hands of the Congress and the Board and the USIA. The Act provides that "No grant may be awarded to carry out this section [Radio Free Asia], unless the Board, through the Director of the United States Information Agency, has submitted to Congress a detailed plan."[24] Thus, in the newly restructured U.S. international broadcasting system, though Radio Free Asia/the Asia Pacific Network is, in theory, not under (or subject to) the public diplomacy considerations of the U.S. government, as promulgated and overseen by the United States Information Agency, nevertheless, it is to be, at least in part, created by this agency.

As illustrated in Chapters 11 and 12, the USIA serves as a gatekeeper at Voice of America. In the arguments presented here, we have presented the proposition that journalistic integrity cannot be maintained when government interferes. From the structure of U.S. international broadcasting as outlined in the Foreign Relations Authorization Act, Fiscal Years 1994 and 1995, the USIA will continue to give oversight to America's radios, to greater or lesser degree, through its continuing presence on the Board, as well as its apparently direct involvement in the creation of the Asia Pacific Network. Further, RFA/APN must "be located within the metropolitan area of Washington, D.C.,"[25] and use the transmitters of the U.S. government (to be determined, perhaps Tinian Island, perhaps the Philippines, or other).

RFE/RL, on the other hand, has managed to elude the direct oversight of the USIA (one of its earlier goals) and was successful in persuading the Congress of the need to be in Europe. Thus, RFE/RL was permitted to move to Prague, rather than be remanded to Washington, D.C. and the direct, physical oversight and direction of the USIA. Further, Section 312 of the Act provides for the privatization of RFE/RL "not later than December 31, 1999, and that the funding of Radio Free Europe and Radio Liberty Research Institute should be assumed by the private sector at the earliest possible time."[26] RFE/RL may yet retain its journalistic integrity.

Despite the long and heated deliberations over the fate and design of U.S. international broadcasting in this seemingly post-Cold War era, the U.S. ultimately chose to ignore the BBC unitary model for transnational radio and opt for what Kim Elliott describes as "more of a Soviet central planning model."[27] Which, as we noted at the time, is "kind of ironic."

CONCLUSION

As demonstrated here, transnational radio has had impact around the world, for good or for ill. In the services discussed here--Vatican Radio, Radio Veritas, the BBC, the VOA, RFE/RL, and the newly created Radio Free Asia/Asia Pacific Network--not only is the nature of journalism an important issue but also the means by which peoples are called into resistance and/or solidarity. As our global village continues to evolve, the part played by transnational radio in the creation of a new world order for the twenty-first century should be carefully scrutinized for its ideological content as well as its incursions, well meaning or not, upon the destiny of target nations. In short, the medium may be the message; but it is the message that will determine how the medium will be designed for future transnational exchanges.

NOTES

1. Chesterton, G. K. *Autobiography* (London: Hutchinson, 1936), 202.

2. Within other contexts and with the economic developments of the past 30 years (NIKs or Newly Industrialized countries, such as South Korea and Taiwan) leading to the Global economy, other divisions may apply--for example, North-South and East-West. For discussion, see Anthony Smith, *The GeoPolitics of Information: How Western Culture Dominates the World* (New York: Oxford University Press, 1980), 13-40.

3. Oddly, in the Socialist/Communist world, as in the religious world, progaganda is not considered to be a negative word or concept. One author has noted, in visits to

China, that office doors in hotels and other institutions carry the wording "Office of Propaganda." In the West, such office door signs usually read "Office of Public Relations," because propaganda is a negative concept, practiced by, within this conceptual framework, "the bad guys." We should also note that Vatican Radio, despite its affinity for propagating the faith, now has an "Office of Public Relations."

4. In Chapter 11, the analysis indicates that among VOA's most grievous errors were the reports of the death of Deng Xiaoping (still alive in 1996), combat between PLA units, as well as the attempted assassination of Li Peng. These errors seem strategic and conducive to further unrest, as well as to the implication of impending civil war.

5. Zhou He, "The Role of the Chinese National News Media and the Voice of America in the 1989 Chinese Pro-Democracy Movement" (Diss. Indiana University, 1992), 298. He cites VOA story CN-128, 6 June 1989.

6. Ibid., 300. From an interview with VOA staff in late November and early December 1989.

7. Ibid.

8. As we write this in June 1996, the Russian process of electing a Russian president has begun. Communist Gennady Zyuganov is challenging President Boris Yeltsin. Yeltsin's presidency and powers are not modeled on the U.S. model--the Russian system has no checks and balances. In short, despite elections, Yeltsin has absolute power as president in this "democracy."

9. This is only one possible scenario.

10. Alex Callinicos, *The Revenge of History: Marxism and the East European Revolutions* (University Park, Pa: The Pennsylvania State University Press, 1991), 74-75.

11. Ibid., 79.

12. Ibid.

13. Ibid.

14. Richard Richter, President, Radio Free Asia/Asia Pacific Network, telephone interview with Street, 14 June 1996, Boston/Washington, D.C. Mr. Richter indicated that at present the plan is to broadcast to these countries in eight languages, and to China beginning in August 1996 in three languages: Mandarin, Cantonese, and Tibetan.

15. Here meaning the Catholic Church only, not to include other denominations.

16. For a discussion of the concept, see Steven Runciman's *Byzantine Civilization* (London: Methuen & Co. Ltd., 1933, 1961), 11-29.

17. Natalie Doyle-Hennin, *The World according to International Radio* (Diss., SUNY Buffalo, 1991), 67.

18. Ibid., 68.

19. Ibid., 222.

20. Ibid., 245.

21. Foreign Relations Authorization Act, Fiscal Years 1994 and 1995, 103rd Congress, 2d Session (April 25, 1994), 200.

22. Ibid., 202. It is unclear from the document whether this version was the final version, or if the Committee of Conference's substitute provision (sec. 307) overrides the senate's amendment. In any case, the International Broadcasting Bureau is within the USIA "to carry out all nonmilitary international broadcasting activities supported by the United States Government other than those described in sections 308 and 309," 58.

23. Ibid.

24. Ibid., 61.

25. Ibid., 62.

26. Ibid., 66.
27. VOA Audience Analysis Division Officer Kim Andrew Elliott, interview by authors, 28 April 1994, tape recording, Washington, D.C. Elliott made clear that his comments were personal opinions only and not necessarily reflective of the Voice of America.

Appendix A

Statutes for Vatican Radio

(*Note:* Because the official version of these statutes do not exist in English, Fr. Kevin R. Locke, S.J., Director of External Relations at Vatican Radio, was kind enough to translate the portions most pertinent to our research. The following excerpt covers the first three sections of the statutes which address the character and purpose of Radio Vaticana, its relationship to the Holy See, and its programming policy.)

1. CHARACTER AND PURPOSE

1.1   Vatican Radio is the broadcasting entity of the Holy See,[1] legally recognized by the international courts,[2] being an instrument of communication and of evangelisation at the service of the Papacy.[3]

1.2   Vatican Radio is a legal entity with headquarters in the Vatican City State.

1.3   The essential purpose of Vatican Radio is to effectively announce the Christian message with freedom and fidelity, and to link the centre of Catholicism with the rest of the world.

   a) By broadcasting the voice and teachings of the Pope
   b) By supplying information on the activities of the Holy See
   c) By reporting on the life of the Catholic Church in the world
   d) By seeking to evaluate present day issues in the light of Church teaching and by paying close attention to the signs of the times[4]

1.4   Vatican Radio also acts as collaborator and consultant to Dioceses or Episcopal Conferences with regard to their broadcasting activities.

1.5   Vatican Radio also has the special task of guaranteeing the recording, amplification, and distribution of sound from all the Pope's public activities, both within Vatican City and, through supervision, outside. Moreover, it has the task of setting up, safeguarding, and managing the Papal sound archive. Whenever this archive is used by third parties, it has the responsibility of protecting the pastoral nature of the recordings and ensuring that copyrights are respected.

2.   RELATIONSHIP WITH THE HOLY SEE

2.1   As an entity of the Holy See, the Vatican Radio[5] is answerable to the Secretariat of State, whose First Section, in agreement with the Second, oversees the Radio Station,[6] which is expected to follow closely the directives it receives regarding its programming, doctrinal, and information content.

2.2   However, Vatican Radio is not the official voice of the Holy See and therefore the content of its broadcasts, which are prepared and transmitted with the speed and timeliness that radio demands, remains its own responsibility. The fact of it being an instrument at the service of the Pope easily leads the general public to attribute an official character to the broadcasts of Vatican Radio. This demands that great care be taken to ensure its concordance with the Church's teaching and with all the activities of the Holy See.

2.3   Two Committees have been set up to oversee relations between the Secretariat of State and Vatican Radio, one is Directive and deals with content, programming, and strategy; the other is managerial and deals with economic, technical, and administrative matters.[7]   Both Committees meet at different times at the invitation of the Secretariat of State or at the request of the Director of the Radio. Apart from these bodies, the Director can count on being able to consult with both Sections of the Secretariat of State whenever the need arises.

3.   PROGRAMMING

3.1   In fulfilling its statutorily defined purpose, Vatican Radio follows the directives its receives from the Holy See as well as pastoral indications expressed in Papal teachings regarding this use of the instruments of social communication for the spread of the Christian message.

3.2   Primarily, Vatican Radio broadcasts Church and religious news and information, taking into consideration the lack of information offered by the various organs of social communication on these subjects. Firstly, the discourses and activities of the Pope and the Holy See are disseminated with the immediacy and speed proper to radio, conscious of the importance of such communications in the formation of public opinion.

3.3   Vatican Radio also deals with political, social, and economic news, and not only that which is of a purely religious nature,[8] its aim being to assist Christians to read in such news the signs of the times[9] and to stimulate them to take a stand and to make decisions in the light of their faith.[10] With regard to the latter, Vatican Radio is careful to proceed with prudent discernment and great objectivity, accurately citing sources and faithfully following the lines laid down by the Holy See.

3.4   Within the limitations and conventions of broadcasting, Vatican Radio offers listeners, especially those who are isolated or whose religious freedom is restricted, to participate spiritually in acts of worship. It also transmits celebrations presided over by the Pope to a wider audience and as a contribution to deepening the communion of the Church with the Successor of Peter.

3.5   Vatican Radio programs dedicate ample space to the various permanent elements of Christian catechesis: the Word of God, ecclesial and patristic tradition, fundamental and dogmatic theology, Christian ethics, the social doctrine of the Church, ecclesiastical history and hagiography, Christian associations, etc.[11] Special attention is paid to ecumenism and to dialogue with the great religions, particularly in those broadcasts destined for areas of the world where there are few Christians.

3.6   Within the limitations dictated by the restricted means and time at its disposal, Vatican Radio also dedicates adequate space to culture, art and music in particular, which is especially suitable for radio. In so doing it is continuing a long ecclesiastical and pontifical tradition.

NOTES

1. Cf. Pius Xi, radio message *Qui arcano Dei* (12 February 1931): AAS 23 (1931), 65-70.

2. Inaugurated on 12 February 1931, Vatican Radio is an active founder-member of UER (Union Europeenne de Radio-Television, with headquarters in Geneva), of URTI (Universite Radiophonique et Televisuelle Internationale, with headquarters in Paris) and associate member of URTNA (Union des Radiodiffusions et Televisions Nationales d'Afrique, with headquarters in Dakar), while in the broadcasting sector it represents the Holy See with UIT (Union Internationale des Telecommunications, with headquarters in Geneva) and the CEPT (Conference Europeenne des Administrations des Postes et Telecommunications).

3. Cf. John Paul II, address to Vatican Radio directors and staff on the 60th anniversary of the Station's foundation (15 June 1991): AAS 84 (1991), 301-304.

4.   Cf. Paul VI, address to Vatican Radio directors and staff on the 40th anniversary of its foundation (27 February 1971): AAS 63 (1971), 225-229. Also John Paul II, address on the occasion of his visit to Vatican Radio (5 February 1980), Teachings III, 1 (1980), 319-323.

5.   Cf. John Paul II, cost. ap. Pastore Bonus (28 June 1988), IX, a 191: AAS 80 (1988), 911.

6.   Cf. ibid., II a 43, 3 , l.c., 871.

7.   The Management Committee (originally defined as "Coordinating Committee") was set up on 27 February 1984, and the General Directive Committee on 7 April 1989.

8.   Cf. PONTIFICAL COUNCIL FOR SOCIAL COMMUNICATIONS, Pastoral Instruction *Communio et progressio* (23 May 1971), 123: AAS 63 (1971), 637.

9.   Cf. ECUM. CONC. VAT. II, Pastoral Constitution on the Church in the modern world *Gaudium et spes*, 11.

10.   Cf. PONTIFICAL COUNCIL FOR SOCIAL COMMUNICATIONS. Pastoral Instruction *Communio et progressio* (23 May 1971), 119: AAS 63 (1971), 636.

11.   Cf. JOHN PAUL II, address to directors and staff of Vatican Radio (15 June 1991), 4 AAS 84 (1991), 303.

Appendix B

Transnational Radio Services throughout the World

Adventist World Radio
Akashvani
American Forces Network
Asian Pacific Network
BBC World Service
British Forces Broadcasting Service
Broadcasting Service of the Kingdom of Saudi Arabia
Canadian Forces Network
Channel Africa
China Radio International (CRI)
Deutsche Welle
Egyptian Radio & TV Union
Far East Broadcasting Association (FEBA)
Far East Broadcasting Co.
Far East Network (AFRTS)
ICRC Radio
Islamic Republic of Iran Broadcasting (IRIB)
KAIJ International
Kol Israel--The Voice of Israel
KVOH
Mongol Radio and Television
Monitor Radio (Christian Science Monitor)
Nexus--International Broadcasting Association
Nippon Hoso Kyokai (NHK--Radio Japan)
Organisme de la Radio-Television Arab Syrienne
Organization of American States (OAS)
Pakistan Broadcasting Corporation
Polish Radio, Warsaw
RAI-International
Radio Almaty
Radio Australia

Radio Austria International
Radio Baku
Radio Bangladesh
Radio Belarus (Radio Minsk)
Radio Bras
Radio Budapest
Radio Bulgaria
Radio Canada International
Radio Denmark
Radio Dniester International
Radio Exterior de Espana
Radio Finland
Radio France Internationale
Radio Free Europe/Radio Liberty
Radio Georgia
Radio Habana Cuba
Radio Intercontinental
Radio Iraq International
Radio Latvia
Radio Marti
Radio Mediterranee Internationale
Radio Miami International
Radio Mocambique
Radio Moldavia International
Radio Nederland Wereldomroep (RNW)
Radio New Zealand International
Radio Norway International
Radio Prague
Radio Pyongyang
Radio Romania
Radio Slovakia International
Radio Station KJES
Radio Sweden
Radio Tashkent
Radio Thailand
Radio Tirana
Radio Trans Europe
Radio Ukraine International
Radio of the United Arab Emirates
Radio Vaticana
Radio Veritas Asia
Radio Vilnius
Radio Vlaanderen International
Radyo Pilipinas
RDP International-Radio Portugal
Russian State Radio Broadcasting Company "Voice of Russia"
Suara Malaysia (Voice of Malaysia)

Sri Lanka Broadcasting Corporation
Swiss Radio International
Tajik Radio
Trans World Radio
U.A.E. Radio and Television--Dubai
United Nations Radio
Voice of America
Voice of Armenia
Voice of Asia
Voice of Free Asia
"Voice of Free China" (International Service, Broadcasting Corporation of
    China--BCC)
The Voice of Greece
The Voice of Indonesia
Voice of Nigeria
Voice of Turkey
Voice of Turkmen
Voice of Vietnam
WHRI--World Harvest Radio
WMLK
WRNO Worldwide
WVHA
WYFR--Family Radio
World International Broadcasters, Inc.
World Wide Christian Radio

NOTE

This list was compiled from Andrew G. Sennitt, *World Radio TV Handbook, 1996*
(New York: Billboard Books, 1996).

Appendix C

Language Services Provided by Vatican Radio

Albanian
Amharic/Tigre
Armenian
Arabic
Bulgarian
Belorussian
Chinese
Croatian
Czech
English

Esperanto
French
German
Hindi
Hungarian
Italian
Japanese
Latvian
Lithuanian
Malaysian

Polish
Portuguese
Romanian
Russian
Scandinavian Sce.
Slovak
Slovene
Somali
Spanish
Swahili

Tamil
Ukrainian
Vietnamese

NOTE

This information was compiled from Andrew G. Sennitt, *World Radio TV Handbook, 1996* (New York, Billboard Books, 1996), 189-190.

Appendix D

Languages Provided by the BBC World Radio Service

Albanian
Arabic
Azeri
Bengali
Bulgarian
Burmese
Cantonese
Croatian
Czech
English (10 variations)
French
German
Hausa
Hindi
Hungarian
Indonesian
KinyaRwanda/KiRundi
Mandarin
Nepali
Pashto

Persian
Polish
Portuguese
Romanian
Russian
Serbian
Sinhala
Slovak
Slovene
Somali
Spanish
Swahili
Tamil
Thai
Turkish
Ukrainian
Urdu
Uzbek
Vietnamese

NOTE

This information was compiled from Andrew G. Sennitt, *World Radio TV Handbook, 1996* (New York, Billboard Books, 1996), 182-186.

Appendix E

Languages Provided by the American Transnational Radio Services

Radio Free Europe/Radio Liberty

Armenian	Kazakh	Serbo-Croat
Azerbaijani	Kyrgyz	Slovak
Belorussian	Latvian	Tajik
Bulgarian	Lithuanian	Tatar-Bashkir
Czech	Polish	Turkmen
Estonian	Romanian	Ukrainian
Georgian	Russian	Uzbek

Voice of America

Amharic	Czech	Khmer	Slovak
Arabic	Dari	Korean	Spanish
Azerbaijani	English	Kurdish	Swahili
Bangla	Farzi	Lao	Tibetan
Bulgarian	French	Pashto	Turkish
Burmese	Georgian	Polish	Ukrainian
Cantonese	Hausa	Portuguese	Urdu
Chinese (Mandarin)	Hindi	Romanian	Uzbek
Creole	Hungarian	Russian	Vietnamese

Radio Marti broadcasts to Cuba only.

The Asian Pacific Network (formerly Radio Free Asia) is scheduled to broadcast to the following countries:

Burma	China	North Korea	Vietnam
Cambodia	Laos	Tibet	

NOTE

This information was compiled from Andrew G. Sennitt, *World Radio TV Handbook,
1996* (New York, Billboard Books, 1996), 121-122 & 321-322.

Selected Bibliography

BOOKS

Aarons, Mark, and John Loftus. *Unholy Trinity.* New York: St. Martin's Press, 1991.

Ambrose, Stephen E. *D-Day.* New York: Simon & Schuster, 1994.

Ascherson, Neal. *The Struggles for Poland.* New York: Random House, 1987.

Ash, Timothy Garton. *The Polish Revolution: Solidarity.* New York: Vintage, 1985.

Barnett, Clifford R. *Poland: Its People, Its Society, Its Culture.* New York: Grove Press Books, 1958.

Barrett, Edward W. *Truth Is Our Weapon.* New York: Funk & Wagnalls, 1953.

Barrett, William E. *Shepherd of Mankind: A Biography of Pope Paul VI.* New York: Doubleday, 1964.

Bateson, Gregory. *Steps toward an Ecology of Mind.* New York: Ballantine, 1972.

Bernas, Joaquin. *Dismantling the Dictatorship.* Quezon City: Ateneo de Manila University, 1990.

Bonner, Raymond. *Weakness and Deceit: U.S. Policy and El Salvador.* New York: Times Books, 1984.

Bowers, J. W., and D. Ochs. *The Rhetoric of Agitation and Control.* Reading, Mass: Addison-Wesley, 1971.

Brandys, Kazimierz. *A Warsaw Diary: 1978-1981.* Translated by Richard Lourie. New York: Vintage Books, 1985.

Briggs, Asa. *A History of Broadcasting in the United Kingdom, Vol. 3: The War of Words.* London: Oxford University Press, 1970.

Brinton, William M., and Alan Rinzler, eds. *Without Force or Lies: Voices from the Revolution of Central Europe in 1989-90.* San Francisco: Mercury House Inc., 1990.

Browne, Donald R. *International Radio Broadcasting: The Limits of the Limitless Medium.* New York: Praeger, 1982.

Brumberg, Abraham, ed. *Poland: Genesis of a Revolution.* New York: Vintage, 1983.

Burton, John W. *World Society.* Cambridge, England: Cambridge University Press, 1972.

Buss, Claude. *Cory Aquino and the People of the Philippines.* Stanford, Calif.: Stanford Alumni Association, 1987.

Calder, Angus. *The People's War: Britain, 1939-1945.* New York: Pantheon Books, 1969.

Callinicos, Alex. *The Revenge of History: Marxism and the East European Revolutions.* University Park, Penn.: The Pennsylvania State University Press, 1991.

Campbell, Paul Newell. *Rhetoric/Ritual: A Study of the Communicative and Aesthetic Dimensions of Language.* Belmont and Encino, Calif.: Dickenson Publishing Co., Inc., 1972.

Cherrington, Ruth. *China's Students: The Struggle for Democracy.* New York: Routledge, 1991.

Chesterton, G. K. *Autobiography.* London: Hutchinson, 1936.

Childs, Harwood L., and John B. Wilton, eds. *Propaganda by Short Wave.* New York: Ayer Co. Publishers, 1972.

Cianfarra, Camille. *The Vatican and the War.* New York: E.P. Dutton, 1944.

Constantino, Renato. *Demystifying Aquino.* Quezon City: Karrel, Inc., 1989.

Dank, Milton. *The French against the French: Collaboration and Resistance.* London: Cassell, Ltd., 1978.

Dawisha, Karen. *The Kremlin and the Prague Spring.* Berkeley and Los Angeles: University of California Press, 1984.

deWeydenthal, J. B. *The Pope in Poland.* Munich, Germany: The RFE/RL Institute, 1980.

Donaldson, Frances. *The Marconi Scandal.* New York: Harcourt, Brace & World, Inc., 1962.

Doyle-Hennin, Natalie Eli. *The World According to International Radio.* Ph.D. diss., State University of New York at Buffalo, 1991.

Dvornik, Francis. *The Slavs in European History and Civilization.* New Brunswick, N. J.: Rutgers University Press, 1962.

Edlund, K., Jon Elliston, and Peter Kornbluh. *U.S. Broadcasting to Cuba: Radio and TV Marti, A Historical Chronology.* Washington: National Security Archive, 1994.

Ehrlich, Blake. *Resistance: France 1940-1945.* Boston: Little, Brown and Co., 1965.

Ellul, Jacques. *Propaganda: The Formation of Men's Attitudes.* New York: Random House, 1965.

Elwood, Douglas. *Philippine Revolution 1986: Model of Nonviolent Change.* Quezon City: New Day Publishers, 1986.

Emery, Walter B. *Broadcasting and Government: Responsibilities and Regulations.* East Lansing: Michigan State University Press, 1971.

_____. *National and International Systems of Broadcasting: Their History, Operation and Control.* East Lansing: Michigan State University Press, 1969.

Fabros, Wilfredo. *The Church and Its Social Involvement in the Philippines, 1930-1972.* Quezon City: Ateneo de Manila University Press, 1988.

Fiske, Susan, and Shelly Taylor. *Social Cognition.* New York: McGraw-Hill, Inc., 1991.

Foot, M. R. D. *SOE in France.* London: Her Majesty's Stationery Office, 1976.

Foucault, Michel. *The Order of Things: An Archaeology of the Human Sciences.* Translated by Alan Sheridan-Smith. New York: Random House, 1970.

Giordano, Pasquale. *Awakening to Mission: The Philippine Catholic Church 1965-1981.* Quezon City: New Day Publishers, 1988.

Gleeck, Lewis, Jr. *President Marcos and the Philippine Political Culture.* Manila: Loyal Printing, Inc., 1987.

Graham, Robert A. *Vatican Diplomacy: A Study of Church and State on the International Plane.* Princeton, N.J.: Princeton University Press, 1959.

Hale, Julian. *Radio Power: Propaganda and International Broadcasting.* Philadelphia: Temple University Press, 1975.

Hanson, Eric O. *The Catholic Church in World Politics.* Princeton, N.J.: Princeton University Press, 1987.

Head, Sidney. *World Broadcasting Systems: A Comparative Analysis.* Belmont, Calif.: Wadsworth, 1985.

Hebblethwaite, Peter. *In the Vatican.* Bethesda, Md.: Adler & Adler, 1986.

_____. *Pope John XXIII: Shepherd of the Modern World.* New York: Doubleday, 1985.

Hernandez, Carolina, and Werner Pfennig, eds. *Media and Politics in Asia.* University of the Philippines Center for Integrative and Development Studies, National Institute for Policy Studies, and Friedrich Naumann Foundation, 1991.

Heyer, Paul. *Nature, Human Nature, and Society: Marx, Darwin, Biology, and the Human Sciences.* Westport, Conn.: Greenwood Press, 1982.

The History of Broadcasting in the United Kingdom. Oxford: Oxford University Press, 1970.

Hofmann, Paul. *O Vatican! A Slightly Wicked View of the Holy See.* New York: Congdon & Weed, 1983.

Holt, Robert T. *Radio Free Europe.* Minneapolis: University of Minnesota Press, 1958.

Hughes, H. Stuart. *Sophisticated Rebels: The Political Culture of European Dissent, 1968-1987.* Cambridge: Harvard University Press, 1990.

Inglis, Andrew F. *Behind the Tube: A History of Technology and Business.* Boston: Focal Press, 1990.

Johnson, Bryan. *The Four Days of Courage: The Untold Story of the People Who Brought Marcos Down.* New York: The Free Press, 1987.

Johnson, James T. *Just War Tradition and the Restraint of War.* Princeton: Princeton University Press, 1981.

Jolly, W. P. *Marconi.* New York: Stein and Day, 1972.

Kedward, H. R. *Occupied France: Collaboration and Resistance 1940-1944.* Oxford: Basil Blackwell, Ltd., 1985.

_____. *Resistance in Vichy France: A Study of Ideas and Motivation in the Southern Zone 1940-1942.* Oxford: Oxford University Press, 1978.

Knight, Frida. *The French Resistance 1940 to 1944.* London: Lawrence and Wishart, 1975.

Kropf, Mathias. *The Clandestine Broadcasting Directory.* Lake Geneva, Wis.: Tiare Publications, 1994.

Kundera, Milan. *The Joke.* Translated by Michael Henry Heim. London: Penguin, 1983.

_____. *The Unbearable Lightness of Being.* Translated by Michael Henry Heim. New York: Harper and Row, 1985.

Küng, Hans. *Infallible? An Inquiry.* Translated by Edward Quinn. Garden City, N.Y.: Doubleday, 1971.

La Libération de la France. Paris: Centre National de la Recherche Scientifique, 1976.

Lernoux, Penny. *People of God.* New York: Penguin Books, 1989.

Lewis, Peter M., and Jerry Booth. *The Invisible Medium: Public, Commercial and Community Radio*. Washington, D.C.: Howard University Press, 1990.

Lipski, Jan Joseph. *Kor: A History of the Workers' Defense Committee in Poland, 1976-1981*. Translated by Olga Amsterdamska and Gene M. Moore. Berkelely, Los Angeles, and London: University of California Press, 1985.

Lopez Vigil, Jose Ignatio. *Rebel Radio: The Story of El Salvador's Radio Venceremos*. Willimantic, Conn.: Curbstone Press, 1994.

Manning, Peter K. *Organizational Communication*. New York: Aldine de Gruyter, 1992.

Marconi, Degna. *My Father, Marconi*. New York: McGraw-Hill, 1962.

Martin, Malachi. *The Jesuits: The Society of Jesus and the Betrayal of the Roman Catholic Church*. New York: Simon & Schuster, 1987.

Maslog, C, ed. *Philippine Communication: An Introduction*. Manila: James B. Reuter Foundation, 1988.

Matelski, Marilyn J. *Vatican Radio: Propagation by the Airwaves*. Westport, Conn.: Praeger Publishers, 1995.

May, R.J., and Francisco Nemenzo, eds. *The Philippines After Marcos*. New York: St. Martin's Press, 1985.

Mercado, Monina, ed. *People Power: An Eyewitness History*. Manila: James B. Reuter Foundation, 1986.

Mesa-Lago, Carmelo, ed. *Cuba after the Cold War*. Pittsburgh: University of Pittsburgh Press, 1993.

Mytton, Graham, ed. *Global Audiences: Research for Worldwide Broadcasting: 1993*. London: John Libbey, 1993.

Perreault, Gilles. *Paris under the Occupation*. New York: Vendome Press, 1989.

Pirsein, Robert William. *The Voice of America: A History of the International Broadcasting Activities of the United States Government, 1940-1962*. New York: Arno, 1979.

Putnam, Linda, and Michael E. Pacanowsky, eds. *Communication and Organizations An Interpretive Approach*. Beverly Hills, Calif.: Sage Publications, 1983.

Rhodes, Anthony. *The Vatican in the Age of Dictators 1922-1945*. London: Hodder and Stroughton, 1974.

Rybacki, Karen and Donald. *Communication Criticism*. Belmont, Calif.: Wadsworth, 1991.

Santos, Antonio Lumicao, and Lorna Domingo-Robes. *Power Politics in the Philippines*. Philippines: Center for Social Research, 1987.

Scannell, Paddy, and David Cardiff. *A Social History of British Broadcasting: Volume One 1922-1939, Serving the Nation*. Oxford, England: Basil Blackwell Ltd., 1991.

Schoenbrun, David. *Soldiers of the Night*. New York: E.P. Dutton, 1980.

Schulz, D. S., ed. *Cuba and the Future*. Westport, Conn.: Greenwood, 1994.

Sennit, Andrew G. *World Radio TV Handbook, 1996* New York: Billboard Books, 1996.

Short, K. R. M., ed. *Film and Radio Propaganda in World War II*. Knoxville, Tenn.: The University of Tennessee Press, 1983.

_____. *Western Broadcasting Over the Iron Curtain*. New York: St. Martin's Press, 1986.

Simons, Lewis. *Worth Dying For.* New York: William Morrow and Company, Inc., 1987.

Singer, Daniel. *The Road to Gdansk: Poland and the USSR*. New York: Monthly Review Press, 1981.

Sison, Jose Maria, and Rainer Werning. *The Philippine Revolution and the Involvement of the Church.* New York: Taylor & Francis New York Inc., 1989.

Skilling, H. Gordon. *Czechoslovakia's Interrupted Revolution.* Princeton: Princeton University Press, 1976.

Soley, Lawrence C. *Radio Warfare: OSS and CIA Subversive Propaganda.* New York: Praeger Publishers, 1989.

Soley, Lawrence C., and John S. Nichols. *Clandestine Radio Broadcasting: A Study of Revolutionary and Counterrevolutionary Electronic Communication.* New York: Praeger, 1987.

Spender, Stephen. *The Year of the Young Rebels.* New York: Random House, 1969.

Stehle, Hansjakob. *Eastern Politics of the Vatican, 1917-1979.* Translated by Sandra Smith. Athens, Ohio: Ohio University Press, 1981.

Street, Nancy Lynch. *In Search of Red Buddha.* New York: Peter Lang, 1992.

Sturrock, John. *Structuralism and Since: From Levi-Strauss to Derrida.* Oxford: Oxford University Press, 1979.

Sweets, John F. *Vichy France: The French under Nazi Occupation.* New York: Oxford University Press, 1986.

Szajkowski, Bogdan. *Next to God . . . Poland: Politics and Religion in Contemporary Poland.* New York: St. Martin's Press, 1983.

Szulc, Tad. *Pope John Paul II: The Biography.* New York: Scribner, 1995.

Thayer, L. ed. *Organization Communication: Emerging Perspectives,* Vol. 1. Norwood, Mass.: Ablex, 1986.

Tunstall, Jeremy. *The Media Are American.* New York: Columbia University Press, 1977.

UST Social Research Center. *The Philippine Revolution and the Involvement of the Church.* Manila: UST Press, 1986.

Walsh, Michael. *Opus Dei.* New York: HarperCollins, 1992.

Walters, E. Garrison. *The Other Europe: Eastern Europe to 1945.* New York: Dorset Press, 1990.

Wang, Fei. *Objective Journalism or Propaganda: A Content Analysis of the Voice of America Mandarin Service's Newscasts before, during, and after the Tian An Men Crisis.* Ph.D. diss., Bowling Green State University, 1993.

The War Memoirs of Charles de Gaulle: Unity 1942-1944. Translated by Richard Howard. New York: Simon and Schuster, 1959.

Whale, John, ed. *The Pope from Poland: An Assessment.* London: Collins, 1980.

Wigginton, F. Peter. *The Popes of Vatican Council II.* Chicago: Franciscan Herald Press, 1983.

Wilkinson, James D. *The Intellectual Resistance in Europe.* Cambridge, Mass.: Harvard University Press, 1981.

Willey, David. *God's Politician: Pope John Paul II, the Catholic Church, and the New World Order.* New York: St. Martin's Press, 1992.

Winkler, Allan M. *The Politics of Propaganda.* New Haven, Conn.: Yale University Press, 1971.

Yallop, David A. *In God's Name.* New York: Doubleday, 1991.

Youngblood, Robert. *Marcos against the Church.* Ithaca and London: Cornell University Press, 1990.

Zhou He. "The Role of the Chinese National News Media and the Voice of America in the 1989 Chinese Pro-Democracy Movement." Ph.D. diss., Indiana University, 1992.

PUBLICATIONS--U.S. GOVERNMENT AND NON-GOVERNMENT

APN Status Report, 13 June 1996.

Baumgartner, Peter, ed. *Shortwaves.* Munich: Radio Free Europe/Radio Liberty, May-June 1993.

Board for International Broadcasting 1993 Annual Report on Radio Free Europe/Radio Liberty. By Malcolm S. Forbes, Chairman. Washington, D.C.: Board for International Broadcasting, 1993.

"China: Kaifang Series Views: Journalism Reform." *Foreign Broadcast Information Service,* March 1993.

The Conference Report (H.R. 2333) of the "Foreign Relations Authorization Act, Fiscal Years 1994 and 1995," April 1994.

Corvera, Bert. "How People Power Erupted." *WE Forum,* 25 February-3 March 1986.

Dabija, Marcia. "Radio Free Europe/Radio Liberty, Inc. Translation." *Europa,* April 1993.

Department of State Appropriation Bill for 1950. Washington, D.C.: U.S. Subcommittee of the House Committee on Appropriations, 1949.

Foreign Relations Authorization Act, Fiscal Years 1994 and 1995. 103rd Congress, 1994.

RFE/RL and Independent Media: A Continuing Partnership. Munich: Radio Free Europe/Radio Liberty. Photocopy.

RFE/RL and the Unfinished Revolutions. Munich: Radio Free Europe/Radio Liberty. Photocopy.

RFE/RL and VOA: What's the Difference? Munich: Radio Free Europe/Radio Liberty. Photocopy.

RFE/RL Audience Handbook. Munich: RFE/RL Research Institute, March 1993.

RFE/RL Audience Summaries: A Status Report on Audience Research Findings in Eastern Europe, the Baltic States and the Successor States of the Soviet Union. Munich: RFE/RL Research Institute, June 1992.

RFE/RL Audience: Who Listens, and Why. Munich: Radio Free Europe/Radio Liberty. Photocopy.

RFE/RL Fact Sheet. Munich: Radio Free Europe/Radio Liberty. Photocopy.

RFE/RL Organization Chart. Munich: Radio Free Europe/Radio Liberty. Photocopy.

Reich, Gene. "Public Diplomacy Report." *Radio Free Europe Transcript,* 18 March 1993.

Responding to the Green Paper. London: British Broadcasting Corporation, 1993.

The Right to Know. Report of the Presidential Commission on International Radio Broadcasting, 1973.

"Surrogate Broadcasting: An Evolving Concept." Munich: Radio Free Europe/Radio Liberty. Undated. Photocopied.

U.S. Advisory Commission on Public Diplomacy. *A Glossary of Terms.* Washington D.C.: 1992.

U.S. Advisory Commission on Public Diplomacy. *The New World of International Broadcasting: Radio.* Washington D.C.: 1992.

U.S. Advisory Commission on Public Diplomacy. *The New World of International Broadcasting: Television.* Washington D.C.: 1992.

U.S. Advisory Commission on Public Diplomacy. *1993 Advisory Commission Report: The Future of US International Broadcasting.* Washington D.C.: 1993.

U.S. Advisory Commission on Public Diplomacy. *Presidential Commission Sees Need for Public Diplomacy in Age of Instant Global Communication*, News Release. Washington D.C.: 1983.

U.S. Advisory Commission on Public Diplomacy. *United States Advisory Commission on Public Diplomacy 1993 Report. By Tom C. Korologos, Chairman.* Washington D.C.: United States Advisory Commission on Public Diplomacy, 1993.

U.S. Board for International Broadcasting. *Forbes Condemns Advisory Group Report*, Press Release. Washington D.C.: July 1992.

U.S. Congress. Senate. Foreign Relations Committee. *Foreign Relations Committee Report on the Foreign Relations Authorization Act. Additional Views of Senator Biden, 1994-1995.*

U.S. Congress. Senate. Senator Russell D. Feingold. *Feingold Praises Advisory Commission Report*, Press Release. Washington D.C.: March 1993.

U.S. General Accounting Office. *TV Marti: Costs and Compliance With Broadcast Standards and International Agreements.* GAO/NSIAD-92-199. Washington D.C., 1992.

U.S. Information Agency. Wireless File. *Commission Urges Merger of US Broadcasting Under Asia.* Washington D.C.: March 1993.

U.S. President. *Report of the Presidential Study Commission on International Radio Broadcasting. The Right to Know.* Washington D.C.: Government Printing Office.

VOA Looking Toward Tomorrow Today. Washington D.C.: United States Information Agency, 1992.

Wearne, P. "David and Goliath Slug It Out in Electronic War." *IPI Report*, May/June 1994.

JOURNALS AND MAGAZINES

Alexandre, Laurien. "Television Marti: Electronic Invasion in the Post-Cold War." *Media, Culture and Society 14* (1992): 523-40.

Amfitheatrof, Erik. "'Spiritual Fruits from the Science of Radio.'" *Variety*, 18 February 1991, 62, 66, 67.

_____. "Unmistakable Message of Love and Peace." *Variety*, 18 February 1991, 66.

_____. "Vatican Wants Radio to Be a Vital Voice." *Variety*, 18 February 1991, 64.

Arana, Ana. "Down from the Hills: El Salvador's Guerrilla Radio Faces Peace." *Columbia Journalism Review* (July/August 1992): 14-15.

Bayer, S. D. "The Legal Aspects of TV Marti in Relation to the Law of Direct Broadcasting Satellites." *Emory Law Journal 41* (1992): 541-80.

Beichman, Arnold. "The Story of Radio Free Europe." *National Review*, 2 November 1984, 29-33.

"Bloc Broadcasting: What to Do." *Telecommunications Policy Review* 9 (March 1993): 1-4.

"The BBC: From a Whisper to a Scream." *The Economist*, 28 November 1992, 66.

Cabrera, Acevedo. "En Frecuencia Modulada: Radios ex Guerrilleras Bajan de las Montanas de El Salvador." *Pulso* (October/December 1992): 16-18.

"Changing Channels: Reforming the BBC Need Not Mean Ruining It." *The Economist*, 28 November 1992, 17-18.

Cuartero, Nestor. "People Power Mobilized by Broadcast Power." *Manila Bulletin* (2 March 1986): 12.

De La Cruz, Jesselyn. "Radio Veritas: ZNN (Radyo Totoo)." *Philippine Journalism Review* 2 (1991): 21-23, 25-26.

Dexter, Gerry L. "The Anti-Castro Broadcasters: Fidel Taking Hits across the Bands." *Popular Communications* (October 1994): 22-26, 31.

Elliott, Kim Andrew. "Too Many Voices of America." *Foreign Policy* (Winter 1989/1990): 113-131.

Elliott, Kim Andrew, J. A. Campbell, Gerard Hauser, and J. Marks. "Unofficial Broadcasting for Politics, Profits, and Pleasure." *Gazette 30* (1982): 109-19.

Escherick, Joseph W. and Jeffrey N. Wasserstrom. "Acting Out Democracy: Political Theatre in Modern China." *The Journal of Asian Studies*, November 1990.

Fotheringham, Allan. "Open-mouth Radio: Shouting Stars." *Business Week*, 5 February 1990, 64.

Garnham, Nicholas. "The Future of the BBC." *Sight and Sound*, January 1993, 26-28.

Gelb, Norman. "John Birt's Revolution: Trouble at the BBC." *The New Leader*, July 12-26, 1993, 3-4.

_____. "The Specter of Censorship: A Watchdog for British TV." *The New Leader*, 27 June 1988, 7-8.

Gonzalez, Hernando. "Mass Media and the Spiral of Silence: The Philippines from Marcos to Aquino." *Journal of Communication* 38 (4) (1988): 33-48.

Goodwin, Peter. "The Future of the BBC." *Media, Culture & Society* (July 1993): 497-502.

Graves, Harold N. "European Radio and the War." *Annals of the American Academy of Political and Social Science* (January 1941): 75-82.

Hebir, J. Bryan. "Papal Foreign Policy." *Foreign Policy* (Spring 1990): 26-48.

Holton, Robert R. "Vatican Radio." *The Catholic World* (April 1970): 7-12.

Jessup, J. J. "Monitoring Cuba--To and Fro." *Monitoring Times*, January 1991, 14-16.

Kircschten, Dick. "Radio Wars." *National Journal* (1993): 865-867.

Knoll, Steve. "The Voice of America: Banned in the Land of the Free." *Washington Journalism Review* (May 1988): 43-44.

Melcher, Richard A. "This Battle of Britain Is Taking its Toll on the Media Barons." *Business Week*, 5 February 1990, 38-39.

"New Signals." *Journal of Commerce*, 1990.

Nichols, John S. "When Nobody Listens: Assessing the Political Success of Radio Marti." *Communication Research 11* (1984): 281-304.

Onder, James J. "The Sad State of Vatican Radio." *Educational Broadcasting Review* (August 1971): 43-53.

Pais, Arthur J. "Anger in India: Blaming the Foreign Messenger." *Columbia Journalism Review* (May/June 1993): 17-18.

Parry-Giles, Shawn J. "Propaganda, Effect and the Cold War: Gauging the Status of America's 'War of Words.'" *Political Communication* (April/June 1994): 203-213.

"Radio Free Europe/RadioLiberty Moves into 1990's." *Broadcasting*, July 1989, 38-39.

Reuter, James B. "The CBCP Owns Radio Veritas." *Philippine Journalism Review* 2 (1991): 24.

"Revisiting the Role of the Government's International Radios," *Broadcasting*, December 1989, 88.

Soley, Lawrence. "Clandestine Radio and the End of the Cold War." *Media Studies Journal* 7 (1993): 129-138.

Third World Studies Center, University of the Philippines, Diliman. "The Church in the Political Order." *Kasarinlan* 5 (1990): 71-81.

Townsend, Cyril D. "The Future of the BBC External Services." *Contemporary Review* (August 1985): 92-96.

"US Radios Seek New Role after the Collapse of Communism." *Journal of Commerce*, 30, (1991).

Van Horn, L. "War of Words: The United States-Cuba Broadcast War Heats Up." *Monitoring Times* (October 1994): 30.

"VOA, RFE/RL Victorious after Failed Soviet Coup." *Broadcasting*, September 1991, 37-38.

Warlaumont, Hazel G. "Strategies in International Radio Wars: A Comparative Approach." *Journal of Broadcasting & Electronic Media* (Winter 1988): 43-59.

Weaver, Carolyn. "When the Voice of America Ignores its Charter." *Columbia Journalism Review* (November/December 1988): 36-43.

Youm, Kyo Ho. "The Radio and TV Marti Controversy: A Re-examination." *Gazette* 48 (1991): 95-103.

Youngblood, Robert. "Structural Imperialism: An Analysis of the Catholic Bishops' Conference of the Philippines." *Comparative Political Studies* 15 (1982): 29-56.

NEWSPAPER ARTICLES/PRESS SERVICES

Binder, David. "College Chief Is Reported Picked to Run USIA." *The New York Times International Edition*, 18 March 1993, A12.

Bitterman, Mary. "VOA Can Do the Job." *The Washington Post*, 5 April 1993, A21.

Briscoe, David. "Commission Proposes Phaseout of Radio Free Europe." Associated Press, 18 March 1993.

Briscoe, David. "Panel Proposes Eliminating Radio Free Europe." *The Washington Times*, 19 March 1993, A8.

Bruns, Joseph. "On the Air Overseas." *Washington Post*, 21 March 1993, C6.

Clemena, Roberto. "The General and the Virgin." *Veritas*, 6 April 1986, 13.

"Cold War Radio Networks on List of Cuts." *Morning News Tribune*, 21 February 1993.

"Commission Recommends End of Radio Free Europe." *The Providence Sunday Journal*, 22 March 1993.

Coquia, Jorge R. "The Church's Mission in a Just Political Order." *Veritas*, 6 April 1986, 19.

Dionne, E. J., Jr.. "Cardinal Sees Pope on Manila role." *New York Times*, 7 March 1986.

Dustin, Diane. "President Looking to Get Power over Overseas Broadcasts." Associated Press, 24 March 1993.

Eyal, Jonathan. "Eastern Europe Still Needs RFE/RL." *Wall Street Journal European Edition*, 1 March 1993.

Francis, Samuel. "Cold War Fossil: Posse in Pursuit." *Washington Times*, 16 March 1993.

"Gorbachev Calls on White House to Fund Radio Liberty." *PRNewswire*, 21 March 1993.

"Gorbachev Fights to Save Radio Liberty." *Washington Times*, 23 March 1993.

Icamina, Paul (1986). "Church Activism in a New Setting." *Veritas*, 6 April 1986: 12.
"Keep the Radios On." *Christian Science Monitor*, 23 March 1993.
Kondracke, Morton. "Hill Should Save Freedom Radios from Clinton Axe." *Roll Call*, 22 March 1993.
Korologos, Tom. "Let's Simplify Our World Radio Role." *New York Times*, 16 March 1993, A20.
Laqueur, Walter. "The Dangers of Radio Silence." *Wall Street Journal*, 4 March 1993.
Martin, Lydia. "Panel Recommends Halting Radio Marti." *The Miami Herald*, 18 March 1993, 6A.
Michnik, Adam. *Guardian*, 1 March 1991.
Mislosz, Czeslaw. "I'd Hate to See Them Go." *New York Times OP-ED*, 3 March 1993.
"Needed Then, Needed Now." *Washington Post*, 8 March 1993.
Orara, Lucy. "A Revered Institution Once Called Radio Veritas." *The Manila Standard*, 4 March 1991, 16.
Pfaff, William. *Herald International Tribune*, 11 March 1993.
"Pope Pius XI Addresses and Blesses the World in His First Radio Broadcast." *New York Times*, 13 February 1931, 14.
"Radio Free America." *Washington Post*, 7 August 1992.
"Radio Free Europe, Liberty May Be Cut." *St. Petersburg Times*, 20 February 1993.
"Radio Station Cancelled." *The Atlanta Journal*, 19 February 1993.
Reye, Fred. "The Four Longest Days in February." *Philippine Panorama Magazine*, 9 March 1986, 5-7.
Sreebny, Dan. "VOA Broadcasts to Its Own Beat." *Washington Times*, 21 March 1993, B5.
"Station Here Helps London to Hear Pope." *New York Times*, 13 February 1931, 14.
"Targeting the Radios." *The Washington Times*, 11 March 1993.
Todoran, Dorin. "Informing Eastern Europe." *Christian Science Monitor*, 24 March, 1993.
Tuch, Hans. "Needed Then, But Not Now." *Washington Post*, 16 March 1993, A16.
"Valuable Voices of Liberty." *The Times*, 17 March 1993.
Wattenberg, Ben. *Washington Times*, 24 March 1993, G4.
Whitney, Craig. "Free Europe's Entreaty: Don't Tune Us Out Now." *The New York Times International Edition*, 19 March 1993.
"World Service Fears Decline over Fresh Cuts." *Guardian*. 21 April 1993.
Woycicki, Kazimierz. "Eastern Europe Still Needs this Message." *Zycie Warsawy*.
"Yeltsin Should Ask." *Wall Street Journal*, 2 April 1993.
Young, Hugo. "Marring a World Class Service." *Guardian*, 28 January 1993.
Zabarenko, Deborah. "Panel: End Radio Free Europe, Liberty." *The Philadelphia Inquirer*, 19 March 1993.
_____. "Panel Phase Out of Radio Free Europe, Radio Liberty." Reuters, 18 March 1993.
Zeller, G. "FOIA Reveals Cuban Clandestine Busted Twice." *Monitoring Times* (January 1995): 92.
Zulueta, Lito. "The Station of Truth, the Station that Cares." *The Manila Chronicle*, 16 March 1991, 10.

INTERVIEWS

Brown, James F., Radio Free Europe/Radio Liberty. Interview by authors, July 1993. Tape recording. Munich, Germany.

Dimitz, Sherwood, Voice of America. Interview by authors, April 1994. Tape recording. Washington, D.C.

Elliott, Kim, Voice of America. Interview by authors, April 1994. Tape recording. Washington, D.C.

Gillette, Robert E., Radio Free Europe/Radio Liberty. Interview by authors, July 1993. Tape recording. Munich, Germany.

Harbaugh, John, Voice of America. Interview by authors, April 1994. Tape recording. Washington, D.C.

Hebblethwaite, Peter, author and Vaticanologist. Interview by Marilyn J. Matelski, March 1994. Tape recording. Chestnut Hill, Mass.

Heil, Alan, Voice of America. Interview by authors, April 1994. Tape recording. Washington, D.C.

Heintzen, Harry, Voice of America. Interview by authors, April 1994. Tape recording. Washington, D.C.

Klose, Kevin, Radio Liberty. Interview by authors, August 1993. Tape recording. Munich, Germany.

Lipien, Ted, Voice of America. Interview by authors, July 1993. Tape recording. Munich, Germany.

Locke, Rev. Kevin R., S.J., Vatican Radio. Interview by authors, May 1996. Tape recording. Vatican City, Vatican.

Lombardi, Rev. Federico, S.J., Vatican Radio. Interview by authors, May 1996. Tape recording. Vatican City, Vatican.

Lyon, Samuel P., Radio Free Europe/Radio Liberty. Interview by authors, July 1993. Tape recording. Munich, Germany.

Marsh, William W., Radio Free Europe/Radio Liberty. Interview by authors, July 1993. Tape recording. Munich, Germany.

Parta, Russell Eugene, Radio Free Europe/Radio Liberty. Interview by authors, July 1993. Tape recording. Munich, Germany.

Pell, E. Eugene, Radio Free Europe/Radio Liberty. Interview by authors, August 1993. Tape recording. Munich, Germany.

Richter, Richard, Asia Pacific Network. Phone interview by Nancy Lynch Street, June 1996. Boston/Washington, D.C.

Shroeder, Terry B., Radio Free Europe/Radio Liberty. Interview by authors, July 1993. Tape recording. Munich, Germany.

Tseu, Betty, Voice of America. Interview by authors, April 1994. Tape recording. Washington, D.C.

LEXIS/NEXIS COMPUTER SEARCHES

"'Active Meddling' in Polish Affairs by Western Intelligence Services." British Broadcasting Corporation World Service broadcast, 12 June 1982.

"Anniversary of Gdansk-Szczecin-Jastrzebie Accords: 'Situation Still Difficult.'" British Broadcasting Corporation World Service broadcast, 5 September 1981.

"Anti-Polish Activity in the West." British Broadcasting Corporation World Service broadcast, 22 December 1982.

"Attempts by Washington and NATO to 'Maintain Anarchy' in Poland." British Broadcasting Corporation World Service broadcast, 18 December 1991.

"Attitudes in Washington: Defection of Polish Ambassador." British Broadcasting Corporation World Service broadcast, 24 December 1981.

"Barcikowski in Szczecin: Warning of Possible Armed Uprising."   British
    Broadcasting Corporation World Service broadcast, 28 August 1982.
Bass, Paul. "Yale Actions Are Criticized." *New York Times*, 5 December 1982, 14.
Chaze, William L., with Harold Kennedy. "The Great Propaganda War." *U.S. News &
    World Report*, 11 January 1982, 27.
"Clearing the Air: A First for Moscow since '80." *New York Times*, 17 November
    1985, 13.
"Confessions of a 'Tygodnik Powszechne' Columnist."   British Broadcasting
    Corporation World Service broadcast, 14 June 1986.
Cwinarowicz, Karol. "Walesa Appeals to Polish Leaders to Share Power."   Reuters,
    15 December 1983.
Dale, Reginald. "Politicians Join Stars in West's TV Salute to Poles." *Financial
    Times*, 21 January 1982, 1.
Diehl, Jackson. "Light from Underground; Polish Publishers Revel in Official
    Tolerance." *Washington Post*, 24 May 1989, D2.
Dobbs, Michael.   "Solidarity Seeks to Salvage Vital Information Network."
    Washington Post, 10 January 1982, A1.
Doder, Dusko. "Moscow Charges Reagan Revives Cold War Tension; President Said
    to Use 'Forgery and Lie.'" *Washington Post*, 31 December 1981.
Engelberg, Stephen.   "The Trail So Far: Testimony Shows That High Officials
    Rejected the Law on Covert Actions." *New York Times* (8 May 1987): A14.
"Events in Poland Explained for Foreign Listeners."   British Broadcasting
    Corporation World Service broadcast, 23 February 1981.
Farquhar, Ronald. "Dateline: Warsaw." Reuters, 28 January 1982.
Geyer, Georgie Anne.   "It's Foolish to Fiddle with Fidel." *Cincinnati Enquirer* (9
    November 1994): A14.
Girardet, Edward. "Afghan Resistance Spells Long Soviet Army Vigil." *Christian
    Science Monitor*, 28 December 1981.
Goshko, John. "Soviets Stop Radio Jamming, BBC Says." *Washington Post* 22
    January 1987, A31.
"Government Spokesman's Press Conference."   British Broadcasting Corporation
    World Service broadcast, 18 June 1987.
Graham, Bradley.   "Polish Report Assails US for Destabilization Moves."
    Washington Post 12 April 1984, A26.
Gruber, Ruth E. "Poland Attacks Western Support for Solidarity."   United Press
    International, 30 October 1982.
_____. "Polish Restrictions on American Relations."   United Press International, 14
    December 1982.
Hatch, Orrin. "Retargeting Radio Resources." *Washington Times*, 30 June 1992, F3.
"Hearing of the International Operations Subcommittee of the House Foreign Affairs
    Committee." Federal News Service, 15 June 1989.
"'Ideological Warfare against Poland.'"   British Broadcasting Corporation World
    Service broadcast, 9 February 1984.
"International News." Reuters, 18 February 1981.
"'Izvestya':   USA's Plans for 'New Large-Scale Operation' in Poland."   British
    Broadcasting Corporation World Service broadcast, 10 December 1983
"Jacek Kuron and 'Outdated' Solidarity."   British Broadcasting Corporation World
    Service broadcast, 5 April 1988.
Kirkpatrick, Jeanne. "Needed Then, Needed Now: Radio Free Europe and Radio
    Liberty Give Information about Internal Affairs That Is Especially Useful
    during This Transition to Democracy." *Washington Post*, 8 March 1993,
    A15.

Klose, Kevin. "What Are the Soviets Afraid Of? Olympic Boycott, Sahkarov Crisis Reveal a New Isolationism." *Washington Post*, 20 May 1984, B5.

"'Krasnaya Zvezda' on West's Continuing 'Subversion' against Poland." British Broadcasting Corporation World Service broadcast, 6 September 1982.

Krauthammer, Charles. "The Hostage-Taking Mind." *Washington Post*, 4 October 1985, A23.

"'Literaturnaya Gazeta' on KOR's London 'Emissaries' and Other Western Links." British Broadcasting Corporation World Service broadcast, 19 February 1981.

Ludwikowski, Rett. "Will the Poles Fight?" *The Heritage Foundation Policy Review*, Fall 1982, 73.

Lund, Chris. "Walesa." United Press International, 11 December 1983.

Manegold, Catherine S. "U.S. Government Broadcasts to Cuba, and Wonders If Anyone Is Listening." *New York Times* (24 August 1994): A14.

"Mr. Reagan, Mr. Casey and the Pope." *Washington Times*, 21 February 1992, F2.

"Polish Government Accuses West of Interference in Elections." Reuters, 29 May 1989.

"Polish Government Rejoinder to West's 'Lies.'" British Broadcasting Corporation World Service broadcast, 5 November 1982.

"Polish Radio Transmits Foreign Radio Broadcasts." British Broadcasting Corporation World Service broadcast, 20 October 1987.

"'Pravda' on USA's 'Unprecedented Interference in Poland's Internal Affairs.'" British Broadcasting Corporation World Service broadcast, 29 September 1981.

"Prosecutors Warn Solidarity against May Day March." Reuters, 28 April 1986.

"Radio Free Europe, Radio Liberty Views Budget Cut." PR Newswire, 15 August 1986.

"Reagan Administration's Anti-Communist Crusade." British Broadcasting Corporation World Service broadcast, 22 October 1982.

Rohter, Larry. "Wielding the Power of the Exiles, A Would-Be Successor to Castro." *New York Times* (8 May 1995): A1.

Rollnick, Roman. "Poland Acknowledges 'Probability' of Accidentally Hitting German Ship." United Press International, 23 June 1987.

"'Rzeczpospolita' Response to Former Union Leaders' Appeal." British Broadcasting Corporation World Service broadcast, 20 May 1983.

Shenon, Philip. "Years of Jamming Voice of America Halted by Soviet." *New York Times*, 26 May 1987, A1.

Siewers, Alf. "US Poles Tell Solidarity: You Are not Alone." *Christian Science Monitor*, 2 September 1988, 5.

"Society and Mass Organisations; Solidarity and the May Day Demonstrations." British Broadcasting Corporation World Service broadcast, 19 April 1988.

"Solidarity Office in Brussels 'Maintained by Western Intelligence Services.'" British Broadcasting Corporation World Service broadcast, 23 February 1985.

"Solidarity's Underground Activities: Police 'Ready to Stop Any Demonstration.'" British Broadcasting Corporation World Service broadcast, 11 November 1982.

"Soviet Press Says West's Radio Give Polish Strikers Instruction." *New York Times*, 19 February 1981.

Stachura, Jadwiga. "Radio Free Europe: After the Victory." *The Warsaw Voice*, 12 June, 1992.

Steinmetz, Johanna. "Poles Honor History, Hear Timely Speech." *Chicago Tribune*, 8 May 1989, 16.

Tagliabue, John T. "Poland Says US Aids Solidarity's Election Campaign." *New York Times*, 31 May 1989, 3A.

____. "Voice of Poland to Go to Munich to Spar with Radio Free Europe." *New York Times*, 22 June 1988, A8.

"Television Programme on Solidarity 'Terrorists.'" British Broadcasting Corporation World Service broadcast, 1 May 1986.

"'Trybuna Ludu' on Radio Free Europe Interview with Solidarity Official." British Broadcasting Corporation World Service broadcast, 12 September 1986.

"Tumanov and RFE/RL Vice-Chairman on Broadcasting Policy." British Broadcasting Corporation World Service broadcast, 21 November 1986.

Turek, Bogdan. "Government Claims Proof of US-Solidarity Links." United Press International, 7 October 1986.

____. "Poland Accuses US of Covert Operations." United Press International, 18 April 1984.

"Turnover at the Voice of America." *National Security Record*, August 1984.

"Walesa Hears Speech On Radio Free Europe." *New York Times*, 11 December 1983, 6.

"Walesa Says Solidarity Plans More Protests." Reuters, 9 March 1985.

"Warning on Polish Protests." *Washington Post*, 24 August 1982, A15.

"Warsaw, Poland." United Press International, 9 October 1984.

Wedel, Janine R. "Solidarity's Caution." *Christian Science Monitor*, 29 December 1989, 19.

"Western Correspondents Functioning as "Letter Box" for Radio Free Europe." British Broadcasting Corporation World Service broadcast, 3 July 1982.

Wiener, Lauren. "Zwack Denounces Recall by Budapest." *Washington Times*, 11 April 1991, A7.

Wisniewski, Walter. "Poland-Mayday." United Press International, 27 April 1983.

____. "Poles Say US Media Violently Anti-Communist." United Press International, 28 April 1983.

____. "Polish Newsman Defects." United Press International, 6 January 1982.

Index

About the Editors and Contributors

Nancy Lynch Street is Professor and Chair of the Department of Communication Studies and Theatre Arts at Bridgewater State College (BSC). In 1985, BSC initiated an educational exchange agreement with Shanxi Teacher's University (STU) in Linfen, Shanxi Province, PRC. That year, and again in 1988, Street was the exchange professor to the Department of Foreign Languages at STU. In the summer of 1988, she received a Fulbright Group Study Grant to study economic development in Korea and Taiwan. In 1990, Street received a second Fulbright Group Study Grant to study Chinese language and culture. Her book relating to these experiences and research, *In Search of Red Buddha*, a study of a Chinese educational work unit during escalating economic and social change in China, was published in 1992. Street returns to China to teach at Southeast University in Nanjing in the Spring of 1997--the year Hong Kong , after 150 years, is released from Great Britain and is returned to China, thus shedding the last vestiges of the Opium War and British imperialism.

Marilyn J. Matelski is Professor and Chair of the Department of Communication at Boston College, where she teaches courses in intercultural communication, mass communication theory, television criticism, broadcast programming, and cultural diversity in the media. She has written eight books, along with numerous journal articles and reviews concerning media and its uses. Some of her previous titles include: *The Soap Opera Evolution, Daytime Broadcast Television Programming*, and *TV News Ethics* (recently translated into Turkish). Her most recent book, *Vatican Radio: Propagation by the Airwaves*, was published by Praeger Publishers, Inc. in 1995.

Miguel Quiachon Rapatan, FSC, completed his MA in Communication (Documentary Film Program) at Stanford University. At present, he is on a study leave from the Department of Communication, De La Salle University, Manila, Philippines and is pursuing his Ed.D. on a Fulbright grant in the

Department of Communication, Computing and Technology in Education at Teachers' College, Columbia University.

John J. Michalczyk is currently Director of Film Studies in the Fine Arts Department of Boston College. From his doctoral work at Harvard University on propaganda and art in the Spanish Civil War, to his most recent study of medicine, ethics, and the Third Reich, John Michalczyk has viewed film in its relation to politics, literature, and the arts. His critical works have studied the films of Ingmar Bergman, Costa-Gavras, Andre Malraux, and a host of French literary and Italian political filmmakers. He is presently completing a film trilogy, "Breaking Barriers," with a documentary on Nazi medicine.

John Spicer Nichols is an associate professor of communications and professor-in-charge of the Media Studies program at The Pennsylvania State University, where he teaches international communications. As a specialist in Cuban communications issues, Nichols has met with President Fidel Castro (most recently in 1994) and most of his top media policy makers and has testified frequently before U.S. congressional committees. He also is the co-author (with Lawrence Soley) of *Clandestine Radio Broadcasting*, which was chosen "Outstanding Academic Book" by Choice, and a contributing author to more than a dozen other books in the field of foreign affairs. Nichols received his Ph.D. in mass communication from the University of Minnesota.

ISBN 0-275-95602-4

90000>

EAN

9 780275 956028

HARDCOVER BAR CODE